Eight Weeks

Eight Weeks

*Looking Back, Moving Forwards,
Defying the Odds*

BARONESS LOLA YOUNG

FIG TREE
an imprint of
PENGUIN BOOKS

FIG TREE

UK | USA | Canada | Ireland | Australia
India | New Zealand | South Africa

Fig Tree is part of the Penguin Random House group of companies whose addresses can be found at global.penguinrandomhouse.com.

Penguin Random House UK,
One Embassy Gardens, 8 Viaduct Gardens, London SW11 7BW

penguin.co.uk
global.penguinrandomhouse.com

First published 2024
001

Copyright © Baroness Lola Young, 2024
The moral right of the author has been asserted

Penguin Random House values and supports copyright. Copyright fuels creativity, encourages diverse voices, promotes freedom of expression and supports a vibrant culture. Thank you for purchasing an authorized edition of this book and for respecting intellectual property laws by not reproducing, scanning or distributing any part of it by any means without permission. You are supporting authors and enabling Penguin Random House to continue to publish books for everyone. No part of this book may be used or reproduced in any manner for the purpose of training artificial intelligence technologies or systems. In accordance with Article 4(3) of the DSM Directive 2019/790, Penguin Random House expressly reserves this work from the text and data mining exception

Set in 13.5/16pt Garamond MT Std
Typeset by Jouve (UK), Milton Keynes

Printed and bound in Great Britain by Clays Ltd, Elcograf S.p.A.

The authorized representative in the EEA is Penguin Random House Ireland, Morrison Chambers, 32 Nassau Street, Dublin D02 YH68

A CIP catalogue record for this book is available from the British Library

ISBN: 978–0–241–59063–8

Penguin Random House is committed to a sustainable future for our business, our readers and our planet. This book is made from Forest Stewardship Council® certified paper.

For all the others whose stories
are yet to be told . . .

Contents

	Author's note	ix
One	A package arrives	1
Two	Back to the beginning	13
	A memory: Visits from Mother	31
Three	Love is conditional	36
	A memory: A visit from Father	69
Four	Recovery/discovery	72
Five	The inevitable	90
	A memory: Daisy	103
Six	Moved on	109
	A memory: A walk in the dark	141
Seven	Taking the long view	144
Eight	A sour note	176
Nine	On the edge	195
Ten	Getting on track	224
	A memory: Christmas	248
Eleven	A fresh start	251
	A memory: A visit with my father	269

Twelve	An invitation	275
Thirteen	A wedding	291
	A memory: A visit with my mother	298
Fourteen	Home	303
Fifteen	Unresolved endings yield fresh beginnings	307
	Acknowledgements	321
	Resources	323

Author's note

To write this book I've had to draw heavily on my powers of recall, and although I've done my best to be specific about dates and events, memory has its limitations. Apologies for any errors resulting from my attempts to reconstruct past events and my experience of them.

Several names and locations have been changed or redacted for reasons that will, I'm sure, become clear.

One: A package arrives

8 August 1951, ▮▮▮▮▮▮▮▮▮: Foster mother states infant was received July 30th. Mother has entered hospital as a student nurse. Foster mother will come to Islington Welfare Centre. Infant having feeds of non-dairy milk.

There it sat, propped up on my desk in my office at The Chocolate Factory in Wood Green, north London. A hand-delivered A5 envelope with my name on it. No return address, and I didn't recognize the handwriting. With no idea of what might be inside, I opened the envelope and shook out the contents – documents and photographs tumbled out in a heap.

I spread the items across my desk. Two passports: one the green of Nigeria, one British and blue. A second, smaller envelope. And a photograph of six women at what looked like a social gathering.

Both passports belonged to my mother, who had died in Lagos a year earlier, in 2005. The British passport had been issued in 1949, the Nigerian one in 1971; their covers had faded and were spotted with age. The second envelope contained an undated handwritten note comprising two sheets of A5 notepaper covered on both

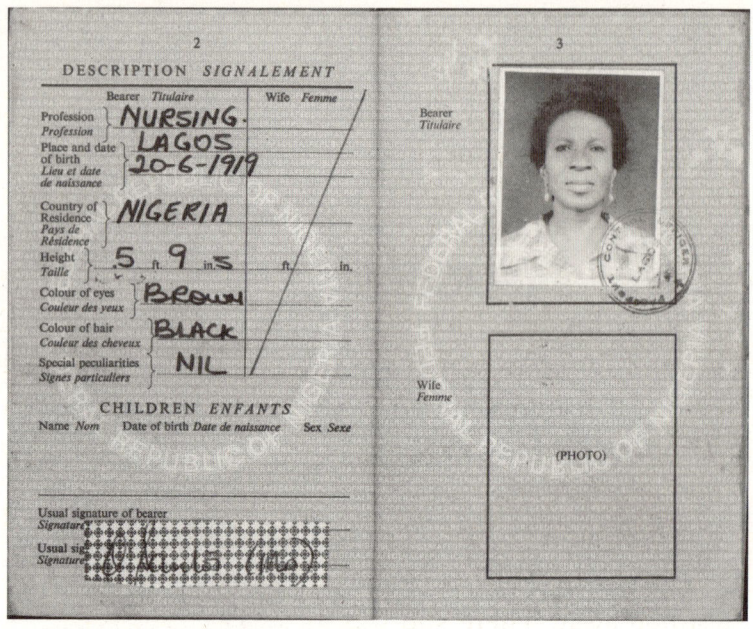

sides with large, semi-legible handwriting, and was signed by a Chief Mrs Obafunke Akinkugbe. The name of the sender and the Lagos address meant nothing to me.

I looked more closely at the photograph. The light exposure made it seem as though the group of women were bathed in the warm rosy glow of a tropical sunset. Above one of the women's heads was a little sticker with 'Mother' handwritten on it, and an arrow pointing down to her face, in case I couldn't identify her unaided.

The envelope's contents created a familiar anxiety. The fear that something of which I was ignorant, and would like to remain so, would be revealed. Something that would disturb the life I was currently enjoying, two years into my appointment to the House of Lords.

I delayed a thorough reading of Chief Akinkugbe's letter for as long as possible, first studying the passports that outlined a story of journeys undertaken, and a life lived unfamiliar to me. I couldn't make sense of a series of visas for trips outside Nigeria, but not to the UK, stamped on the blotchy pages of the green and blue booklets. I stared at the little portrait photograph in each. My mother. I had never owned a photograph of her, and I tried to match the woman in the photos with the facial features buried a mile deep in my memory. Was it vain of me to want to see if I was reflected in my mother's eyes, her cheekbones, the shape of her jaw? I searched her face, her expression, trying to read who she was, get a sense of her character, but her half-smile gave nothing away. There she was, bejewelled and gazing at the photographer, bottles of Coca-Cola and a 7Up waiting on the table. I had no idea who the other women seated with her in the group photograph were.

I turned my attention back to the handwritten note. It contained a brief sketch of the years my mother had spent in London just before I was born. Some of the names mentioned were hazily familiar, others were not known to me. Williams, Adekunle, Makanju, Young, Santos. Place names jumped out too – Earl's Court, Osogbo, Lagos, Aldershot, Leyton and Epping Forest – emphasizing a connection between Nigeria and England, Lagos and London.

Over the decades, I'd been fed scraps of information about the past. Dribs and drabs culled from random, unverified sources passed on to me by distant relatives.

Unexpected visits of wealthy Nigerians had punctuated my life from around the 1970s; they would come to London to stay in their apartments in well-to-do areas like Marble Arch, St John's Wood, Chelsea and Hampstead, or to stay in posh central London hotels. They'd pass me slivers of information and, if I was lucky, a ten-pound note, then off they'd go, seldom to be seen again. Almost inevitably, the most recent tale told would contradict the previous one in some aspect.

Chief Akinkugbe's letter did little to clarify the picture. The choppy phrases, the names and dates dropped in without elaboration, had the feel of someone taking notes over the phone while the person on the other end of the line told a jagged story. As I read it, I imagined her standing in her kitchen, phone receiver nestled between her chin and her shoulder as she searched for a pen and notepad.

I couldn't help feeling a pang of frustration when I came to the end of the note. The unspoken promise of the package was that I'd find answers, if I could only fit the pieces together, but my expectations had been raised only to be let down with a jolt. Yet another incomplete story, which left me with the questions that had haunted me throughout my life: how had my parents met? How had I come into being? And why hadn't they wanted me?

Perhaps it was pointless to try and revive that painful history. Even though in the past I'd sought answers, finding out the truth about why my mother and father had acted in the way they did was a task for which I had little appetite. In my professional life, the desire to know as much as possible, to see the full picture, had always been an important driver for me. But in the matter of my family history, that compulsion to know was a source of upsetting, contradictory feelings.

What I knew about my parents was this: my mother, Yele Santos, was a widow with two sons living in Lagos when she began a relationship with my father, Maxwell Young. I don't know when but I would guess around the late 1940s, after her husband died in 1944. Yele and Maxwell agreed that she would travel to London to train as a nurse and wait for my father to join her. He was also coming to the UK capital with the aim of studying microbiology. Reunited with Maxwell in west London, Yele became pregnant with me – and found out that my father had already married someone else in Nigeria. Maxwell had a wife and a daughter who was two years old when I was born. The daughter's name was Shade.

I was born on 1 June 1951 in St Mary's Hospital, Paddington. Six weeks later I was handed over into the care of Daisy Vince, a registered foster mother in her late sixties who had looked after many children over the years. I had no idea at the time, of course, but I would end up staying with her until I was fourteen years old. Throughout my early childhood at Daisy's house in Tufnell Park, each of my parents came to visit me, independently of the other, on a handful of occasions. By the time I was twelve years old, both Yele and Maxwell had returned to Lagos to live their separate lives, and I would not see either of them again until many years later, when I was an adult. My father had a stroke and died in June 1994, and I learned of my mother's death through a circuitous route involving Shade and other, previously unknown, relatives in 2005.

Over the days and weeks that followed, I tried to put the envelope and its contents to the back of my mind, and focused instead on my still relatively new position as a member of the House of Lords.

There had been so much for me to learn since my introduction ceremony in July 2004. I was one of the beneficiaries of the Labour government's reforms of the House of Lords: as well as cutting down the number of hereditary peers, the idea of so-called 'people's peers' was established, enabling those with no party political affiliation to become part of the country's law-making machinery. Entering the House of Lords by this route entailed applying, and being interviewed several times, and eventually vetted. The process was long and similar to that of the appointment of a chief executive at a large, well-known organization. As with those roles, you might be approached and asked to apply, or you might take the initiative and apply yourself. Encouraged by friends and colleagues, I applied and was accepted the second time around.

As members of the House of Lords (or peers, as we're often called), we aren't employed by Parliament or anyone else, and, unlike MPs, we're not paid a salary, but we may receive an attendance allowance. It had been made clear to me that our main task was to scrutinize legislation, but the number of hours I dedicated to the role, and the frequency with which I should attend parliamentary sittings, were left to me. As an independent crossbench peer, unlike those members who belonged to a political party, I was not subject to the discipline of a party whip. When I first started, several peers advised me not to make being a member the centre of my life, while others suggested I should simply observe how everything worked for a while, to orientate myself. I followed both pieces of advice.

As well as getting to grips with the rituals and procedures, I had to find my way around the building. Easier said than done for someone with my poor sense of direction. There are miles of passageways in the Palace of Westminster, in which the Houses of Parliament sit, and there are more staircases than you'd like when you're late for a vote and the lift is slow. There are over a thousand rooms too.

I joined the House with no legal training, and no experience in party political machinations, so there was a lot to absorb. While I'd always been an avid reader, I'd had to learn that skill all over again when scrutinizing new legislation proposed in bills, or the proceedings of a select committee. If I wanted to play an active role in Parliament, developing legislative literacy would be essential.

During my first two years in the House I'd been surprised by the number of bills proposed by the government to which I'd felt a connection. I'd assumed there would be few opportunities to contribute, initially, but both the *Human Tissue Act* (2004), which provoked heated debates about the transfer of human remains from museum collections, and the *Children Act* (also 2004), establishing the role of the Children's Commissioner, related to different areas in which I had an interest. I'd assumed that my experiences would lead me to get involved in laws relating to children, families and the care system. But I hadn't imagined that my background in the cultural and creative industries – I'd set up an arts and culture consultancy in 2004, served as Head of Culture at the Greater London Authority, sat on the boards of trustees of the National Theatre and the National Archives, and chaired judging panels of literary prizes – would also prove relevant quite so quickly. Debates about the status of human remains in museum collections took place both in the sector and in Parliament.

While I'd long been interested in the relationship between political activity, cultural and creative practice and cultural theory, my participation in the Lords signified a new level of political engagement and understanding, underpinning the campaigning and activism in which I'd been involved before my appointment.

Despite my best efforts to remain focused on my work, the contents of the envelope kept calling to me while they awaited my return. I pored over the writing and the images, seeing something new each time.

Shortly after I was introduced to the House of Lords, an elderly fellow crossbench peer quoted an old saying containing a truly offensive racial slur, in my presence. Difficult though it might be to believe, I think he had been trying to make me feel welcome by 'joking' with me. I recalled this incident as I continued my study of the contents of the package. Trying to fill the gaps in my knowledge of my parents' lives with only the outline of a narrative before me, I wondered how, back in the 1950s, each of us had coped with similar racist insults – they as adults and me as a child.

On a phone call with my friend Sally, I brought up the subject of the package and its contents. Sal and I had been at Parliament Hill Comprehensive School together from 1962 to 1969. She was one of three lifelong friends I had made during those years – Sally, Jo and Anne. We were the self-styled 'Parlets', still friends more than six decades later.

I told Sal how frustrating it was to have been sent a tantalizingly small part of the whole picture.

'You do know you're entitled to see the records from your time in care, don't you, Lo?' she said.

I was stunned. I had never considered there was such a possibility.

'The council are legally obliged to share them with you. Get on to Islington and see what they have.'

'Seriously?' I tried to take in the implications of what Sal was saying. How had I not known about this before?

In the years that followed our conversation, I would learn that my experience was not uncommon. It was the 1989 Children Act that enshrined the right of anyone who'd spent time in the care system to access their records. A laudable decision, but making sure that everybody affected by the law was aware of their rights was another matter. There are those who still do not know about it – I've met care experienced people in their fifties and sixties who had no idea that it was their right to access their case notes.

'It may not be straightforward, given the time that's passed,' Sal continued. 'The files could have been lost or destroyed. And, even if you find them, names and events may be heavily redacted. Also, bear in mind that you were in care in the fifties and sixties – some of the language they used then would be totally unacceptable today, especially around race.'

I smiled wryly to myself as I thought of the elderly peer who had obviously not received the memo on that subject.

After a pause, Sal said, 'To be honest, the chances of you finding anything from that period are pretty remote. When I was still working for Islington, a room where old files were stored was flooded by a leaky washing machine in the flat above.'

Thinking about all those lost histories saddened me, and I wondered if my past had floated away on a tide of scummy grey water. I considered Sal's remarks: the social workers I'd encountered would have had no idea that one day I'd be reading what they'd written about me. Later I would learn that some of them deliberately destroyed care records, believing that to do so enabled care leavers to move on with their lives. They might have thought it an act of kindness, but I see it as woefully misguided, an abuse of power. These historic missteps in keeping children's care records safe meant that I needed to manage my expectations about what I might be able to find.

The reality was that the prospect of me finding anything at all, let alone something that could resolve my feelings about my history and my parents, was as distant as ever.

'It's still worth a try though, Lo.'

Sal was right. For as long as there was even a faint possibility that I might find a record of my life in care, I couldn't ignore it. I had to follow the trail. We hung up and I was left with doubts and anxieties. What if there was something truly disturbing in those notes – something I'd forgotten about? Or had never known? I had few photographs of myself before the age of about twenty-four, so it wasn't difficult to pretend childhood had bypassed me altogether. Would it be better or worse if there was no record at all of Lola Young's experiences as a child?

Over thirty-five years had passed since I'd left the care of the London Borough of Islington. A part of me felt fortunate that I hadn't experienced the abuse that others have had to endure in their childhood and adolescence, and I was also aware that having had a degree of stability early on in my life was helpful. But the idea that I had somehow been lucky was not apparent to me as a child, or a teenager; I'd viewed myself as unwanted and unlikeable.

In the interests of completeness, I wanted to know

the missing details that might help explain the absence of parents in my life. Without that knowledge I realized I wouldn't be able to make sense of the random collection of puzzle pieces I'd been sent from Lagos, along with the snippets I'd collected over the years. What was more, since the 1980s, with the discovery that the presence of Black people in Britain could be traced back to Roman times, I'd come to appreciate the importance of our individual and collective histories. As far as possible, I needed the whole picture, because whether I chose to engage with it or not, my past experiences had shaped the woman I had become. The arrival of the mystery package had stirred up old hurts, that was obvious, but perhaps there would be some resolution – even some comfort – in discovering why my parents had left me behind in London.

Two: Back to the beginning

20 July 1952, ▉▉▉▉▉▉▉▉: Well & happy. Has won a prize at a baby show recently.

1 November 1956: Bright child. Likes attending school. Has never been a miserable child but has until recently been rather solemn.

Sal's revelation about the care records should have spurred me to action straight away, but something held me back. I needed to think through how I would feel if my detective work came to nothing. Best to spread it out over time so as not to make the process too intensive; I mustn't over-invest in the search to the detriment of other parts of my life. After all, I'd managed to get this far without even knowing that the records existed.

So it was some months after my phone conversation with Sal that I contacted Islington Council by email, giving them details of my time spent in the care system. Their first reply took several weeks to arrive and indicated that this was not going to be a straightforward search because of the length of time that had elapsed. I'd told them of the period I'd spent in children's homes outside London and they responded that I should approach the local authorities responsible for those areas – Hertfordshire and Middlesex.

No, I said, these were Islington Council-owned homes.

No, they said, Islington didn't have children's homes outside London.

Yes, I said, they did and I'd lived in them.

Check with London Metropolitan Archives, they insisted. They'll have the records for Hertfordshire and Middlesex.

I knew what I'd experienced, and I knew what I remembered, but just to be sure I wasn't somehow mistaken about all the different places I'd lived in, or how the system worked, I emailed London Metropolitan Archives and I asked if they had records from that era relating to the care system.

No.

Of course they didn't, I thought.

You should try the London Borough of Islington, they said . . .

With my expectations raised and then dashed to the ground, I took the decision to put my quest on hold again. It was an emotionally draining situation and I had more than enough to keep me occupied working out how I could make a positive contribution in the House of Lords.

When I look back on those early years in Parliament, it's clear that my childhood experiences played a part in how and why I involved myself in particular issues. Now that I had a platform from which to persuade and cajole, to influence, I focused on who was likely to miss out as a result of passing a given piece of legislation, accepting the findings of a committee report or policy paper. I threw myself into my cultural consultancy business at the same time as building a presence in Parliament, taking on contracts that exposed the inequalities embedded in the way systems were built, and proposed how to address them.

Between 2004 and 2011, I was involved in select committees, spoke on topics such as the abolition of the transatlantic trade in enslaved Africans, and co-produced an event to mark its bicentenary; I founded an All Party Parliamentary Group on Ethics and Sustainability in Fashion, the first of its kind, before sustainability became more or less mainstream; I visited schools, giving talks; I contributed to a new law that criminalized forced labour and domestic servitude; I spoke at academic, policy-based and political conferences and seminars, and worked with cultural practitioners and theorists, as well as parliamentarians in the UK and around the world. It was a busy, productive period.

Through postgraduate study, which I'd loved, I'd gained critical and analytical skills, and I now found the act of linking theory, practice, policy and politics a challenging and exciting environment in which to work. That thrill connected with my love of reading and writing, the joy of which has remained with me from my first years at school. The various aspects of my working life were beginning to click together, enabling me to maximize impact; what I learned outside Parliament reinforced what I learned inside the institution, and vice versa.

While I was thinking about the politics of culture (and the culture of the political sphere), every now and then a stray thought about the search for my care notes would pop into my head. At this very moment, they might be lying under a pile of tatty folders in a rusty filing cabinet at the back of some forgotten Islington office along the Holloway Road, waiting to be revealed. I had to set aside my initial disappointment at not receiving the records as soon as I asked for them, and be more realistic. I would restart the hunt, and if I couldn't find them after a sustained, determined search, then I'd forget all about it and be no worse off.

On a friend's recommendation, I contacted the Care Leavers' Association (CLA), a Manchester-based organization that supports care experienced people when they leave the system. I told the CLA the story of my search so far, and they advised me to go back to Islington Council. They gave me some pointers on how to formulate my request.

So it was that after a few brief introductory email exchanges, on 5 August 2011 – some five years after I'd first learned about care records – I received the following email.

Dear Ms Young,
Thank you for your prompt response in sending the completed access to records application to me. I regret

to inform you that we are currently operating with a significant backlog. It is therefore necessary to place your application on our waiting list before being processed. Your application has been entered at number 35 on our waiting list.

The access to records process involves locating any relevant files, reading through these files in detail, contacting family or professionals who have contributed to the files in order to obtain their consent to share their information with you, and finally making a copy of the files for you. We recommend that applicants attend our office to collect their copies – you are welcome to bring a support worker or friend with you if you wish to read through the files in our offices.

Alternatively we can arrange for files to be sent via recorded delivery mail but we encourage applicants to have support networks in place as reading through these files can be a difficult experience.

I will be in contact to advise you whether we have located any files regarding you, and will endeavour at this point to give you an estimate of completion time.

If you have any queries or concerns in the meantime, or you would like an update on the progress of your application, please feel free to contact me using the details below.

Kind regards,
Access to Records Officer Children's Social Care
Islington Council

Given that I had been number 36,000 on the waiting list for an Arsenal season ticket, I thought my patience would stretch to however long it took for Islington's bureaucratic wheels to turn.

I thought endlessly about what the records – should they ever turn up – might contain. Would they match my earliest memories? Would I need to think of a different way of telling that story? However many gaps and absences there'd been in telling others about my childhood to date, I'd always felt confident about what I did know: where and how certain events had taken place, my age at the time of a specific incident. Now I had to face the possibility that while everything I thought I knew might be confirmed, it might equally be turned on its head.

Daisy Vince, the white foster mother I would grow up calling 'Mum', was nearly sixty-five years old when my parents handed me over to her. As I grew up in her care, Daisy would tell me many times that I was just six weeks old when I arrived at 207 Tufnell Park Road. I knew this pronouncement must be significant, because of the number of times she repeated the story, but it was also meaningless, for what does a five or six year old know about being any age other than the one they are at that particular moment?

The imposing Victorian terrace in which we lived stood on the corner of Tufnell Park Road and Huddlestone Road, in north London. One flight of steps led down to the basement, and another led up to the main front door over which, printed on glass, was the word 'Stalheim'. Somebody told us it was a German word meaning prison, but I later discovered it was the name of a village in Norway. The four-storey house belonged to Daisy's family and was divided into separate flats. Daisy lived in the basement occupying four rooms, and on the elevated ground floor lived two middle-aged single women. The rest of the house was occupied by Daisy's daughter, granddaughter, and eventually great-grandchildren.

Our flat had direct access to the garden, and was made up of a kitchen, a front or living room, one bedroom and a scullery. Daisy and all of us who were fostered by her slept in the same bedroom.

Daisy told us she was a widow and that her husband had died in the war: I was about ten when she let this slip and it didn't occur to me to enquire about the name of her spouse, or to which war she was referring. Several decades later, thanks to a friend who was interested in genealogy, I found out that the truth was rather more complicated than Daisy's simple statement suggested, but I'll come to that later. For the moment it's enough to say that Daisy Vince was the birth mother of Evelyn, who lived on the second floor with her husband, Liam Flanagan. By the time I arrived on the scene, in the summer of 1951, Evelyn was in her mid-forties. Evelyn and Liam had a daughter, Julie, who lived on the top floor with her husband, Terry Andrews. They were married in 1954; I was three years old and wore a red 'siren suit' (as the all-in-one hooded outer garment was called then) to the wedding. That's my earliest memory. I was captivated by the confetti that fell like snow and covered the bride, the groom and the pavement outside the church.

As a registered foster mother, Daisy Vince was well known and trusted by what was then London County Council authorities. She was also one of the few in the area who would take in Black children. When my mother and father turned up at her door in the summer of 1951, she had been fostering for several years. Some children would stay for a few months; others spent their entire childhoods with Daisy and only left when they moved into rented accommodation or married. I wonder whether they were curious about where they'd come from, or whether they simply knew enough to be grateful that they'd ended up with Daisy Vince. I have vivid memories of Jack and Sidney, in particular, as they returned to Tufnell Park Road every year for Christmas lunch. Sidney would blink rapidly for several seconds, a kind of nervous tick, though he was always fun, cracking jokes, indulged by everyone when he expressed what were then considered outlandish ideas such as vegetarianism and yoga. Jack was rather more strait-laced and conventional, handsome in a distant movie star sort of way. He too was fun and was a willing Father Christmas year after year. Sidney and his wife, Jeanette, and Jack and Gillian with their son, Oliver, came laden with presents, and without them Christmas would have had a very different feel.

Tufnell Park Road was long and straight and led to Holloway Road, the main shopping area, with the department stores Jones Brothers and James Selby. The neighbourhood around Tufnell Park, Archway and Kentish Town marked our geographical boundaries, with an occasional foray into Camden Town or Parliament Hill Fields. Daisy was well known in the area, most likely due to always having various children or babies in tow. Local shop owners would greet her in the street, as would the police officer on his beat. The pet shop on Junction Road was a regular haunt, and the back-street route to it took us past a railway line. As kids we loved waving at the trains as they approached and tooted, steam billowing behind the engine as it caught in the wind. If we were lucky, a passenger would spot us and wave back, their acknowledgement curiously thrilling.

Tufnell Park wasn't posh, but it did have an air of quiet gentility. Nonetheless, notoriety wasn't far away. Holloway Women's Prison, its castellations giving it the air of a fairy-tale medieval castle, was burdened with the horrors of incarceration and hangings. Nearby, its male counterpart, Pentonville, stood behind a deceptively bland wall on Caledonian Road. To complete this triangle of criminality, the former home of an infamous killer, cloaked in ordinariness, was located between the two prisons. I have a vivid recollection of my primary school head teacher regaling Daisy and me with the story of how she'd refused to let her school be named after nearby Hilldrop Crescent because of its association with the murderous Dr Crippen. Perhaps growing up with all this talk of crime influenced my choice of reading. I always preferred thrilling tales about the adventures of intelligent, brave detectives – usually male, but not always – to the stories of girls who played lacrosse and ate midnight feasts in boarding schools.

When I first arrived at Tufnell Park Road, there were two other children being looked after by Daisy: Richie and Lynne. Even without a photograph to refer to, I can still recall Richie's features in my mind's eye. Describing what he looked like to someone else is more difficult. He was just a boy – older, bigger and stronger than me; sometimes an amiable joker but just as often my tormentor. When I look now at a photograph from about 1956, I can see a sadness in his eyes that matched my own. Or perhaps it was a wistfulness, a yearning to be someone and somewhere else. He would run away on several occasions from the boarding institution in Stony Stratford where he'd been sent after some escapade or other. Eventually we managed a peace of sorts, though our relationship couldn't really be characterized as a close friendship. Richie had been with Daisy since he was a baby; only Lynne had lived with Daisy for longer. She would have been in her early teens as I started primary school. Sleeping in a cot, I joined Richie, Lynne and Daisy in the bedroom in the cool, north-facing rooms in the basement. I called Daisy 'Mum'. I knew she wasn't my mother, of course, but I tried not to think about that complicated situation too much. Lynne and Richie also called Daisy 'Mum', and this made it feel normal.

Bath night was a palaver and took place about once every two weeks. Daisy would fill two big saucepans, a bucket and the kettle with cold water, then light the gas stove in the scullery, and put the tin bath by the fire in the front room. Sometimes, after I'd started school, I would get a turn in the proper bath upstairs, where Miss Enderby and Miss Asher lived. They were nothing to do with Daisy's family and, although Miss Enderby was friendly, Miss Asher didn't speak to us much. I liked the tin bath best though, because Daisy made sure the water didn't scald me. When Lynne bathed me upstairs, the water was too hot, and I cried.

Being taken to visit the primary school I would be joining at the age of five was exciting beyond description.

Even now, I can see myself running up and down Huddlestone Road like a hyperactive puppy, as Daisy watches on, smiling. I remember that I overheard the conversation between Daisy and Mrs Kemp about Dr Crippen, but I hadn't any idea what it all meant.

I'd learned how to read before I started school, or perhaps it was just that I can't recall a time when I couldn't read: if true, it must've been either Daisy or Lynne who taught me, and I know they encouraged me to enjoy the stash of books I had at home. Richie had a large number of comics and, although he taught me how to box, I can't imagine him having the patience to help me with my reading. I relished reading his comics – especially *Superman* and the *Eagle* – as much as I loved reading books. This skill, of being able to read just about anything put before me, meant that I made short work of the Janet and John books at school and looked forward to returning to my storybooks waiting for me in the sideboard cupboard in our kitchen. This was the place where I kept all my books and games and jigsaw puzzles; my version of a library. My handwriting skills couldn't match the high level of my reading ability: my exercise books were always untidy and I had to have a rubber by my side at all times.

Daisy said I was clever, and her opinion of my intellect had been reinforced for me by her often-repeated assertion that Africans were more intelligent than white people. Her perception might have been influenced by the fact that several of the Black parents who sought her services were professionals or university-educated. It may also be that, like me, she'd read an article in the *Daily Mirror* in 1958, when I was seven, in which author and journalist Keith Waterhouse wrote about West African students journeying to England in the quest for knowledge and skills to take back home. By contrast, I don't think any of Daisy's friends or relatives had stayed in school much beyond the age of fifteen.

Imitating the quintessentially upper-class officer's posh voice, such as we heard in 1950s films like *The Dam Busters*, Richie would say to me, 'You're British. Remember you're British, Lulla.' It nearly always made us all laugh since Richie wasn't at all posh himself, and at the time I had no understanding of ironic references to the British Empire. I'm not sure that Richie did either. It was a remark drawn from too many viewings of Sunday afternoon films set in the former colonies, and the jingoism of post-war comics. Along with Daisy and everyone else at Tufnell Park Road, Richie pronounced my name so that it sounded like 'Lulla'. Teachers and school friends called me 'Lola' to rhyme with 'cola'. No one other than my mother or father pronounced 'Lola' as it was said by Nigerians – to rhyme with 'dollar'.

Starting school meant having children of my own age to play with. I had longed to join the groups of girls and boys clad in their bottle-green jumpers who walked past our house every weekday afternoon. So much so that after the interview with Mrs Kemp, I'd asked Daisy if I could stay the night at school. However, my first day at Tufnell Park Primary School was a bewildering mixture of emotions. I was accepted by the other children – even if I was suspicious of their motives for choosing me to be the witch in playtime dramas – and I received multiple invitations to my new classmates' homes for tea. The brown-skinned girl-witch who raced around the playground, and whose touch caused her friends to 'die', was something of a novelty. When Daisy asked me how my first day at school had gone, I told her I had played with lots of girls, and that I had fallen over and hit the back of my head on a stone step. But I hadn't cried.

Around the middle of 1956 – when I was five years old – a new baby arrived at the house, and I was no longer the youngest. I was told that her name was Kayin, that she was one year old and she was my cousin; her mother, Mrs Taylor, was my aunt. This was confusing, as the other aunts and uncles in my life were Daisy's relatives – sisters, brothers and cousins – and they were white and lived in Southend-on-Sea. When she dropped Kayin off, Mrs Taylor tried to talk to me, but I was too shy to reply. Before she left that day, she gave me a shilling – intended, perhaps, to soften the blow of losing my place as number one in Daisy's affection. It didn't work.

Kayin's outgoing personality was evident from the start. At one, she was a bundle of lovely smiles and a mass of hair. She established herself as the centre of attention the moment she arrived, and I knew straight away that she'd be the favourite now. Daisy wouldn't want me any more; she had a happier, more attractive child to look after.

The day of Kayin's arrival was momentous for me, though I'm sure no one else present at the time found it any more remarkable than any other weekday. I remember how Mr and Mrs Hunter and Adam, our next-door neighbours, gazed adoringly at Kayin, exclaiming how beautiful this new baby was. It was clear to me that after only being with us for five minutes, Kayin was already everyone's favourite little girl. That day set the pattern: I could sense that the people who'd been interested in me before now only had eyes for her. And I thought they were right to prefer her. The evidence was clear: Kayin's mother came to see her. Kayin's mother was there, she existed, she was real. My mother and my father had each only visited me once or twice a year, and they never sent me birthday or Christmas cards or presents.

Daisy and Mrs Hunter would often talk over the fence

that separated our gardens. Mrs Hunter's face was white like the colour of bleached flour, while her husband was Jamaican and nut-brown. He wore those fashionable sideburns that reached out to his cheekbones, ending in a little point. They had a son some years younger than me, named Adam. The Hunters would have known about my situation, I'm sure, as Daisy would have told them about the lack of contact with my parents, along with potted histories of all the children she looked after. I remember, one time, Mrs Hunter looking over the fence and saying to me, 'Never mind, my mother and father don't come and see me any more either.'

'Don't they like you?' I asked.

She laughed and said, 'It's my husband they don't like.'

As I grew older, and Daisy confided in me, she told me that Mrs Hunter's parents had ignored her ever since she married the handsome Jamaican.

My initial feelings of suspicion and resentment towards Kayin eventually gave way to a tacit recognition that while neither of us was actively content in our situation, we could help each other make the best of it. We had been thrown together in an environment that required solidarity rather than jealous competition.

Kayin saw her parents regularly, and once they'd bought a house and were freed from the strict 'no children' policy of their rented accommodation, she would sometimes stay with them over the weekend. I developed a sense of responsibility for the girl who seemed so much younger than me, and we became sisters and even surrogate parents. The experiences we carried with us from the house in Tufnell Park bound us together, and we remain close friends today.

Our kitchen had a big window looking out into the garden, framing the borders filled with hydrangeas and hollyhocks, Daisy's favourite shrubs and perennials. Amid all the plants, there was a path leading to a child-size replica Swiss chalet. Kayin and I used to play there in the summer, the musty smell inside noticed but not deterring us from holding dolls' tea parties. Evelyn didn't like us using it, claiming it wasn't intended for us to play in. But who else would it have been for? Kayin and I were the only children old enough to play on our own. Julie's children were too young, and besides, as they lived on the top floor of the house, their mother wouldn't have been able to supervise them from afar. Other children had Wendy houses, I knew, but not even Sarah Westwood, my best friend throughout most of my time in primary school, had anything like our chalet to play with. Viewed through my innocent eyes this was an important benchmark, because the Westwoods appeared to have endless wealth and could have afforded several play houses in the expanse of their garden.

Behind the back wall of our garden there was an orchard, where Richie was allowed to climb over the wall and collect the apples. It couldn't be seen from the road, and it wasn't attached to a house there, so we thought of it as a secret garden. When I asked Daisy if I could go over the wall with Richie, or even on my own, she told me I wasn't allowed to. Although I could have taken advantage of her poor eyesight and rheumatic legs, being a mostly obedient child I resisted the temptation to climb over the wall and search for a tree big enough to live in like the one I'd read about in *Hollow Tree House*.

On sunny days, we'd be outside most of the time, ignoring the abundance of scented flowers and flourishing bushes to concentrate on other, more exciting things. I loved the garden – loved examining leaves and worms we called 'blood suckers'. I liked digging out the slime from the slots in the drain with sticks, and I'd show the mucky substance to Kayin, taking care not to daub dirt on her nice dresses. I hoped that one day she'd want to explore the drain's treasure trove with the same levels of enthusiasm and concentration as me. I tried to feed the worms that lived beneath the surface of the soil with drain-slime, but I couldn't see where their mouths were located. We also had a garden swing, so there was plenty to do, and we'd make up stories and songs. We really didn't need anyone else.

As far as I can remember, Daisy didn't allow me to have school friends round to our house for tea or to watch television, not even Sarah Westwood. The Westwoods must have had some knowledge of my situation – perhaps they'd seen Daisy at a parents' meeting, or found out through the parent grapevine. I do know that when I went to Sarah's house for birthday parties (one of the few times Daisy would allow me to visit friends outside of school), her family always ensured I won a little pouch full of coins or a nice toy in the games we played. They also donated the ten pounds needed to pay for me to go on the school trip to Devon, and I suspect Daisy felt that these acts of generosity were a pronouncement on her inadequacy. Or she may have been trying to protect me, by not exposing me to unattainable aspirational lifestyles. It could have been that the Westwoods represented a middle class towards whom she held some resentment, seeing them as intellectually pretentious and people who would regard us as charity cases. Whatever her reasons, Daisy restricted my visits to my friends' homes and didn't welcome other children to come and play in our house. The time I spent on my own was put to good use reading and sketching, and making up stories. I became self-sufficient to an extent, perhaps as a way of denying the insecurity I felt regarding friendships.

When I went to school, I think at first I must have assumed that other children lived in circumstances similar to mine. It didn't take long for me to grasp the fact that my friends lived with their parents, and their households weren't subject to inspection visits from health visitors or welfare officers like Miss Boardman.

A memory: Visits from Mother

January 1958: *seven years and eight months old*

Mum says I have to go for a walk with my real mother today. Mum says I've met her before but that was years ago, I think. I can't remember much about her, except she's very tall.

My mother and I walk to Kentish Town. I run along by her side, holding her hand. She walks really fast.

She says she has a surprise for me as we go into a shop and up some stairs. I'm excited now. Perhaps there are toys up there. Or games to play with other children, like the ones at Sarah's birthday party.

But when we get upstairs, we only find a man fiddling with some things with his back to us. Mother points at a big black chair, a bit like a dentist's chair. The man tells me to sit down on it. It must be made for very tall people because my legs don't touch the floor.

I want to know what the surprise is, and I ask my mother because I can't wait any longer.

The man turns around and he's holding something in one hand. I don't like his face. It reminds me of Uncle Harry, who's married to Mum's twin sister, Aunty Vi. When he visits us, Uncle Harry spits horrible yellow stuff into the fire, and eats hard-boiled eggs with his fingers, like they're apples.

The man tells me to keep still, and I try to do as I'm told. I'm pressing my lips together very tight, so my head doesn't move. I feel something cold in my ear, then something like burning. It hurts, and I can't help moving.

'Ow!' I shout.

The man tells me again to keep still. He pushes a metal thing through my ear.

A trickle of blood runs down my neck. It doesn't hurt as much as when Richie stuck a red-hot poker on my leg but I can't help shouting, 'Ow!' again.

The man takes the thing from my ear and mops the blood with cotton wool.

He moves round to the other side of my head and does the same thing to my other ear. I don't cry out this time, because I don't want to make him cross. Then he takes out two golden rings from a little tray. He puts one in each ear, mops the blood again and washes his hands.

I'm not looking at my mother's face, but I see her give some money to the man. I'm not crying, because it doesn't hurt now, it just feels funny.

As we walk back to Tufnell Park Road, I ask her if that was the surprise, and she says, 'Yes.' She's smiling.

There's a funny, sweet smell of bath cubes and talcum powder that sticks to my mother's skin; I try to sniff it as we're walking along. It's nicer than the Wrights Coal

Tar Soap Mum uses to wash us. I don't think it's really got coal or tar in it because it's bright yellow. I don't like it at all, especially when Mum makes me use it in the toilet.

Three months later

Mum sits on her couch, and Mother stands by the fireplace. Her face is sad and angry at the same time.

Mother sees I'm not wearing the gold earrings she gave me as a surprise, and she'll be upset about that because that's the only present she's ever given me. She wanted to make my ears look nice. But I had to go to the doctor because there was yellow stuff coming out of the little holes in both my ears and the doctor said that was bad, he said that my ears had been poisoned because the earrings weren't made of real gold. That's why I'm not allowed to wear them any more.

My mother asks me if I want to go on a journey with her. I say I don't know. When I look at Mum, her eyes are watering.

'Your mother wants to take you to Nigeria,' says Mum.

'Do you mean for ever?' I ask Mum.

I'm not exactly sure how you get to Nigeria, but I know it's in Africa and that's across the sea.

We learn about other countries at school in our geography lessons.

Our teacher points at a pink blob on the map of the world. 'This country is called Nigeria and it belongs to the Queen of England. It's where cocoa beans come from, and they're made into chocolate,' the teacher says, all the time looking at me.

Mother says, 'Yes, Lola. I'm going on a big ship on a long journey across the sea to another city just like London, called Lagos.'

My mother, Nigeria . . . I don't know. There are things I don't like about living in Tufnell Park Road: like when Mum tells me off. And I hated it when Richie burned my leg. And when he uses me as a punch bag to practise his boxing. And when Mum and Evelyn shout at each other when they're having a row.

The good things that I like about living with Mum are when I go to school and see my friends, Sarah Westwood and Robert Green; when Richie teaches me a new card game; when we have fish and chips on Friday night, and suet pudding and treacle for Sunday lunch; I like it when Lynne's boyfriend comes round and tells us jokes and what it's like to fly in an aeroplane.

I don't want to go to another country with my mother, but Mum says it's not nice to say words that are hurtful to people, but maybe it's not so bad if you just think them and keep quiet. I don't want to go to Nigeria because I don't know if I like my real mother. Does that mean I'm not a nice person?

Mum's sniffing and pointing her chin up to the ceiling, as if there's something really interesting up there. Then she stares at the Toby jugs with their ugly old men's faces, and her eyes are all wet. And she's stroking Trixie the cat really hard, making tracks in the thick fur from her neck all the way down along her back to the end of her fluffy tail.

Mother tells me that I'll be happy when I go with her, back to her home. 'Come with me, and see all your aunties and uncles. They are very excited, waiting to see you,' she says.

I'm trying to think about what she's saying, about going with her.

My mother hasn't told us where her home in London is. Why doesn't she take me there to live with her? Mothers and fathers are supposed to look after their babies until they grow up, unless they die and go to heaven, then a kind aunty or uncle looks after their children, and they're called orphans.

I don't want to leave Mum, and all the friends I have at school. I wish that Mum would stop stroking Trixie so hard.

'I want to stay here,' I say. Mother doesn't say anything, so maybe she doesn't mind if I don't go with her on the ship after all.

Mum lifts her glasses and rubs her eyes with her crooked, knobbly fingers. She gets out a handkerchief and blows her big nose on it.

I sit down next to Mum and tickle the cat's tummy.

Now Mother is sitting in the armchair, staring into the fireplace. The fire is nearly out, I'll have to put more coal on it soon. I look at my mother's face and try to memorize her eyes, nose and mouth for the next time I see her.

Then she's gone.

'Don't worry, Lulla, she'll be back one day,' Mum says.

Three: Love is conditional

September 1958: Mother returned to Africa.

10 September 1958: Father (married man) called to see child and left a box of chocolates.

Almost five years had elapsed between that first, revelatory phone call with Sal, and the email from Islington Council in August 2011 confirming they'd received my application for access to my records. My ambivalence about delving into my past had stalled me from taking action, but I had finally acknowledged to myself that if I didn't engage fully in the hunt, I would be creating a fiction: pretending that my past no longer mattered to me.

A huge 'what if...' was waiting, ready to jump out from those notes should they ever end up in my possession. What if my search produced something terrifying – something that would suspend gravity and leave me unmoored? What if I'd misremembered everything? No matter that Kayin could corroborate much of what I recalled at Tufnell Park Road, and that some of the impact of my experiences had been observed by my friends.

While these fears remained, I was now determined to get through the process quickly. Get it over and done with, and prepare to deal with the consequences. I responded within the hour. About a month later, on 1 September, I received another email.

> Dear Ms Young,
> Unfortunately our archivist is experiencing some difficulty in locating files relating to you. I wonder if you know of any other names that you or your parents may have been known as? I have asked her to check again under the surname Vince as you mentioned that you were under the care of a Mrs Vince for a number of years.
>
> Any other information which you feel might be relevant would be very welcome.
>
> Kind regards,
> Access to Records Officer Children's Social Care
> Islington Council

I supplied all the information I could dredge up – as many names as I could remember. Daisy and her family, Lynne and Richie, Miss Boardman the welfare officer, and of course Kayin.

In those intervening five years, my work as a member of the Lords had also intensified. In 2009, I'd worked with Anti-Slavery International and Liberty to criminalize domestic servitude and forced labour in the UK. One of the aims of the campaign had been to convince the then Labour government that there was a need for a new law now as we began to realize the extent to which abusive, exploitative labour was a reality in twenty-first-century Britain.

While reviewing the evidence and meeting with survivors, I also came to understand how being a member of the House of Lords enabled me to highlight key issues and propose legislative and policy solutions. My perspective was informed by a blend of my experience of childhood vulnerability, which gave me personal knowledge of financial and emotional precarity, and my academic background, which had taught me to identify when and how words, historical references and images combine to normalize assumptions and prejudices. The narratives that emerge from such assumptions can fuel bad policy-making, and undermine effective policy frameworks. I learned how to work with fellow parliamentarians, even if I didn't agree with some of their political positions. With the power of the House of Lords to convene and galvanize key stakeholders, I figured out that I had a unique opportunity to effect positive change.

I relished the challenge of working with charities, campaigning organizations, businesses and individuals with lived experience, and was invited to chair inquiries into a range of social issues. Although the subject matter wasn't always directly focused on the care system, the consequences of our society's failure to address the inadequacies of how we care for our young people were never far away. Whether examining the over-representation of young Black and/or Muslim men in the criminal justice system, or investigating the causes of poor outcomes for vulnerable girls and women, many of the people concerned had had multiple encounters with the care system in one way or another. Disproportionate numbers of former and current care experienced individuals and families appear in the troubling data of mental health and homelessness services, as well as the criminal justice system – providing clear evidence of systemic failures.

Listening to survivors' testimonies during this period, I would sometimes feel drained of energy as the sense of responsibility for trying to bring about change weighed heavily on me. Since then, I've tried to strengthen my mental and emotional core by being disciplined about preparing for these difficult encounters, making a big effort to understand and gauge the potential unintended consequences of policies and legislation. Those with lived experience should be at the centre of policies intended to improve their circumstances, and have a platform from which to speak themselves.

I knew that the uncertainty surrounding the search for my files was another factor in feeling hollowed out emotionally. It was another two months before I prompted Islington Council for an update on their search.

The response from Islington, received on 17 November, was swift, though not encouraging.

> Dear Ms Young,
> Thank you for your email, and my sincere apologies that I haven't chased this up since. I was waiting for

advice from our senior archivist for any other routes which may be helpful.

We certainly don't seem to be able to locate files relating to you in our archive. However, it may be an idea for you to contact the local authorities where the two Children's Homes in [. . .] and [. . .] were located in case any care responsibilities were shared with them.

I'm afraid the only other option that I can think of is for us to read through your cousin [. . .]'s files. As you were both in care together at one point, there is a small chance that there may be some information relating to you contained on her file. I imagine that this will not be much consolation, as you were expecting to find far more information, and again I can only apologize that we are unable to provide that for you.

I have attached some information about an organization offering support around Access to Records and information about your rights should you be dissatisfied with the service.

If you'd like to discuss this further, or if you'd like me to obtain and read through your cousin's file, please let me know.

Kind regards,
Access to Records Officer Children's Social Care
Islington Council

Kayin's files? She had never even been in the care system – she'd been privately fostered. I didn't see how there could be any notes relating specifically to her. And there was no way that I was going to waste time trying to track down the children's departments from Middlesex County Council, or from Hertfordshire County Council. Their records would have been in the London Metropolitan Archives, and I'd already tried emailing them to find out if they held the relevant records, with no success. Islington Council may have lost their institutional memory about how they'd dealt with the children in their care; I hadn't. Those homes in Middlesex and Hertfordshire had been owned and administered by Islington. And I'd already found out for myself about the Care Leavers' Association and emailed them for advice, which was to pursue Islington. All in all, very disappointing. They were, after all, meant to be the repository for the official records of thousands of children and young people. The image of the leaking washing machine that Sal had told me about resurfaced to remind me that there might be nothing to find.

All I had were distant memories.

This is how I remember encounters with my mother: three or four times over the course of seven years, a stranger – a spectral being, without facial features – came to see me. She liked to take me out, so we would walk up Tufnell Park Road. She clutched my hand as I urged my five- or six- or seven-year-old legs to keep up with her long stride. Other than the day she took me to have my ears pierced, I'm not sure where we went on those excursions or how we spent our time together.

And then there was the day my mother asked me to go with her to Lagos.

When she returned to Nigeria, in 1958, with a suitcase and no child – that is, without me – did anyone ask her about the missing daughter? After all, she'd written home about her pregnancy, according to a distant relative. The ghost of the small girl, last seen at seven years old, must surely have preoccupied my mother for some while after the long sea voyage home.

The scraps of information I'd received just after I entered the House of Lords weren't enough to put a coherent story together: how was I to find enough pieces of the puzzle to understand what had happened to her before and during her pregnancy, and after giving birth to her first and only daughter? It was an odd feeling, the idea that I knew more of the life stories of the strangers I met who were survivors of trafficking, or domestic abuse, than I did my own mother's. Yet I believe that it was not knowing about my mother, and the experiences I had after she left London, that enabled me to understand a little of the loss that survivors felt.

Before I received the email from Islington Children's Services in November 2011, I was already beginning to think the search would be fruitless. Like the mysterious package I'd received five years earlier, the promise of fresh information about my parents and my early years was both distant and tantalizingly close.

There was only one person who had shared the experience of being fostered with Daisy Vince and who was able to confirm some of what I remembered from those days in Tufnell Park: Kayin Taylor. We have always kept in contact, though on occasion a year might pass between meeting up.

I was told when she arrived that Kayin was the daughter of a cousin of my mother's. Whereas the council paid for Lynne and Richie's upkeep, Kayin's parents made regular payments to Daisy for her. Neither of my parents did – I knew as much from Daisy – so there was no financial incentive for Daisy to keep me. Richie was in and out of Daisy's home, taken to a Fegan's institution for young people in Stony Stratford, only for him to run away back to Tufnell Park Road on several occasions, sometimes with a fellow escapee. I often fretted over my situation, wondering if it would be my turn next to be shipped off: I had no idea where Stony Stratford was, but the name alone sounded terrible, and hard-hearted.

That feeling of being on the verge of being sent away was particularly acute when Daisy gave me a really bad telling-off. There are two occasions I remember in particular.

One morning, Evelyn, Daisy's biological daughter, had harangued me about something or other. She didn't like me, I was certain of it, and as Kayin and I sat on the stairs that day, I said as much to her. I can't be sure whether she fully understood what I was talking about – she was only about six years old at the time – but she knew who I was referring to.

'I hope she dies,' I said, and Kayin agreed.

How were we to know that just at that moment 'she' was coming downstairs to hang her washing in the garden and overheard us chatting?

Evelyn tore into our scullery and we heard her shouting at Daisy, saying she shouldn't have to put up with children like us in her own home. I couldn't hear what was said but the angry tones had a familiar rhythm to them: Evelyn shouting and Daisy responding angrily, but in a low voice.

There were times when it seemed that Daisy and Evelyn were only able to communicate through arguing with each other. Sometimes they wouldn't speak to each other for days, weeks even, after the initial dispute. I didn't like it, finding it unsettling. I might have had a vague idea that their arguments were often something to do with me, but I had no insight into why Evelyn might resent me so much. After all, she was always generous towards both Kayin and me when it came to Christmas and birthday presents.

If I thought that Daisy might have been sticking up for me on that particular day, and that it meant I was going to avoid a severe scolding, I was mistaken. After Evelyn returned to her flat upstairs, the familiar refrain of 'I've only got my widow's pension' rained down on me. I was sure my time was finally up. I'd be sent away. Like Richie. Needless to say, Kayin escaped a telling-off, but I had to concede she'd barely participated in the damning conversation.

The other occasion that left me distraught, and fearing for my future, I can recall in striking detail.

My black school shoes were all the proof Daisy needed.

The last time it had happened, she'd said I mustn't do it again. That afternoon, my badly scuffed black leather lace-ups were evidence of my disobedience: fed up with playing a witch with the girls, I'd played football with the boys during lunchtime. It wasn't such a bad thing to do, was it, kicking a ball around?

Daisy was angry on two counts. First, girls weren't allowed to play football in the playground or in the park – or anywhere, as far as I could see – and second, because she really did have very little money, and I was well aware that neither of my parents made any significant contribution to my upkeep. She said it was already bad enough because now, at eleven years old, I was growing so quickly and always needing new clothes – and what had I been thinking of, ruining my shoes by kicking a ball around with the boys?

Daisy kept on and on, going over the same old ground, about money problems. There came a point when I no longer heard individual words, just an angry voice, like when she was arguing with Evelyn. My nose was running – how I hated that sticky cascade of snot! And I couldn't stop crying. By the time she'd finished, I'd started hiccoughing and I walked slowly towards the front door. I opened it, thinking I should run away before I was sent away. I stood there for ages, my runny nose making one of our improvised handkerchiefs – made from scraps of an old sheet – damp and sticky. But when I looked out of the door, I shrank into myself, scared of the encroaching darkness, unable to think of anywhere to run away to. Instead, Daisy packed me off to bed early as punishment for my transgressions. The hiccoughs and runny nose had gone, but the feeling that Daisy – and Evelyn – were close to having had enough of me lingered for days afterwards.

Kayin's mother was a midwife, working at what was then the Royal Northern Hospital on Holloway Road, and I was in awe of her. Mrs Taylor's distinctiveness in a grey world intrigued me. She seemed to shimmer and glow, with her make-up and carefully dressed hair. Her voice, her laugh, her gestures – all seemed to come from somewhere different to everyone else. The only other regular visitor to Tufnell Park Road was the child welfare officer, Miss Boardman – but she was white, like everyone else we saw. There had been one other Black mother who came to see her child, a boy Kayin and I nicknamed Smelly Melly due to his foul-smelling nappies, but Daisy was his childminder rather than foster mother, and it was a short-term arrangement. We lived in a white world at home and at school, so Kayin's mother was different in so many striking ways from the seven or so adults who populated our daily lives.

Daisy may not have aligned herself to any specific political party, but she enjoyed reading the newspaper every day and would sometimes make a political statement along the lines of pensions being too low or bemoaning the high price of beef. She would rarely discuss with me the articles she read and, as far as I can remember, she never commented on racial issues, but she did help crystallize one thing for me. I'd joined the Brownies at the age of seven and had been unable to understand why the white girls who'd joined much later than me had completed their full enrolment into the charmed circle of the Second Tufnell Park Brownies Group almost straight away.

Each time I came home after a session led by Brown Owl, Daisy asked me if I'd finally been enrolled, and each time I said no. When she said they were delaying because I was 'coloured', the pieces of an ugly picture slotted into place for me.

That Brown Owl hadn't liked me, I'd already guessed, and now Daisy's observation cleared up why that might be so, but it created another problem at the same time. If Brown Owl's dislike of me was grounded in hatred of my skin colour, what was I to do? This skin was mine: it was who I was, and it never occurred to me that I should want it to be otherwise, in spite of the racist taunts I endured.

So perhaps it's no surprise that whenever I saw Kayin's mother, my secret thought was that we could have been mother and daughter. But it wasn't just that she was Black and from Nigeria like my mother. And it wasn't because they looked alike – after a couple of years' absence, I'd have been hard put to identify my actual mother in a group photograph of other Black women. It was my longing for a proper mother and father, which if not quite projected on to Kayin's parents was amplified by their presence in Kayin's life. I found it hard to accept that Kayin's mother visited her, took her out and paid Daisy on a regular basis. Neither Daisy nor Evelyn ever had cause to complain about Kayin's parents.

It's not easy to explain, even to myself, the nature of my various longings – what I wanted from any of the adults around me. I wondered about many aspects of my life: I wondered why my 'mum' was an elderly white woman. I also wondered how it was that, unlike me, my school friends appeared to be treated as though they were special by their parents, their aunts and uncles. On the surface, Kayin seemed to be in a similar situation to me, except that her mother would visit once a month. After they moved into their own house in Drayton Park, Kayin's parents would have her to stay the weekend with them two or three times a year. Although at least once I went with Kayin to her parents' flat in Chalk Farm, I don't ever recall being invited to stay for the weekend.

Perhaps I couldn't have articulated it at the time but, looking back, I think I always knew my life at Tufnell Park Road with Daisy couldn't last for ever, and unlike the other children I knew, I had no prospect of a secure future. I had the idea that every child in the entire world outside of Tufnell Park Road – and the home for bad kids in Stony Stratford – had a happy, 'normal' childhood.

In the mid-1950s it wasn't unusual to come across an unattended baby soaking up the sun outside in one of those prams that resembled a Roman chariot. There was one I saw often on the route I walked to and from primary school. Sometimes the baby would be gurgling, sometimes snuffling while asleep. I didn't know the family but, if no one else was around, I would stop and stare at the child. I wondered at the carelessness of it; any passing stranger could run off with the lone infant, never to be seen again. I was catastrophizing before the word had been created. In spite of the way the baby had been left on its own, I felt jealous because I was sure that it was loved in a way that was alien to me.

Thinking about that little child basking in the sunshine reminded me of a baby who had been brought to Daisy to be cared for when I was around the age of eight or nine. I could see that he was a perfect candidate for adoption – six months old, a boy, with light blond curls and blue eyes. Daisy was looking after him while the council searched for potential parents. She said that if she'd been younger, she would have adopted him herself.

I would take this baby out on my own to do the shopping or collect our wash bag from Westerns Laundry in Campdale Road. This involved crossing main roads and manoeuvring a pushchair almost as tall as me. None of the adults around me seemed to find it remarkable or think I was too young for such a responsibility.

Leaving babies outside in their prams – and me doing the shopping with a six-month-old baby in tow – was just what happened. Were people more relaxed about safeguarding their children back then? I remember an occasion when Daisy was approached by a young man who claimed to be making a film about the 'brotherhood of man' or some such theme, and he wanted me to be in it. I must have been about seven or eight at the time. The filming was taking place about a mile or so away, in Waterlow Park, and there would be bubbles and balloons. Daisy waved me off as I clambered into his van. Perhaps she trusted him because we went to the same park for a picnic so often that she couldn't imagine me being in any kind of danger there. Returned unharmed, I sensed she had been in a state of high anxiety once she realized she'd let me go off with a complete stranger.

It didn't happen that often, but it was exciting when it did. Kayin's mum would come to take us out for the day. I remember one particular afternoon when we were all going to the funfair on Hampstead Heath. Not Daisy, of course – just me, Kayin and her mum.

We heard the noises before we saw where they were coming from. Incomprehensible shouts, screams and squeals, music that sounded like a circus had come to town. There was a ghost train, of course, and a hall of mirrors that pulled your body into fantastical shapes and made you look long and very thin, or short and very fat, plus a merry-go-round and rides, and sideshows where you could win a teddy bear.

We walked around for a while before Kayin's mum took us over to a bingo stall. She gave me a shilling for us to spend while she played the game with other customers. She sat down on a stool at the counter, focusing on the numbered card in front of her.

Kayin and I have retold this story between us countless times. Sometimes our memories play tricks on us, bringing out a fresh detail or reviewing a fact that it turns out couldn't have been true.

Whenever we speak of the events of that day, our reminiscences are punctuated with laughter, though we weren't laughing at the time. I thought I'd been about eleven years old at the funfair, but Kayin was sure I was only nine, which would have made her just five years old. I know I did feel responsible for her, and if I had been eleven, and Kayin seven, the situation would have felt quite different.

We left Kayin's mother vying for the big prize, having agreed we'd go on a ride, then meet her back at the counter where she sat.

There was a huge wooden ride with several rows of seats, facing each other; it was filling up with adults and teenagers. There were no other young children on their own like us, as far as I could see, and perhaps this should have been a warning signal to my nine-year-old self. I held Kayin's hand very tight, so we didn't get split up, and I checked that I could see Kayin's mum sitting on the stool. She was still there; I could see her bright dress with orange and yellow flowers on it.

The man in charge of the ride took the money from me and asked whether we were by ourselves or with an adult. I don't remember responding but I do recall him taking our money without hesitation. The man told everyone that this was the most thrilling journey any of us would ever have.

The Swinging Yacht. It was like a giant cradle with rows and rows of seats. We sat facing the people in the other half of the 'boat', which hung on giant poles attached to a large metal frame.

Kayin distinctly remembers the man working the machinery saying there was no need to be scared, we would all be fine. But when the yacht began to swing backwards and forwards, Kayin and I screamed. The higher we swung, the more we screamed. Higher and higher the unstoppable monster went. We swung one way, we rushed downwards, expecting to be flung to the ground and killed. In the other direction we went, going up, up to the sky, pinned back in our seats. We went backwards and forwards like this, over and over again. We screamed and screamed and cried and begged the man to make the ride stop.

But he just laughed and said, 'Don't worry, it won't fall, and neither will you . . .'

When the ride finally came to a halt, I knew I'd never go on another fairground ride again in my life. Or a boat.

'Told you you wouldn't fall!' the man said, laughing.

Kayin remembers that last comment vividly too, filling in what I'd forgotten.

Our throats were sore from screaming. We made our way to the bingo stall, only to have to face another, different horror. Kayin's mum wasn't there.

Where was the flowery dress with its bright colours that had been so easy to see before?

I tried to keep calm, and held Kayin's hand more tightly.

We were well aware that we shouldn't talk to strangers, and Daisy had told us that if we ever got lost we should ask a policeman to show us the way home. But there weren't any around that I could see.

We went round and round in circles, looking out for that bright summery dress among the grey of our surroundings. Until I decided we were wasting our time. We would just have to make our own way back to Tufnell Park Road. I was worried, but I thought we couldn't be all that far away – Daisy had taken us to Parliament Hill Fields, which were adjacent to the Heath, many times.

Somewhere in the back of my mind it was Kayin's mum's fault that this had happened, but I also wondered if making our own way home was the right thing to do. My courage only lasted so long. I was acutely aware of my responsibility for the little girl by my side.

We passed Parliament Hill Lido, having left the fields of Hampstead Heath behind, and crossed a main road.

We walked on our tired legs for what felt like hours, and I still had no idea where we were. We were hopelessly lost, and I could feel myself beginning to panic. I thought again how we had often been told we shouldn't speak to strangers, but then there was a man walking towards us, and he looked kind enough. What made me feel I could trust him? Desperation. We'd been wandering around for a long time, and I knew Kayin's mum would have realized by now that we had somehow missed each other.

I asked the man with the kind face for directions to Tufnell Park Road. It was a long way for little girls to walk, he said, and quite unexpectedly he gave me sixpence to buy some sweets from a shop down the road. He took us there, and I thanked him, and then, chewing our Toff-o-Luxe, I followed the directions he'd given us.

Kayin and I have often discussed the kindness of that stranger. For all children, the ways of adults are mysterious, and Kayin and I had been subject to the vagaries of grown-ups who had disrupted both our short lives. What he did that day was such a small gesture, and of course we have no idea about his character outside that one meeting, but when we recollect the vulnerability of our position as Black children, lost and on our own, during the 1950s – a time of racist slogans and graffiti, being called names in the street and in shops – that man's small act seemed significant to us somehow.

I was relieved – as much for Daisy as for us – that we weren't all that far away from home. Even that young, I felt some responsibility for Daisy's well-being. I knew that if Kayin's mum got to Daisy before we did, Daisy would be very anxious for our safety. Evelyn often reminded me of her mother's age and that I should be helping out with household chores and shopping, especially since there was no regular payment coming in for my upkeep. In fact, I had already taken on many of those tasks, and didn't need reminding of Daisy's increasing frailty.

When we reached the junction of Lady Somerset and Fortess Road, I recognized where we were. Undaunted by having to navigate the complicated coming together of five main thoroughfares, we skipped across the zebra crossing on Brecknock Road, past the hut outside Tufnell Park tube station, where my classmate Bryan Hardy helped his father sell newspapers. On familiar ground now, we ran down Tufnell Park Road, all the tiredness gone from our legs, and we were home. The possibilities of what could have happened to us that day were not hard to imagine.

Over the years I became convinced that Daisy had been cross with us at the time, as well as being angry with Kayin's mum for letting us out of her sight. In my mind's eye, I could see her display the testiness that came with concern. But Kayin remembers otherwise. She distinctly recalls Daisy suggesting I should write a story about our adventure called 'The Day We Got Lost on Hampstead Heath'. I would have been pleased about that, I'm sure – to be recognized as a budding writer.

As we moved into winter 2011, I was still waiting for news of my care records. In the absence of any official documentation, I'd organized a memory walk with Kayin, and we traipsed around our old neighbourhood, recalling our day at the fair, trying to weave other snippets from our memories into a seamless narrative.

One of the mysteries I was hoping to solve once I got hold of my records was that of Daisy's motivation for looking after so many children for decades. Perhaps she'd experienced something in her childhood that had led her to empathize with children whose parents had let them down. I didn't know the answer to that question, and neither did Kayin. It's too easy to speculate, to make judgements based on little knowledge, and I didn't want to fall into that trap.

As we approached the large house we had lived in for so long, we spoke again about the mystery of Daisy's background. We realized how little we knew, and resolved to try and find out more, though how we'd do that we had no idea.

We walked 'the railway way' from Junction Road to Tufnell Park Road, noting the changes to the shops, the new flats and so on. Kayin reminded me how our neighbours – not the Hunters, but the family on the other, Huddleston Road side of our house – reacted when Daisy told them that I'd passed the 11 Plus. These neighbours were brown-skinned, not from Africa or the Caribbean, but from Mauritius. Daisy had been proud of my exam success and told them how smart I was. Our neighbour told us that her daughter had passed too, and implied there was nothing exceptional about being a high academic achiever in their household.

The remark didn't dent Daisy's pride in my achievement, which makes me wonder now why I'd always been convinced that Daisy didn't really like me. Or perhaps that's not quite right. The truth was I could see no reason why Daisy should like me or wish to stand up for the child whose parents had slipped quietly out of our lives.

My best friend, Sarah Westwood, also passed the exam and accepted a place at Camden Grammar School for Girls, while I chose Parliament Hill Comprehensive School. I must have been reading about the attempt to shift to a more egalitarian education system, exemplified by comprehensives, when we were looking at secondary school choices. Comprehensives were still a relatively new development in 1962, and I had been quite clear about not wanting to go to what I saw as a snobby grammar school.

Shortly after we started at our new schools, Sarah and her parents invited me to her birthday outing to see the musical *Oliver!* in the West End. I had always liked Sarah's mum and dad; I remembered them both as warm and friendly, and generous towards me too. Though going to the theatre was a treat, and I loved the songs, the music, the tragedy and the comedy of the show, I knew it was the end of my friendship with Sarah. In the company of her new classmates, I felt ill at ease, conscious that I was from somewhere else. I could see we had very different experiences of the world through the way these other girls talked, the clothes they wore, their self-confidence already firmly embedded in their personalities.

I'd lost my friend and her family when I opted to go

to Parliament Hill School, and I sensed that I was unlikely ever to see Sarah again.

Throughout my early childhood, Daisy made attempts to explain my situation to me: the reasons why I lived with her, rather than with either of my parents. She told me that my father was married to Joan, and they lived in a flat in Streatham, south London. They had a daughter whose name was Shade – pronounced Sha-day – who was two years older than me. So, Shade was my half-sister, our shared father binding us. I hadn't known what to make of the idea of a newly acquired sister.

Daisy's explanations had gone over my head for the most part, it had all been too complicated. My birth mother, Yele Santos, had left for Lagos in 1958, with Daisy claiming the separation from my father was the consequence of arguments between them, and that they'd divorced. That had been the reason why my mother returned to Lagos on her own. It's fortunate for Daisy that I was ignorant in these matters, as the timings – of Shade's birth, my birth, my parents' 'marriage' and 'divorce', and my father's marriage to Joan – didn't quite work. My younger self was unable to do the maths, and I accepted what she said at face value. Though for most of my life I never had a photograph of either parent, when I conjured up images of my father, it was easier to fill in his features than my mother's. As my mother had done, my father would appear sporadically to take me out for walks. But what we talked about, or where we went, I can't remember. In fact, although I'm sure he came to Tufnell Park Road four or five times before returning to Lagos, I can only really remember two of his visits. I must have crammed every tiny scrap of visual information about him I'd ever had, or imagined I had, into these memories.

I remember a man, a stranger, who was cold as ice. A tall, thin, dark brown iceman who wore a grey overcoat and a checked neck scarf, which he kept on all the time, even though a roaring coal fire radiated warmth to every corner of the living room. Somehow he filled the space with his presence, trying to assert his authority where it wasn't wanted. There we sat – Daisy, me and him – in the front room at Tufnell Park Road, exchanging a minimum of words.

So it was a great surprise when he announced he was taking me to my interview with the head teacher at Parliament Hill School. After we'd walked there, as we looked around the gym and the classrooms, he issued his orders: 'Stand up straight!' 'Walk like this!' 'Don't speak like that!' He held my hand at arm's length, as though he wanted to keep his distance, as if I might have an infectious disease. And yet when we were in the headmistress's office he spoke about me as though he was a real father, someone who saw me every day. Someone who knew me.

I wished that Daisy had accompanied me to my new school, even though that would have raised eyebrows, as teachers would have struggled to understand the relationship between the elderly white woman and me. My father knew nothing about my life, my hobbies, my health or favourite subjects, and he had no real answers to the questions posed by the teachers. I can only speculate about why he decided to take an active role in my life for once. Perhaps it was his way of demonstrating that he had some control over me, or maybe he wanted Daisy to know he could fulfil his parental role when necessary. My memory of his demeanour that day is of a man at ease in the situation, without any apparent embarrassment about his lack of knowledge about his daughter.

I had an inauspicious start to life at Parliament Hill School in the autumn of 1962.

The flooring of Morant Hall in Parly Hill's Old Building was dark wood. On this cool, wet autumn day, the smell of damp clothing mingled with floor polish.

'Lola! Lola, over here!' Linda from my old primary school was calling me to join her. I walked towards where she and other girls I didn't know were sitting. Halfway across the huge hall, I slipped, skidded across the floor and fell on my backside. I felt the whole of the new first year burst out laughing.

Feeling graceless and stupid, I laughed too.

Despite my clumsy entrance, I quickly settled into life at Parliament Hill. The walk from Tufnell Park Road was easy enough at first, but when Acland Burghley School was rebuilt, my route took me past the entrance every day, at about the same time as their school day ended. That's when my walk home took on a different flavour and on many occasions I was subjected to racial abuse. I tried to avoid passing the groups of boys amassed outside their brutalist concrete building but I didn't always have the energy to take a more circuitous route home. Our distinctive uniform of grey velour bowler hat, purple blazer and grey skirt made us prone to ridicule and abuse as well.

Our school backed on to Parliament Hill Fields and Hampstead Heath, though we were in any case well stocked with open spaces within the school's perimeter: we had the use of several tennis courts, the standard asphalt playground decorated with a rose arbour, and grassy banks.

I'm not one for rose-tinted spectacles or manufactured nostalgia, but one evening when I was still hunting down my care notes, Anne, one of my old school friends, and I did have fun going back over some edited highlights of our years at secondary school.

I remember making friends with Anne Kauder quite early on in our Parly Hill careers: we shared a liking for sport and soul music, and both of us had a streak of mischievousness mixed with a sense of humour in our personalities.

On that balmy evening in 2011, as we reminisced, Anne recalled that we were generally well behaved in the classes taken by our more formidable female teachers. We may have cowered under the steely glare of our English teacher, Miss Ross, for example, but we had no qualms giving poor old Miss Medway a torrid time during her geography lessons.

The two teachers were very different in appearance, the contrast of their generational styles stark. Miss Ross was in tune with the mood of young people in what was about to become the Swinging Sixties. This was evident in her deliberately restricted palette of beatnik black and dark grey pencil skirts and baggy black polo-necked jumpers. Miss Medway, on the other hand, favoured box-pleated, calf-length tweed skirts, cream-coloured crinkly blouses and moss-green round or V-necked cardigans.

Miss Medway's thick-lensed glasses with their pale rims sat unobtrusively on her nose, the colour merging with her pink-white skin tone, while Miss Ross's spectacles announced themselves loudly, their emphatic black rims set against the thick, light beige foundation covering her face.

Miss Medway was a gentle woman, powerless in the face of our mischief, especially on the days when Anne initiated an exploration of the classroom on our hands and knees. I suppose it was vaguely appropriate for a geography lesson, as our activity consisted of any number of us crawling on all fours 'exploring' between desks, while Miss Medway droned on about how rubber was tapped in the country we now call Malaysia. Glad of the distraction, I joined Anne and the others making their way around the classroom, like lab mice navigating a maze. (The time I spent on this activity instead of concentrating on what Miss Medway was saying had a knock-on effect when it came to my failure to grasp the simplest geographical concepts. In an exam paper I explained that when it was winter in the northern hemisphere, it was winter everywhere. It was just that south of the equator they had really warm winters.)

We would never have pulled a stunt like that on Miss

Ross, who had once shut my fingers in the classroom door in an attempt to stop me from leaving. Nor was it unusual for her to throw chalk at us for the smallest transgressions, while Miss Medway could only manage to throw us despairing glances.

Anne was always thinking of ways to create a bit of mayhem in the classroom. In maths she demonstrated her leadership qualities early on, and with devastating impact.

The early sixties television sitcom *The Rag Trade* had been very popular. Paddy, played by Miriam Karlin, was the female shop steward and union rep in the clothes factory where the programme was set. When the factory owners upset the workers, Paddy blew a whistle and shouted, 'Everybody out!' That was the signal for the women who made the clothes to leave their sewing machines and go on strike. Anne loved the show as much as the rest of us, and one afternoon, while we waited for Mr Potter to take our maths class, she took it on herself to organize us.

We were supposed to stand up when a teacher came into the classroom as a sign of respect. But on this particular day, Anne had other ideas. She told us that when Mr Potter entered the classroom, Jo had agreed to blow a whistle, after which Anne would shout, 'Everybody out!' and we'd all put our chairs on our desks and sit on the floor. I couldn't believe it. It was an audacious plan to propose in a school that prided itself on its serious, academic and respectful culture, but we all agreed to take Anne's lead anyway.

It could have been that Anne's parents' activism had rubbed off on her, transmuting at that time into a relatively mild act of rebellion in the classroom. But it wasn't as if we had a specific political motivation for our actions: we were only in the first year of our secondary school careers.

Whatever the impetus, the minute Mr Potter walked through the door into the classroom, Jo blew the whistle and Anne gave the order. We put our chairs on our desks and sat on the floor. Rather than shouting at us, Mr Potter's cheeks went very red, drawing even more attention to his large, protruding ears, which remained resolutely white. He was the only male teacher in the whole school and was perhaps a little scared of the thirty-two girls sitting down in protest before him, albeit amiably. As with my geography lessons, I really should have been paying more attention to my studies, as this was another subject that made little sense to me, and a few years later, I would find myself unable to muster a GCE O level in the subject.

I liked so many girls in my class, it was a joy to be with them in lessons and during breaks. It was so different to primary school. I know that many children find the transition from primary to secondary school difficult, but I preferred the anonymity of the over 1,000 girls who attended Parly Hill. It may seem contradictory, because I did stand out as one of only a few Black girls there, and I drew some unpleasant comments from both girls and teachers as a result. But my fondness for those girls in my class was reciprocated. I was delighted, for example, to share the fantasy of creating a pop group together with a classmate. I hadn't been able to compose music but I could write words to fit the tunes in my head:

> You'd better save your love, boy,
> For someone new.
> You'd better save your love, boy,
> Because I don't want you
> To give your love, boy,
> To me . . .

All the pop groups at the time were boys, but we thought we should form a band anyway. It never occurred to me that there might be musical talent in my family – otherwise I might have made the effort to learn the piano or the guitar, so that I could write the music in my head as well as the lyrics. It wasn't until many, many years later that I learned my father had played the trumpet in his youth.

While I had a hankering to perform, there were also many times when I yearned to be invisible: for example, during our primary school journey to Devon, where I was stared at by the locals for the whole week; or when sitting in class listening to a colonial adventurer talk about 'darkies' living in 'the jungle', all the time casting me sideways looks; or when a Parliament Hill science teacher explained that I was no good at science because I didn't understand English. Throughout my childhood in the 1950s and 60s, then on into the 70s and beyond, I hated being constantly 'seen' through racialized lenses.

These experiences, and many more, put me in the spotlight in an unwelcome way. I absorbed them all, just as I did the conviction that I must either be invisible to, or disliked by, my mother and my father.

Daisy Vince may have recognized the problem with Brown Owl but that didn't translate into a wider understanding of the dynamics of racism. She was left mildly outraged after a news broadcast on the civil rights movement in the USA – not something many people had grasped in this country in the 1960s. And yes, she'd misunderstood or perhaps misheard what they'd been chanting at a political rally, but it was the nature of the misperception that was telling.

As far as Daisy was concerned, she'd heard the activists shouting, 'White Man Must Go!' The reality was they were actually chanting, 'One Man, One Vote!' The fear embodied in Daisy's misidentification of what was actually being said upset me, and I tried in vain to explain to her how Black Americans had systematically been denied the right to vote. But my twelve-year-old self hadn't the words, the knowledge or the confidence to challenge the woman to whom I owed so much.

I didn't know it then, of course, but I'd been trying to counter centuries of rhetoric developed and honed during European colonialism and the British Empire, a rhetoric that had shaped British people's thinking about themselves and 'others'. Like so many people who had grown up during the rapid expansion of Britain's empire, Daisy had little knowledge of the far-reaching and enduring impact of British imperialism and global racism. The spreading of these ideas had been aided and abetted by films like *Sanders of the River*, which we watched on television often, in spite of my embarrassment at seeing images of Africans in grass skirts and speaking in broken English. My horizons had been expanded by my reading, whether that was literature about possible fantastical fictional worlds of the future, or the brutal reality of the USA in the twentieth century, described in books by James Baldwin and Richard Wright, among others. But I was only a child trying in vain to explain Jim Crow laws and apartheid. Mostly, what I knew came from what I'd seen on television news programmes and read in newspapers: Black people in South Africa and Black people in the USA being beaten and attacked by white people with faces contorted by anger, dogs set on them by the police.

Terry Andrews, my foster mother's grandson-in-law, voiced the thoughts of many from his generation brought up on Britain's enduring imperial fantasies. Terry would make comments that were so patently ludicrous that, even as a child, I remember being appalled at how people could be duped into believing such obvious untruths. There was no logic, and certainly no science, to the claims he and others like him made. He stated with complete confidence that the soles of Black people's feet and the palms of our hands were pale because we moved around on all fours in the 'jungle', and that Africans chewed their food in front of their teeth (don't ask me how), due to the shape of our mouths. The strange thing is there appeared to be no malice underpinning his remarks; I think he believed these assertions were simply statements of fact. Similar themes – the result of Britons' 'scientific knowledge' about racialized differences – had been evident when white nurses and midwives checked Black babies for tails in the 1950s.

Maybe I shared my unease about what I saw and heard, and how I experienced it, with the adults in my life; I don't remember doing so or, if I did, I can't recall getting any sort of response. But thanks to the local library, and to the library at Parliament Hill School, in the writing of the African American authors I read, I found an immediate connection to, and explication of, the destructive force of racism.

A memory: A visit from Father

1963: *twelve years old*

He's sitting on one of the easy chairs in our front room. His legs are crossed and stretched out in front of him, taking up space so no one can get past. I can't feel the warmth from the fire now because he's blocking it.

He's been to see me four times in twelve years. Does that sound like a father who's interested in my future? I don't think so.

He says to Mum, 'I'm going back to Nigeria.' Then he turns to me and says, 'You're to come with me.'

Mum says nothing, just looks at him.

I'm shocked. What does he mean?

'Mum? Do I have to go?'

Looking down at the floor, I catch sight of a shiny black beetle as it comes out from under the skirting board. I look at my father's feet. His long thin legs are crossed at the knee now, and one foot dangles in mid-air. His shoes are as black and shiny as the beetle's armour. What if the creature decides to go on an adventure, crawling across his shoe, gripping his sock, and on, up his leg –

'Lola, I'm talking to you.' My father makes a tutting

sound and looks across at Mum, his eyes blaming her for my bad manners.

I'm still thinking about the beetle. They are forever nipping out from the wall beside the fireplace. Mum says we should stamp on them.

My father's face is softer now, and he's smiling. 'We've had some good luck with reference to your travel costs: a family member has offered to pay for you,' he says, sounding pleased with himself.

He speaks like that, using words like 'reference' as if he's in a court of law. That's what he does now: he used to be a doctor but now he's a lawyer.

My mother came to our house, and in this same room said I should go to Lagos with her. That was more than five years ago and I've not heard from her since then. My father's words make me think they're both the same — trying to make me choose, so I take the blame if anything goes wrong. In my mind, I shout at him, *You don't mean it. I know you have a daughter you care about and it isn't me.*

I want to stay with Mum in the place I know, with the friends I've made in my new school.

There are bad things that happen in this country that I don't speak to Mum about. There's the name-calling, and the horrible things about coloured people that get painted on the walls. Those things upset me. But what if I go to Lagos and everyone there hates me because I'm from London, and I don't speak Nigerian, and I don't have any new clothes or nice hair like Shade? Everyone will know Shade's mother isn't my mother. What if I turn up in Lagos and my mother treats me like a stranger?

'I want to stay here, with Mum,' I say.

There's a long silence. Mum hasn't said a word yet.

Can he force me to leave Mum and go with him and his family? I'd run away if he did. Or, if he does get me to Nigeria, I'll come back to London when I'm twenty-one and can do what I want.

Mum asks him for some money for my food and everything.

My father's voice brings me back to the present, claiming that he's 'already contributed funds towards her current uniform'.

That's the first I've heard of it. Although, like my mother used to, he slips me half a crown to spend when we go for a walk.

Mum says nothing. She knows I'm going nowhere with him.

Four: Recovery/discovery

1962: Talk of Lola going back to Nigeria with Father.

2 February 1962, ▮▮▮▮▮▮▮: All well. Margaret (called Lola) is sitting 11 Plus exam: HM [headmistress] at school says she is brilliant. School Care Committee phoned me for mother's address in Nigeria as they wish to contact re Margaret's future education.

28 March 1962, ▮▮▮▮▮▮▮: Case is known to Nigerian Government.

The email I'd received from Islington Council on 17 November 2011 had not been encouraging, and I felt frustrated by what seemed like a never-ending process that was going nowhere. After all the time and emotional energy I'd expended in pursuing the elusive record of my time in care, I felt let down by an inadequate filing system and the lack of institutional memory, which led to the failure even to admit my records existed. It was hard to keep in check the emotional turmoil that resulted.

From having known nothing about the possibility of getting hold of the documents, I'd dragged myself through hope, expectation, desire and dread. I read and reread the passage that seemed to extinguish all hope of finding my care records.

> We certainly don't seem to be able to locate files relating to you in our archive. However, it may be an idea for you to contact the local authorities where the two Children's Homes in [. . .] and [. . .] were located in case any care responsibilities were shared with them.

But I'd already contacted the London Metropolitan Archives who would have held records for those counties, and they'd told me that they had none that were relevant. The statement in the latter part of the email, that there might be something of use in Kayin's file, was no real consolation, since there was no apparent reason why there would be a file in her name in the first place.

Entering a busy period of work, which included planning round tables on labour exploitation in the global garment industry, I decided to throw myself into reading research papers and articles on the subject in preparation. But a week later, on 24 November, when I checked my non-parliamentary email inbox, my eyes were immediately drawn to the sender of the email that had arrived at 10.16 that morning: the Access to Care Records Officer for the London Borough of Islington.

> Dear Ms Young,
> I have just returned to the office today and am pleased to say that, using the surname [. . .], our archivist has

provided me with one file which contains documents relating to your care from 1951 to 1970. Although [. . .] is named on the file, at first glance it appears that the file relates to you. (Perhaps [. . .]'s [your cousin's] information was separated at some stage so that you both had separate files.)

Your application is now at number 13 on our waiting list to be processed. We will contact you again once it reaches the top of the list. However, if you have any immediate questions, or would like to discuss this further, please let me know.

Kind regards,
Access to Records Officer Children's Social Care
Islington Council

The news came as a complete surprise to me and I was stunned. I'd been working on the assumption that there was little, if anything, to be revealed of Islington Council's role in my childhood. I wasn't sure how to feel about this, unclear whether I'd be able to withstand an onslaught of fresh information about my past. I wondered what to do next. I didn't want to be trapped in a perpetual cycle of desire for revelations about my past that turned into dread of new discoveries and threatened to challenge my memories of my childhood.

I rationalized that I couldn't allow myself to be derailed by something that was not yet within my grasp; there was not much I could do about it, I would just have to wait and see what turned up. So I did my best to file the news away and tried to forget about it. I continued with the projects I was working on, as the rate of progress felt slow. Whether the subject was the over-representation of young Black men in the criminal justice system or the mental well-being of the baby boomers' generation, these were issues that weren't going to disappear, and I still had a commitment to address them.

By March 2012, it occurred to me that I should be more proactive, so I wrote to the access to records administrative officer and asked for an update. On 5 April I received the following reply.

Dear Lola,
My apologies for the delay in responding to you as I have been out of the office. I have actually begun processing your file. I have made a copy of the original file and am currently reading through this to 'process' it in accordance with the Data Protection Act.

I would hope to have this completed in the next week. Can you remind me if you expressed a wish to attend the office to collect your file or whether you wanted it sent by registered post?

Kind regards,
Access to Records Officer Children's Social Care
Islington Council

So this was it. The long wait, and its attendant uncertainty, would soon be over. Some of the missing pieces of the puzzle that could tell the story of my early life would soon be put in place.

Of course I was going to collect the file in person – there was no way I would entrust that precious material to any mail delivery service.

The Children's Social Care office was just off the Essex Road, an area familiar to me from my teenage years in north London. April brought a cool wet spring in 2012, with wave after wave of torrential, wind-driven rain, and this particular day was no exception. Inside-out brollies could be seen scattered on the ground and discarded in bins, and my hooded coat provided only limited protection for the half-mile or so walk from Highbury Fields. By the time I arrived, I was soaked through.

After years of false starts and delays, I now needed to have that record of my time in care in my possession. I was ready. As I showed my identification to the receptionist, I observed the mundane nature of the building, which looked just like any other office – yet I was as nervous as if I was preparing to take an exam. I might be about to access a set of papers that would illuminate every corner of my childhood, or I might discover that Islington had found nothing of any substance. Either would be damaging in its own way.

Nerves and imagination working overtime, I waited for someone from administration to appear. To alleviate the tension, I thought how the opening bars of the theme from *Jaws*, filled with dread and menace, would be an appropriate accompaniment as the council officer descended the stairs into the reception area. Then, finally, I was face-to-face with the official I'd been in email contact with for almost a year. My eyes went immediately to the black box file in her hands, that's all I could see. I don't recall her appearance, except that she was probably in her late twenties or possibly early thirties. We must have conversed, though briefly; I seem to remember she mentioned something about having embarked on postgraduate study, but I have only the vaguest recollection of our meeting, in spite of the build-up to that moment. I'd literally imagined a faceless bureaucrat, hadn't 'seen' the person behind the emails at all. Nothing about her or the interior of the building indicated how pivotal this meeting was. Even the file itself was just the standard office accessory, still seen on desks up and down the country.

At the handover, all the 'what ifs' I'd been thinking about were running round the racetrack in my mind. Then the time came for her to officially hand over the unwieldy box file to me, along with some leaflets about support available. While I appreciated the effort it had taken to locate the paperwork, I was impatient to start reading the documents I had just been given. 'The Life and Times of Lola Young' was now in my hands.

There was one empty seat left on the lower deck of the bus that would take me home. Soaking wet, I sat down. I should've waited before starting on the files, I knew that. But I felt compelled to open up my Pandora's box, there and then, as the bus made its slow way through rush-hour traffic. A gloomy sky and the dirty windows filtered the late-afternoon light, making it difficult to read the fading, photocopied papers. But after what it had taken to get to this point, nothing was going to deter me.

The box file was perched on my lap, too big to fit in my work bag. I thumbed through the documents, hoping the answers to my questions about my family and my early life would leap off the pages. Soon enough, I found a record of my birth parents placing me in the care of a stranger.

Surname	Christian name(s)	Date of birth	Place of birth	Sex M or F	~~Legit or~~ illegitimate	Religion
Young	Margaret	1.6.51	London	F		

With foster mother as indicated below.

Surname	Christian name(s)	Address	Date of reception
Vince	Daisy	207 Tufnell Park Road	30 July 1951

Name and addresses of responsible parent(s):

WIDOW Mother SANTOS 290 Portobello Road (West African)/10 TAIWO STREET LAGOS NIGERIA BRITISH WEST AFRICA

Father? SANTOS YOUNG Somewhere in Streatham (co-habiting)

My first name was officially recorded as Margaret – something I'd known since finding my birth certificate in a drawer in Daisy's house when I was fourteen – but everyone always called me Lola, which was my second name. Most people pronounced it as in the song, popular at the time, 'Whatever Lola Wants, Lola Gets' (oh, the irony) from the soundtrack of the musical *Damn Yankees*. Margaret Young sounded so much more English than I ever thought I could or wanted to be. Many years later, I would find out that I was named after a relative of my father's.

These notes were quickly followed by further records. I skimmed through, occasional details catching my eye.

8.8.51
Mother has entered hospital as student nurse. Vigorous infant. Content . . . Dry skin. To apply olive oil.

2.10.51
Infant sleeping in pram in garden. Gaining in weight. Clean and well cared for. To start bone broth.

Every page I read – each densely packed with scrawled handwriting – made me hungry for more. I tried to picture myself in a Roman chariot-style pram in the crisp autumnal air, while Daisy put sheets through the mangle, squeezing out the last drops of Sunlight soap and water. I imagined a dark grey fifties sky, with clouds ready to cover the city in cool rain.

The smell of damp wool alerted me to a body leaning

over my shoulder. I looked up and caught a woman peering down at my lap. I wondered if she could read the pages spread precariously across my legs. If so, perhaps she could help me interpret the handwriting, some of which was virtually illegible.

The handover of 'the infant', me, to Mrs Daisy Vince, the foster mother, had taken place on 30 July; I'd been born on 1 June, so here was a first small correction to the version of events I'd been told. One of Daisy's repeated refrains to me had been, 'I took you in when you were only six weeks old.' The dates in the records showed this was not quite right: it was eight weeks. Eight weeks. It meant I had been with my mother for two weeks more than I'd always believed. There wasn't a way of allowing that thought into my head, because I'd never thought of myself as having been born like other children. If I thought about it at all, I imagined I'd been born at six weeks old and immediately handed over to Daisy. But whether I'd been with my mother for six or eight weeks, it was still an unbearably short time. As I looked at the form I felt a pang at this stark reminder of just how young I'd been when I was put into foster care.

The note about me being illegitimate was not news to me, although it had been a shock when I'd first discovered this on my birth certificate at about fourteen years old. Daisy had a habit of repeating the few facts she knew about me, and the story she often told was that my mother was a nurse and my father a doctor, and that they had divorced. The birth certificate told a different tale. I saw straight away that my mother and father had not been married when I was born – at least, not to each other. I still remember the nervous feeling in my stomach at reading this contraband information. My suspicion is that Daisy had told me an untruth to spare me the stigma of being labelled illegitimate. In the 1950s being labelled 'illegitimate' was not a neutral statement of fact but a value judgement, as was 'bastard'; both terms were inexplicably used viciously against children. The labelling meant something too, especially to those who were religious; I remember at school overhearing some girls saying that those 'born out of wedlock' couldn't be baptized, and if you weren't baptized you couldn't go to heaven. Not that it bothered me: I'd given up on religion before I started secondary school. Neither did it do much to change what I thought of my parents, as by then I'd long since given up on them too.

The record of my early years was handwritten, while, later on, more of the pages were typed. Sal had mentioned the possibility of redactions, and I guessed that the blank spaces where there should be names and comments were the outcome of the Data Protection Act mentioned in the email from Islington Council. The blanked-out details were suggestive but they might also be red herrings – I'd have to wait and see.

The number of documents surprised me. A dossier so large, it barely fitted into the box file. The official record of my early life, from babyhood to young adulthood, in the care of the London Borough of Islington, had the potential to be more complete than I'd imagined. A window into a different world in so many ways.

The slow pace of the traffic mirrored the speed at which I was able to assimilate the implications of the material before me. I skipped through more documents. I knew some of them might challenge or confirm my memory of some significant moments – revealing the callousness and thoughtlessness of some, the kindness and generosity of others. Whatever revelations were to come, however difficult the emotional upheaval they might cause, I had to believe it would be worthwhile in the end.

Later that evening, I stared at pages and pages of handwritten documents spread across my kitchen table. The pages weren't numbered and, although roughly in chronological order, the sequence of events wasn't always clear. Disappointment flooded through me as I contemplated them, my clothes still damp from the earlier soaking, until I reminded myself that I hadn't even begun to scratch the surface of the contents. It was far too early to assess their significance – I was coming to conclusions having done the bulk of early reading sitting on the number 38 bus, for goodness' sake. I would have to read everything thoroughly. That was the only path ahead.

The first time I was seen by a council official, while in the care of Mrs Daisy Vince, was in August 1951.

> General condition: Satisfactory
> Feeding: N.D.M
> Vaccinated: No
> Clothing : Adequate

There was a record of subsequent visits.

8.8.1951, 2 months 8 days: Vigorous infant. Content.

[. . .]

4.1.1952: Big baby. Firm muscles, cutting teeth. Happy and contented. Sleeps well. Mother & father visit.

29.9.1952: Child shows good progress. Walks, talks. Sleeps well. FM says Mother took her to see friends at Sloane Square and she cried all the time.

9.12.1952: Doing well. Mother present at this visit. Child will not go to her probably because she is now used to white people instead of coloured.

'Big baby. Firm muscles.' At six months old, really? Had Miss Boardman, the child welfare officer, poked and prodded me as though I were a laboratory specimen, to come to that conclusion? And what about the gratuitous 'probably because she is now used to white people instead of coloured'? No point in getting upset by her observations – there was a long way to go, and I recalled what Sal had said about social workers writing comments, unaware that one day a new law would entitle the subjects in question to read their reports. I was sure there'd be other, more upsetting judgements to come. For now, I needed to hold back my indignation for the sake of my sanity.

Comments were recorded once a month until I went to school in 1956. They became less frequent as I entered my teens, replaced by the occasional two-page summary of my life – as though so much had happened that all the detail couldn't be absorbed without an aid for whoever was expected to read the paperwork.

It was strange to read those descriptions of myself as an infant. I wasn't officially in care at that time but, as two of the others living at Tufnell Park Road were, I'd been swept up into the official record, to be regularly monitored by the child welfare department.

'Has foster mother undertaken care of children previously?' a printed form enquired. Miss Boardman responded 'all her married life'. It was another clue that drifted into view, then out and away again, as no other details were given.

When Kayin and I speculated about Daisy's background we were always intrigued by the house in which we'd lived, which was spread over four floors, with generously proportioned rooms and a decent-sized garden. One puzzle the notes partially cleared up concerned whether the house was rented or owned by Daisy. Noting that our flat's sole bedroom was damp, Miss Boardman urged Daisy to 'speak to the relative who owns the house'. Said relative wasn't named, though I suspected it was Evelyn.

That suspicion was later confirmed in some of the documentation a friend was eventually able to unearth about Daisy Vince for me. From what I discovered about Daisy's life prior to my arrival in it, I imagine that grief would have played a significant role in the development of her character.

Daisy's father had died when she and her twin sister, Violet, were about five years old; their younger sister, Irene, had been just two years old, so neither she nor Daisy and Violet would have had many memories of their father. I learned of other tragedies, involving mental ill health and the loss of two husbands, but I realize this is not my story to tell. In the end I've accepted that looking for one single answer to the question of what motivated Daisy to foster and adopt so many children – there was certainly little financial incentive – will always only ever be speculation.

In all the notes I found only one critical observation of Daisy's care towards us: Miss Boardman recorded that Daisy did not take me to Islington Welfare Clinic (IWC) often enough for my health check-ups, commenting on the poor attendance several times.

My foster mother's constant presence in my life from when I was two months old meant that I had far more vivid recollections of what she looked like, how she spoke, her quirks and foibles, than the parents I saw for a day or two each year they were in London. Several entries in the notes supported the memory.

1.4.1954: Father has visited!

It's the exclamation mark that gives away the social worker's impression of my father, along with 'he does not give any [financial] help'. It wasn't only my father. Miss Boardman notes that in December 1953 my 'mother did not send even a toy and no card'. That point about there being no Christmas card or present was echoed each year for Christmas and birthdays. Even so, at Christmas time, Miss Boardman would find me surrounded by presents, happy and content. Daisy made sure there were plenty of exciting gifts for me to unwrap, so I didn't need to dig too deeply into why my father sent me a box of three handkerchiefs in January 1955, or chocolates in September 1958. Either a bit late or too early for formally recognized occasions.

Many of the early entries were banal, in an everyday sort of way. 'Child doing well', 'child seems happy', 'child doing well at school', 'child is content', and so on. Perhaps that was so when I was a baby, but as I got older, I would go on to be labelled 'solemn', 'serious' and even 'sulky' by anyone who cared to pass comment.

By the age of eleven, or maybe twelve, I had accepted that I would have to live with the brutal truth that my parents didn't care about me. To cope, I found ways to comfort myself: I became quite independent, able to amuse myself with whatever books or other reading material I could lay my hands on, or with a sketch pad and paints. When I was older, as a teenager, I would go to the cinema on my own. Having understood that adults could not be relied upon, my strategy was to protect myself by being self-sufficient.

I hated the idea of being thought of as weak, because that would have left me exposed and vulnerable to the whims and preoccupations of the adults who determined the shape of my life. That was my understanding of power dynamics at home, at school, on the street: if you didn't look out for yourself, no one else would.

When Daisy and her daughter, Evelyn, argued, a part of me suspected it was all my fault, and that exposed my vulnerability. The only way Evelyn would be placated was if I left, or if my mother paid what she owed. The first option was unpalatable, the latter unlikely. Now I picked up a piece of paper with a note dated a matter of weeks after Daisy died, in 1965. It outlined a conversation between my social worker and Daisy's daughter, Evelyn, in which Evelyn readily admits to being 'anti-colour'. My social worker at the time wrote:

> At one time there was considerable pressure on Mrs Vince through [. . .] to get the Nigerian Embassy to pay the cost of Lola's fare back to Lagos, and to put the responsibility squarely with the parents.

Not so unreasonable, you might say, especially the note about 'responsibility', but I'm glad I had no inkling of Evelyn's feelings towards us during that unsettled, difficult time in the summer of 1965. A sudden realization came over me: even if my mother or father had paid up, that wouldn't have satisfied Evelyn. She would have much preferred it if I was 'returned' to Lagos, as though I were a faulty appliance to be taken back to the shop. Like Islington Council – who almost always referred to me as African or Nigerian, occasionally coloured, never Black – Evelyn's view was that, despite having been born in London, the idea that I was British was unthinkable.

If having Daisy and Evelyn argue over me was a source of shame, it nevertheless meant that they acknowledged my existence. With my parents it was a different story. Once they had returned to Lagos, it seemed I had become invisible to them. Neither of them wrote to me after they'd left England. That was how I remembered those years, anyway. I had an address for my mother but I had no inclination to write to a woman I didn't know, and who didn't acknowledge my presence in the world. No address for my father had been passed on to me.

After spending the evening sifting through the contents of the box file, I went to bed, retracing the details I had read so far, over and over, as I waited in vain to fall asleep. On the basis of my first look at the material, I had found little to alter my conclusion that the essence of my life in foster care and the care system had been uncertainty, subject to the whims of moody adults and to the unexplained situations in which I found myself, the flow of kindness and affection randomly turned on and off. Perpetual change was the key motif of my teens, and I hadn't needed a box file full of frequently illegible notes to tell me that.

I was also disappointed to find that, despite the initial appearance of completeness, there were big gaps in the documentation. For example, there wasn't a word about my parents' lives in the months or weeks, let alone years, leading up to my birth. They had no presence and therefore no official history before 1951, apart from references to their academic achievements, which seemed to count for something, though what that was I've no idea. I'd hoped for – really needed – something more substantial than a hastily written note and a couple of old passports, but as far as I could see there was nothing officially recorded by child welfare services that could help me learn more.

They had been here, in London, in the late 1940s, through the 1950s, and then they had left. And that was that.

Five: The inevitable

25 January 1963, ▮▮▮▮▮▮▮▮: Margaret [Lola] shares a bedroom with Mrs V and two other females. Mrs V has hesitated in the past to approach the CH/Dept in case they could remove Margaret, who is very much attached to her despite the inadequacy of the accom. I explained to [. . .] that this Dept could not take any action unless asked to by Mrs V or Margaret's parents, since the child is not in any danger, moral or otherwise.

When the going gets tough, I get walking. Taking a route that encompassed some of my old haunts, I started in Upper Street, and continued past Highbury Corner, and on to Highbury Fields. Just beyond Highbury Barn, I walked past The Gunners pub on the corner of Elwood Street and Blackstock Road. I needed to gather my strength before digging deeper into the box file to look in more detail at the reports about me in the late 1960s. I knew that this neighbourhood would feature heavily in those care notes.

Resisting the temptation to carry on down Elwood Street to take in the view of the old Highbury Stadium,

I cut across to Green Lanes, via Mountgrove Road, my memory jolted as I took in the Brownswood Road library. There's something about this stretch of north London that I find comforting in its familiarity, even though it's always changing. There are the libraries I've borrowed books from, and mostly returned; the houses where friends lived; the houses where I've lived. It's almost as if my legs have decided that whatever I might want to do, I should prioritize revisiting the sites where notable memories were formed.

The social history of the area is evident in the variety of architectural gems: large Victorian and Edwardian terraces are sprinkled between housing developments from several decades, evidence of previous attempts to achieve social integration with limited success. I note the fact that houses, although dominant, are now more likely to be divided into flats than occupied by single families as they were when I lived here. But the shops are still a bustling mixture: supermarket-style grocery stores, barbers and numerous cafés and restaurants reflecting a range of cuisines. In the four decades since I've lived here, buildings have disappeared and been replaced, others have been repurposed. Yet in spite of the changes, I still recognize and identify strongly with this corner of the capital.

Back home, I opened the box file and began excavating the official version of my past, once again. Over the years, I'd managed to stitch together a reasonable narrative about the facts of my parents' leaving, their payments for my upkeep, their visits and so on. At the start of the quest for my records I'd been concerned that I might have been way off the mark with, for example, my recall of how old I was when each parent left this country and the number of times they'd visited me at Daisy's home in Tufnell Park. But my first forays into the reports demonstrated that my memory had served me quite well. Regarding the big events and when they took place, in most cases I had only been out by a year or two. Most cases, but not all.

The notes from the final months of 1962 reminded me of what a brutal winter we'd had that year. Across the whole country, snow and ice prevailed for several months, causing no end of problems. Daisy suffered a fall that left her largely housebound, which meant that I did the shopping and any other errands that required leaving the house. She was no longer able to attend parents' evenings at school, which was frowned upon at Parly Hill, seen as a dereliction of parental responsibility. When Lynne attended on Daisy's behalf, my teachers seemed mystified as to the identity of this young white woman, and her relationship to me.

In the summer of 1963, a few months before her seventy-seventh birthday, Islington Council recognized that Daisy Vince was struggling with fatigue and ill health. I read an entry from Miss Boardman noting that she'd urged me to help out with the household chores. It was a lot of responsibility for a twelve-year-old, but I also know that it's nowhere near what many children caring for parents and siblings with complex needs are facing today. Although Daisy was now only looking after Kayin and me – a relatively light load compared to what she had been used to – the notes make it clear that she was in need of a break.

So Kayin and I were sent away for a two-week holiday, our destination a temporary foster home in the East Sussex countryside. I remember the two of us being deposited at Victoria train station by a council welfare officer, before travelling together unaccompanied on a train to Shoreham. The social worker had told me which station to look out for, then off we went.

It was my first ever holiday, apart from the school trip to Devon. At twelve years old I may have been an adolescent, but I had rarely ventured beyond our immediate north London neighbourhood, and I found the train journey unnerving, convinced I'd miss the stop, and worrying that we'd end up who knew where.

Much later, when we compared notes on our experiences that summer, Kayin could remember everyone's names that we stayed with during the trip. I couldn't, but that didn't matter now: I had the official record of it before me. The foster mother responsible for looking after us had been called Mrs Miller; she was to meet us at Shoreham station. She had a son called John, who was a little older than me.

Seeing it all in black and white, I find my own memories slowly returning. The day after we arrived, we could see that there wouldn't be much to do in the middle of the countryside on our own, and so we went for a walk. Ahead of me, I could see Kayin making her way through a field of wheat: I wasn't going to let her out of my sight. Suddenly I heard her squeal. I caught up with her and, following her gaze downwards, I saw hundreds of shiny black beetles scuttling past our feet, their hard cases making scratchy sounds as they brushed against the wheat stems. We pranced away like show ponies, lifting our knees high and squealing with horror at the thought of those creatures getting inside our open sandals.

Otherwise the holiday passed in a blur. My memory was that it had rained a lot, and this much was confirmed when I came across something I had not been expecting: a copy of a letter in Daisy's distinctive handwriting.

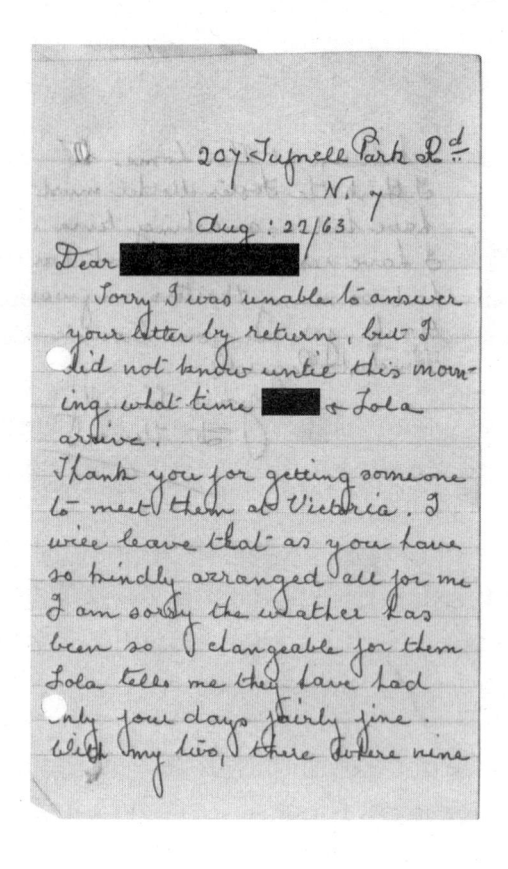

> 207 Tufnell Park Rd
> N. 7
> Aug: 22/63
>
> Dear ▮▮▮▮
>   Sorry I was unable to answer your letter by return, but I did not know until this morning what time ▮▮▮ & Lola arrive.
>
> Thank you for getting someone to meet them at Victoria. I will leave that as you have so kindly arranged all for me I am sorry the weather has been so changeable for them Lola tells me they have had only four days fairly fine. With my two, there were nine

> children at this home so
> I think the Foster Mother must
> have had a smashing time.
> I have rested a bit but have
> had so many visitors, anyway
> thanks for all your trouble.
> Kindest Regards
> yours Sincerely
> D. Vincent

As I read it, I could hear Daisy's voice in my head loud and clear. I could see her beaky nose and her blue-rinsed hair, and I could picture her picking up a biro to compose the letter.

The proprietorial way she'd referred to 'my two' – that is, Kayin and me – struck me as a revealing indication of how differently I felt about our relationship; I would never have assumed that Daisy would suggest there was such a bond between us. I had often retreated into my shell as a child, not wanting to invest in the idea of permanence. It occurred to me that there might be more documents like this to come: handwritten by people who weren't Islington Council officials. It was something I hadn't anticipated – finding a document not only about me, but written by Daisy.

There was one incident Kayin and I had never forgotten from the Shoreham holiday, and I was braced to come across a detailed account of it in the notes. It took place on the night we played cards – just us kids. The adults were watching television in the other room.

John Miller looked at me and said, 'You're a cheat.'

I punched him in the face before I knew what I was doing.

He cried out, and Mrs Miller came into the room, saw her son with his hand over his eye.

I wanted to cry because, in that moment, I didn't know who I was or why I'd done such a thing, and I expected to be punished. I had cheated, and I'd lied about it, and I'd hit a boy whose mother had been kind to us. John just looked surprised. His eye was already swelling up.

At the time I was convinced that Mrs Miller would call Islington Council or even the police. She would tell them to come and take me away. The mad Black girl from London who'd just punched her son in the eye. But she only asked that we apologize to each other, then acted as though nothing had happened.

Later, once I'd returned to London, I was mortified by my bad behaviour, and wished I could apologize to the family. But there had been no repercussions, and now, as I read through my file, I could see that Mrs Miller hadn't reported the incident to the authorities. There was no reference at all to my violent outburst – the first time I had ever lashed out with rage at someone. I was surprised, thinking that this was just the sort of incident that would have been noted. I felt the shame of my actions, embarrassed that I would have been so offended by John's accusation. The only thing I can think of is that we'd been sent off on holiday around the time my father left for Nigeria, though I don't recall his departure having such an impact on me. In any case, that wouldn't have been an excuse for my bad behaviour.

What I did find in the notes was a comment from Miss Boardman saying she was impressed to hear that I was in the process of writing a storybook for Kayin. I have always loved writing. Before I was old enough to be allowed out on my own, my favourite ways of occupying myself were writing, reading, drawing and singing along to music with Kayin. We were immersed in popular culture, watching plays on television, listening to sitcoms on the radio, serenading ourselves by singing along to the film soundtrack of *South Pacific*, miming to Frank Sinatra, Ella Fitzgerald and Ketty Lester. This musical feast came courtesy of Lynne, who after she'd left Daisy's had given us her record player, and some records too. We had an out-of-tune piano in the living room, on which Daisy could just about play 'Chopsticks'.

The pianists Russ Conway and Winifred Atwell were two of Daisy's favourite performers. The stylish, immaculately coiffured Atwell was making history and we looked on, transfixed by the speed and dexterity of her hands on her battered piano. She was the first Black artist to have a number one hit in the UK singles charts, and was distinctive for being from Trinidad, rather than the USA, where most of the other well-known Black performing artists came from.

These thoughts and many more rose to the surface, and I began to realize what a potentially rich resource the care notes represented in terms of provoking memories. Even if I wasn't going to find all the answers I'd hoped for, I might be able to flesh out my story in other ways.

By Christmas 1964, both Lynne and Richie had left Tufnell Park Road to live their adult lives. Lynne had married Len, and Richie was no longer a bad boy; he'd become an apprentice printer and had a steady girlfriend. As was tradition, Lynne, Richie and several other adults who had once been children in Daisy's care would come round to Evelyn's flat in Tufnell Park Road for a late Christmas lunch and stay for the rest of the day.

That Christmas morning I woke up to find presents stuffed into a pillowcase at the end of my bed. I always opened my presents very slowly, to make the excitement last as long as I possibly could. I waited for Kayin to wake and start opening her gifts; no patient unwrapping for her, she got straight down to work.

Lynne had bought me a Kodak camera. It was a real camera, not a toy. And a roll of film was wrapped up in the same package. Daisy tutted and said that Lynne shouldn't have bought me a present that would require me to spend more money later on. Money I didn't have.

I put the camera back in its box and placed it on a shelf in the wardrobe I shared with Daisy and Kayin.

Mum came into the bedroom pushing a toy pram. Tucked up inside was a beautiful doll with dark brown skin and lots of curly black hair, just like one I'd seen a girl hugging in the butcher's one Saturday. That girl had stared at me for ages. Even though I was too old for dolls, I could see hers was different. The ones I used to have were always white, with straight brown or golden blonde hair. That day was the first time I'd ever seen a 'coloured' doll, nestled in the arms of a white girl who couldn't stop staring at me.

The pram and the doll were for Kayin, from Evelyn and Liam. They'd given me a 500-piece jigsaw puzzle and a painting-by-numbers set, which I loved. Even though Evelyn never seemed to like us very much, she always showed generosity towards us at Christmas.

Christmas lunch followed the same pattern every year and was a spectacular affair: enough food to make a sturdy table sag; Christmas crackers to pull; turkey and mince pies and blue-flamed Christmas pudding to eat. Fifteen people were seated at the table, all ready to enjoy the feast and the entertainment that would follow. Each time someone arrived, there would be loud greetings. Daisy's family included her actual relatives as well as the adults she'd adopted or fostered as children, who returned each year at Christmas time.

Daisy never really disclosed much about the children she'd looked after many years ago. She told us that Sidney had been with her since he was a little boy, though

I wasn't ever entirely clear about his origins; his persona was quite different to everyone else's, but I don't think I'd ever been that curious about his past. According to Daisy, Jack had been adopted as a boy, but as for the circumstances, I've either forgotten or never knew.

I couldn't be sure which one of June and Derek had been looked after by Daisy, but because they weren't present, I wasn't so curious about their background. They had moved to Australia shortly after they married. It saddened Daisy that they didn't ever come back to England to visit: she had to make do with the rare occasions on which they called from their home thousands of miles and twelve hours away.

Jack and Sidney were probably in their forties at most, though of course to us they seemed almost as ancient as Evelyn. Jack and his wife, Gillian, had a son called Oliver. Jack had been known to appear dressed as Father Christmas, while Gillian always looked well groomed and faintly glamorous; her bright red lipstick and highly styled auburn hair made her stand out from the other women present. Daisy thought Gillian was 'all airs and graces'. I liked Jack's husky voice, and although we only saw him at Christmas time, he was ever present, his image captured in a framed photograph in the front room.

Sidney and his wife, Jeanette, were my favourite of all Daisy's former foster children. Sidney made us laugh by standing on his head in the hallway, explaining that it was a position in yoga, while Jeanette looked on smiling. I couldn't say we were any the wiser for Sidney's explanation, and though I found it curious that they both ate nut roast instead of turkey, because they were vegetarians, no one seemed to view this as outlandish behaviour or made judgemental comments.

Evelyn did all the cooking, a mammoth task for so many people; her husband, Liam, had the job of carving the turkey. Cutting the slivers of meat occupied both hands, and I think that might have been the only time I saw him without a cigarette between his fingers, or hanging from his mouth. Daisy often urged him to give up smoking, as it was already known in the 1960s that smoking was bad for people's health, but that never stopped Liam. He was one of those smokers who would light his next cigarette from the still-glowing end of the previous one. He seemed content with his habit and its effects on him: his cough, easily identifiable as belonging to a dedicated smoker, preceded him wherever he went, and his cigarette fingers were stained walnut brown. The rattling in his chest when he coughed sounded as if there was something drowning in his lungs that wanted to escape.

Terry poured brandy over the Christmas pudding, then set light to it. As the blue and yellow flames covered the dish, we all said 'ooh' and 'ahh', like we did when we watched the fireworks on Guy Fawkes Night. Once the pudding and mince pies disappeared, we'd get the Monopoly board out. There would be an argument about who played with which token, as usual. Then it would be time to sing and dance to the 'Hokey Cokey', 'Knees Up Mother Brown' and 'Auld Lang Syne'.

I remember Daisy looked tired, that Christmas of

1964, as though all her energy had drained out of her. She sat and watched us, hardly saying a word.

As I went deeper into the file, I became increasingly nervous. I could see papers relating to the mid-sixties coming into view. This had been an especially difficult period, and I felt I might be sullied by the material – that it would spring some emotionally painful bear traps. What if I wasn't adequately prepared?

I decided that, rather than face that possibility at home, I would take the papers away with me to read. I'd not long been in my flat and I didn't want to feel it had been contaminated by the toxins that were potentially waiting to spill from the files. Instead, I told myself, I would confine whatever unpleasantness emerged from those sheets of paper in a different location. Until then, I'd put the file away, out of sight, for when I was ready.

But this didn't stop the contents seeping into my thoughts and dreams.

A memory: Daisy

June 1965: *fourteen years old*

An unearthly moan, then a sound like someone choking. At first I think it's part of my dream. It's early, not even time to get up for school yet. I poke my head out from under the blankets, and straight away I know something's wrong.

When I look across the room, I can't make sense of what I'm seeing. Mum's not in her bed. I leap up and rush over, to find her slumped on the floor.

'Oh, Mum,' I cry. 'Mum, Mum, Mum.' I try to help her up, on to the edge of her bed, but I'm not strong enough, so I put a pillow under her head where she's fallen.

Still in my nightie, I race up to Evelyn's flat on the second floor, taking the stairs two at a time. I'm panting now, terrified by what I've seen. Mum has a lump as big and as round as a ping-pong ball on her forehead. *I don't like it*, I think, as I try to get rid of the image from my mind. *I don't like it at all.*

I knock on Liam and Evelyn's bedroom door, shouting at the same time.

'Mum's fallen out of bed. She's got a big lump on her forehead!'

Before I finish telling her what's happened, Evelyn whooshes past me in her dressing gown and slippers, moving so fast I worry she'll fall down the stairs. Liam appears in the doorway; he's in his pyjamas, a half-smoked cigarette between his fingers.

He asks me what's going on, and I repeat what I just told Evelyn.

'Oh Lord,' he says.

I'm back in our bedroom and Evelyn is leaning over Mum, talking to her in a quiet voice. Liam is here now and Evelyn tells him to go upstairs and phone for an ambulance.

Liam leaves, his breath rattling as he tries to hurry. Evelyn's body is shielding Mum, keeping her out of my sight; Mum's not saying anything, just moaning every now and then.

Evelyn turns to me and says in a kind voice that I should get ready for school.

I crane my neck to try and see how Mum looks. Has she been knocked out? She's only just come back from hospital. I was just getting used to having her back again.

My mind is full of dread.

I take my uniform and my school things from the bedroom. I'll wash in the scullery as usual and get dressed in the kitchen. Better not go back to the bedroom. Evelyn will take care of Mum.

The kettle's whistle lets me know the water for my morning wash has boiled; I wonder if Mum can hear it. When she came back from the Whittington, she seemed depressed and everyone said she was 'out of sorts'. Now she'll probably have to go back to the same hospital again.

I walk to school and try not to feel scared.

When Mum comes back from the hospital this time, she's not right at all. I don't know whether it's because she banged her head so hard when she fell or what, but she's not the same. Liam and Evelyn and Terry and Julie stand around in our front room while Mum lies on her couch. They look like they're ready to have their photograph taken for a family portrait, except they're not smiling.

Mum can't speak properly, but I know she understands I'm in the front room with her, because she says my name, over and over, 'Lulla, Lulla, Lulla.' It's like a chant, like she's using my name to beat out a rhythm. 'Lulla, Lulla, Lulla.'

If I was on my own, I could have said something – let Mum know that it's all right, Lulla is here. But I can't speak to her with everyone around, keeping guard. Mum seems to like it when I stroke her hand; her skin is very soft, and thin, like the colour and feel of damp tissue paper. Her veins stand out as though someone has woven blue wool under her skin. Her knuckles are all knobbly.

Evelyn and Liam and Terry and Julie are all saying the hospital sent her home too early. They talk about Mum in front of her as though she's not there any more, as though she's gone away. In a way she has, because she doesn't sound like the same person; she doesn't look you in the eye like she used to.

And still, all she says is, 'Lulla.'

Evelyn says that Mum is going to have to go back to the Whittington, to the hospital that sent her home too soon.

One week later

Skipping and running from Tufnell Park tube station, duffle bag over my shoulder, I'm hoping Evelyn will have some good news.

Today I've been competing with girls from across Camden in the long jump and sprint races at the running track. I managed just under fifteen feet in the long jump, and I've got a certificate to prove it. A personal best.

Before I cross Lady Margaret Road, I stop to think. How could I be happy about getting a certificate, when Mum's lying in hospital waiting to come home? Any idiot can be good at running and jumping. She's probably wondering why I haven't visited her, but children aren't allowed to go and see patients on their own, and no one has offered to take me. It's nearly a week since I last saw her.

My key is in my hand, ready to open the door to our basement flat. I stand still for a moment, imagining I will see Mum sitting on the couch in the front room as usual.

She's still not home though. The whole place feels like it's been emptied of air, no trace of any of us. I peek inside the bedroom. It's not our bedroom any more. It's just a room. That's not our kitchen, or our scullery or our dresser. It's just a big emptiness, filled with useless furniture.

As I go upstairs to Evelyn's flat, where I've been staying, I hear low voices coming from the front room. The room where we have the Christmas parties. Where Sidney and Jeanette eat nut roast, Jack plays Father Christmas and there's a tree as high as the ceiling.

I open the door and I see Evelyn, Liam, Julie and Terry. Mum's great-grandchildren, Michael, Clare and Steve, are also sitting around the dining table. Their voices go quiet when I enter the room.

Food is laid out on the table: ham, cheese, salad and apple pie. Everyone is already on their dessert. Evelyn says that I should sit down and help myself to some apple pie, and I do; I'm very hungry after running around all day.

The children – Michael, Clare and Steve – are looking down at their plates. The adults look at each other or out of the window or up at the ceiling. I don't look at anyone but carry on eating.

Then Evelyn says, 'Lulla, I'm really sorry but Mum passed away earlier today.'

I spoon more apple pie on to my plate. Still no one looks at me. I drop the spoonful of pudding on my plate, letting go of it clumsily, so small pieces of custard-covered apple splash on to the tablecloth.

Evelyn says that she's sorry and that everyone is very sad.

I stare at my plate, not speaking.

I get up slowly from my chair, saying nothing as Evelyn takes my elbow and steers me into the room where I've been sleeping while Mum's been in hospital. The window overlooks the garden: Mum's favourite plants are just beginning to flower. I don't know what to say to Evelyn. Tears run and I can't stop them.

Six: Moved on

22 July 1965, ▮▮▮▮▮: The remainder of the home as before – clean, comfortable, very pleasant and family-like.

26 October 1965, ▮▮▮▮▮: Generally I am pleased & hopeful that this home will provide and care for Lola.

In 2012, I was asked to chair the Young Review, the aim being to improve outcomes for young Black and/or Muslim men in the criminal justice system. At more or less the same time I took on the role of chairing Agenda, formed to build an alliance of women's organizations that would challenge policy makers and politicians to take a more effective, holistic approach to supporting vulnerable girls and women. The negative impacts of the care system on children and young people and their families were implicated in both reviews.

Through this work, I was again speaking directly to victims and survivors, in prisons, mental health services and institutions, and in communities, trying to absorb and channel my emotional and intellectual responses into practical policy recommendations. What I had been reading about my younger self was refracted through the lenses of the people I encountered while gathering evidence, and vice versa. My reading of the care notes and reflections on my experiences underwent subtle changes as I became more familiar with the subject matter of the two reviews.

There was another facet of my work that emerged directly from gaining access to my care records. Islington Children's Services invited me to speak to an audience of social workers and data protection officers who dealt with the release of care records from across the country. They wanted me to share my experience of locating and accessing care notes and where I thought improvements to the process might be made. A representative of the Care Leavers' Association was present at the event, and after a brief conversation, we agreed to meet and discuss how we might collaborate on a campaign they'd been working on.

Meanwhile, I was reckoning with the prospect of reading all my records in full and in chronological order. I had blocked out the Easter break for the endeavour, and was trying to prepare myself for what might be to come. But before then, whenever I found myself unoccupied with work, I couldn't help returning to my memories of the period immediately after Daisy's death.

I was officially taken into care on 18 July 1965, at the age of fourteen.

On the June afternoon when I learned that Daisy had died, I knew everything was going to be different. At first, in the weeks immediately following her death, I shuttled between Lynne and her husband Len's flat in Kentish Town, and Evelyn in Tufnell Park, but I knew this wasn't a long-term option. Lynne's health wasn't great and the couple wanted to have children of their own soon, rather than delaying. Evelyn and Liam were constantly concerned about their daughter Julie's health and had no obligation to look after me. Kayin had left to live with her parents several weeks earlier, when Daisy had been admitted to hospital the first time, and she was now living with them in Drayton Park, between Holloway and Highbury.

I didn't realize it then, but being formally taken into care signalled that the last scintilla of the relationship between me and my parents had disappeared.

Every time I met with Mrs Bould, my new child care officer, a different potential home seemed to have appeared on the horizon, always just out of reach. I remember her as a warm person, and she helped me understand that I had entered a whole new world; it was a different set-up compared to when Lynne, Richie, Kayin and I had all been under the watchful eye of Miss Boardman, the welfare officer. I was now an individual in a different system. Where Miss Boardman had been distant and officious, Mrs Bould was a younger, more modern woman — but still an alien presence in my life. Mrs Bould seemed more like the parents of my closest friends, who I'd glimpse every now and then. Strange beings living strange lives, with ideas and lifestyles entirely different from what I'd observed in Tufnell Park

Road. I'd known though not fully understood the adults in my closed little world, their moods and vagaries, but now I was in uncharted waters.

Daisy had died in early summer, and in August arrangements were made for me to go and live with Kayin and her parents in Drayton Park. I had been surprised and relieved when Mrs Bould informed me that they had offered to take me in. While I hadn't really known the Taylors, I was grateful that I wasn't going to be sent to a children's home. Lynne was also pleased that I was going to live with Kayin's family – Len and I hadn't been getting on well at all. I remember him telling me off on one occasion because I'd said I'd rather watch tennis on the television than go for a drive to the countryside. Lynne said she thought I'd have a better life with Kayin's parents because they'd encourage me to study.

Mrs Bould told me that Mr Taylor had been taking a lot of trouble to decorate the room I would share with Kayin, and I gathered from Lynne that the council would buy me some new clothes. A new life, or at least a new phase of my life, was beginning and I didn't know whether to be excited or terrified. Everything felt unreal: the knowledge I'd never see Daisy again; moving away from Tufnell Park; going to live with Kayin's parents. My conception of familial relationships was unsurprisingly a little confused, because although I had always accepted Kayin as my cousin, I couldn't quite acknowledge that her parents were related to me and were now to be called 'aunty' and 'uncle'.

The list of the clothing in my possession just after Daisy died was noted by Mrs Bould.

Present wardrobe
　1 winter coat – given by [. . .]
　1 pair all-purpose shoes
　MOSTLY CAST-OFFS FROM OLDER FAMILY MEMBERS & SADLY IN NEED OF REPLENISHING
　1 pair old slippers
　1 suit
　1 skirt
　2 dresses
　1 nightgown
　2 bras, pants, petticoats
　& school uniform

The evidence of Islington's capacity to fund a decent set of clothing came as a surprise to me at the time. In August 1965, Mrs Bould's notes recorded an anticipated spend of £30 5s to buy me a complete wardrobe of clothes. That was to buy two of everything. Brand new. I'd never imagined before that it was possible to buy so many clothes all at once.

As a young teenager, I was acutely aware of my deficient wardrobe. It marred the anticipation of the few occasions when I had been allowed to meet friends after school or at weekends. I can't recall having a single new item of clothing bought for me apart from a nightdress, which terrified me with its continually sparking static electricity. I spent countless hours dreaming up and drawing the fashion trends I most coveted, taking inspiration from television shows and magazines, as well as from my friends, and I fantasized about becoming a fashion designer.

So an excursion to Jones Brothers on the Holloway Road with Kayin and her mum – now my Aunty Iyinoluwa – was a real treat. Armed with an Islington Council Purchase Order, we had the run of the girls' clothing department in the store. The most luxurious, expensive single item we bought was a cardigan costing – the records confirmed – an extravagant £2 12s 6d.

Kayin's parents' house was a large terrace, built over three floors, close to Highbury Fields. The back of the house overlooked the garden, and beyond that was Westerns Laundry. The house compared favourably with the facilities at Tufnell Park Road, though I missed the womb-like security of living in the basement.

A room shared with just one other person, a proper bath – albeit unconventionally located in the kitchen – and a wardrobe full of new clothes could not, of course, make up for the chasm left by Daisy's death. There was a cavity in my being where there should have been an emotional reaction to these unsettling events. Perhaps this was, in part, due to not having been allowed to go to Daisy's funeral earlier in the year. I don't recall protesting about my exclusion. In fact, I don't think I even heard about it until after the event. I do remember feeling my banishment as painful. I didn't know whether or where she'd been buried or, if cremated, where her ashes had been scattered. Mr and Mrs Taylor barely acknowledged the reason I'd come to live with them, and I had no idea how to talk about my loss with school friends.

The image of Daisy reclining on her couch, murmuring the one word over and over again, was lodged in my mind: Lulla, Lulla, Lulla, Lulla, Lulla. A disturbing, ever-present morbid chant. I could still hear Terry, Daisy's grandson-in-law, claiming that she hadn't really been saying my name at all. According to him, Daisy had been reciting the names of her pets. It was as if he – and by extension, all members of the real family – refused to acknowledge that I'd been on Daisy's mind, no matter that it was clearly befuddled. But I know what I heard.

Daisy Vince would have reached the age of seventy-nine in October of 1965 – the month I moved into Guernsey Street with the Taylors.

A letter from Mrs Bould that I'd found in my first foray into the box file of my records, and which was sent on 14 October 1965, after she'd visited me at the Taylors' home, gives a flavour of my mood. It brought a strong surge of emotion when I first read it.

> Dear Lola,
> I was sorry to see you so tired and worried by all your schoolwork last Thursday. I know only too well how hectic life gets near and during examination time. If you find all your sports activities and homework too much to cope with, perhaps [. . .] would see your teacher or headmistress and ask what other arrangements could be made . . .

With the change from the health visitor via child protection social worker to the child care officer came a shift in language from one that was detached and formal, based on quasi-anthropological observation, to a more individualized connection. This was a welcome development, as my relationship with Mr and Mrs Taylor began to deteriorate before it had a chance to be properly established.

Living with Kayin's mum and dad – my aunty and uncle – did not turn out to be anything like the fantasy of family life I had hoped it would be. Their approach to my life and how I should live it went against the grain of much of what I'd known with Daisy. I wasn't prepared for their kind of strictness, their adherence to rigorous table manners, being forced to go to church, the deference they felt they were owed automatically as adults. Tensions between us began to emerge, and I desperately felt the need for someone who would look out for me.

From June 1965 onwards, when Daisy died, I'd felt hollowed out. Kayin and I both found aspects of our lives with her parents difficult after the years spent with Daisy, not because we were feral children but because the changes in our lifestyle were unsettling and much too rapid. That transformation was exemplified by our diet, which in the blink of an eye switched from sausages and chips to fufu and pig's trotters.

One of the reasons I liked Mrs Bould was that she seemed to listen and hear what I said – she talked with me rather than at me. She would ask me what I was doing at school, and what I'd enjoyed reading when I'd been with Daisy. This wasn't something I'd misremembered either. Her notes on my character were more complimentary than any of the others who wrote about me; yes, she described me as a 'worrier' but she also said I had a good sense of humour, that I worked hard on my school subjects, as well as being good at sports.

She must've seen I was in need of cheering up though, and, having noted my interests, on one memorable evening she took me out for a meal – at a theatre-themed, proper restaurant – in the West End, followed by a film.

On our way from the restaurant to the cinema, I spotted a huge, brightly lit clothes shop on the opposite side of Oxford Street.

Mrs Bould saw me staring and asked if I'd like to take a closer look.

The shop was Peter Robinson's. It was closed, but I could still see the mannequins in the window with sleek, dark and shiny hairstyles, cut into geometric shapes, similar to the way stars like Cathy McGowan wore their hair on pop music programmes. The mannequins wore miniskirts and bell-bottom trousers in dazzling black and white patterns. I'd read about 'op art', and now I was actually seeing it.

My love of fashion predated this first trip to Oxford Street, but seeing it all staged before me opened up the idea of a world where it was possible to dream anything into existence. Up until then, I'd only seen pop stars or celebrities in clothes like these – not ordinary girls. But if you had money, it seemed, you could buy the latest clothing and become whoever you imagined yourself to be.

Mrs Bould knew that I loved sport, especially athletics and tennis, and that I had expressed an interest in training to become a PE teacher. So, at the cinema, we watched *Tokyo Olympiad* – Kon Ichikawa's impressionistic portrait of the 1964 Olympics.

The film was an extraordinary event in itself to my unworldly eyes – a little like watching paintings come alive, mixed with theatre and dance. The camera's focus on the rivulets of sweat on the athletes' bodies made me feel I should pass them a glass of cool water. I was gripped by the spectacle of the athletes filling their stomachs from plates piled high with chips and rice and hunks of meat. I marvelled at the presence and talents of the Black women and men from across the African continent and from the West Indies, as well as from the USA.

When we left the cinema, I bombarded Mrs Bould with questions. About films, about fashion, about everything. All these novel experiences had been crammed into one night.

We drove back to north London, and the West End faded into the distance. I'd seen so little of the outside world under Daisy's care that the whole evening had been an adventure, almost like going on holiday, and I wished I could capture everything I'd learned that evening. I tried to console myself with these thoughts. I might not have spoken about it to the Taylors or to Mrs Bould, but I'd been missing Daisy. All that Mrs Bould and I had seen and discussed that night suggested the possibility of a life in the future very different to the one I'd experienced so far.

Mrs Bould pulled up outside the Taylors' house, and the front door swung open as soon as I stepped out of the car.

Aunty Iyinoluwa was standing in the doorway, waiting, arms folded.

'*Ah, ah*, Lola,' Aunty Iyinoluwa said, once we were inside.

She was upset with me because it was 9.30 p.m. and she said that girls under eighteen shouldn't be out after 9 p.m. I thought that perhaps she hadn't realized I'd been out with my child care officer, and I told her that Mrs Bould had brought me back in her car.

Aunty Iyinoluwa said that a person in such a responsible job should know better.

I said goodnight and went upstairs to bed.

I had known I would be confronted by outdated views on race when I first began delving into my files – and considered myself adequately prepared. I'd studied nineteenth-century theories of race, eugenics and British imperial cinema, so I'm not easily shocked by either historic or contemporary racist language and sentiments.

The initial reference to me being a 'big baby' with 'firm muscles' introduced a theme that recurred in various forms over the years. I'm described as both 'a tall, well-built lass' and 'a large Nigerian girl'. My size requires further comment.

> Whilst we have been exceptionally fortunate in being able to make provision for this girl, there is one problem which we have been unable to overcome. Lola is a big girl, 5′ 8″ and well built ... Her school uniform ... is satisfactory, but her other clothing is quite inadequate.

One council official went further and described me as being 'large, so well developed that you might mistake her for a grown woman'. I was just over fifteen years old at the time.

Today, we talk of the 'adultification' of Black children – the assumption whereby notions of innocence and vulnerability are not deemed applicable to young people from certain communities. I was by no means the tallest girl in my class, nor the largest in any dimension. The individual comments on their own aren't the issue: it's the fact that they're embedded in a particular narrative that focuses on Black physicality as a marker of difference. Another example, this time the social worker's comments, is in response to questions on a form.

> Lola is of above average height and tends to stoop in order to make this less evident. She is not superficially attractive except when she smiles. She is above average intelligence and is also extremely good at games and athletics and represents the school in tennis, hockey and athletics.

This isn't just a question of semantics. Adultification has real-world consequences – as many of us have learned in our interactions with the authorities, and especially in encounters with the police. I remember one such incident when this was made painfully clear to me as a teenager.

When I'd lived with Daisy, the walk from Tufnell Park Road to Parliament Hill School had taken me about thirty minutes, and I'd always enjoyed that time to myself – apart from when I had to pass groups of jeering boys. From the Taylors' house the journey was more complicated and involved public transport.

Gospel Oak Station was a few minutes' walk from the gate at the back field adjoining Parliament Hill School's New Building. From Gospel Oak, it was a short trip straight to Highbury and Islington station and a ten-minute walk from there to the Taylors' house on Guernsey Street. This particular day, I hadn't been feeling well and at lunchtime I asked my form teacher, Miss Armitt, if I could be excused lessons and leave school early. My nose was blocked, I felt hot; my stomach hurt too.

In many respects I was a cautious child, and I'd always paid attention to the warnings of adults: don't talk to strange men; don't walk down alleyways, day or night; never take a short cut across fields on your own. So as the train came into Gospel Oak station, I ignored my body aching with flu and ran along the platform looking for a carriage with several passengers inside, just to be on the safe side. There weren't many people around but I managed to find a full carriage just before the train moved off.

At Camden Road, everyone stood up to leave as though they were all travelling together or they'd all received a secret signal, and the carriage emptied out. Except, that is, for me and one other passenger. The guard blew his whistle, and the train moved off.

I will be safe, I said to myself, and studiously avoided looking directly at the man on the long seat opposite. I could see his ghostly reflection in the window when I stared out, his pale image superimposed on the passing houses and gardens and railway yards. He was a large man with short dark hair and glasses, his belly overhanging the thin plastic-leather belt cutting him in two.

The two of us, on our own. We were on the long stretch between Camden Road and Caledonian Road and Barnsbury, and with no linking corridor I couldn't change carriages until the next stop.

I remember silently telling myself, *Don't look at him, don't speak to him. Don't make him think you want to talk to him.* I knew not to do that. There was only one more stop after this – I just needed to be safe until then.

He said, 'It's a nice day, isn't it? Lovely weather.'

I couldn't see his expression properly behind the thick lenses of his glasses. I wanted to be able to read what was in his eyes. Perhaps a man who commented politely on the weather wasn't going to try and hurt me? I was in my school uniform, for goodness' sake, just a schoolgirl. Still, I didn't reply, instead I continued to stare out of the window.

In a different voice he said, 'Those are nice stockings you're wearing.'

Now I knew something was wrong.

I told myself to keep quiet and shrink into as small a space as possible; to press my legs together; lean into the corner by the door, ready for when it opened; hope that when the train slowed down, he would get out, or someone else would get into the carriage. I just had to make it to the next stop.

As the train began to slow down I felt relief. I'd survived being alone with this stranger.

But the man reached across to where I was sitting and quickly used one hand to part my legs, while shoving his other hand up my skirt. He ran out of time to do anything else and, with the train still moving, he pulled away, flung open the carriage door and ran at top speed up the stairs from platform to street level, and out of view.

I felt sick with shock. Clutching my school satchel, I half stumbled on to the platform, crying out and sobbing in fear and disgust.

Through my tears, I saw blurred faces appear at the windows along the length of the train, necks craned, men and women straining to see what the commotion was about. A woman on the platform came towards me and put her arm around my shoulder, and I told her what had happened.

The woman called a male guard over and he ran into an office on the platform. He was going to call the police, he shouted. I hadn't had any bad experiences with the police at that time; the only exchange I'd had was with an officer on the local beat who'd asked me why I wasn't at school one day. I'd explained that Daisy couldn't leave the house so I was posting a letter for her.

The woman who'd stopped to help me said she'd seen a man rush from the train and up the stairs to the street. Other passengers nodded in agreement.

The train huffed and puffed, as the driver waited to see how the scene would unfold.

The stationmaster asked me a question. I couldn't speak.

The police arrived.

At the police station, I was interviewed in a poky office decorated with piles of folders, ashtrays and dirty teacups. The bin was stuffed with crumpled notepaper and snack bar wrappers.

A female uniformed police officer listened as I told her what the man had done. The man. The words, the hands. I stared at her nicotine-stained fingers as she tried to convince me that nothing much had happened.

In answer to her question about my parents I told her that I was fostered, and she seemed interested to hear that.

I gave the officer the Taylors' phone number.

The policewoman's brown-tipped fingers reminded me of Liam, Evelyn's husband. Even though she was much younger than him, her fingers had already reached that same dense colour.

The officer's lack of interest in my plight was disconcerting. She sucked in the smoke as her biro hovered over her notebook, but in my memory I don't see her writing anything down. I remember her asking me if I was sure the man had actually touched me.

I give her a description of him, and the thought crossed my mind that I might see him around Holloway or Drayton Park. I hated to think he might live round our way.

The policewoman kept referring to Aunty Iyinoluwa – Mrs Taylor – as my mum. And I kept telling her she wasn't.

She left the office to phone the Taylors.

I'd been sure that this would be a waste of time: neither Aunty Iyinoluwa nor Uncle Tolu would want to visit the police station, and they would most likely be at work anyway.

When the officer returned, she said she'd spoken to my 'foster mum' and told her to inform my school about what had happened. The policewoman said that Mrs Taylor hadn't known what school I went to, and asked me to tell her.

This had been upsetting, and prompted my tears to restart: how could Aunty Iyinoluwa not know this simple fact, when I'd been living with her for months? It made me feel that I was surplus to requirements at Guernsey Street, someone the Taylors couldn't be bothered with.

The policewoman offered me a lift back to Drayton Park in a police car but I told her I'd rather walk.

'I didn't feel well,' I replied, when Aunty Iyinoluwa asked me why I'd left school so early.

Inside, I raged at her and asked her why she wasn't trying to comfort me instead of wanting to know why I wasn't at school – the school with the name she couldn't remember.

I crept into bed and fell asleep.

When I first looked through my care notes I found nothing recorded about me having been assaulted on the train, so it appears that neither I nor Mrs Taylor reported the matter to Islington Children's Department. With hindsight, I would guess that I hadn't felt comfortable about the prospect of confiding in a social worker, but the fact it hadn't been deemed significant by the Taylors made me realize that they didn't know how to relate to teenage girls in general, and me in particular. Mrs Bould noted how they'd found it difficult to adjust their thinking and change their lifestyle when Kayin returned to them and they started to foster me.

In April 1966 I went on a school trip to Norway: a trip I recorded in a journal that, miraculously, I still have, somehow managing to keep it safe with me during all my changes of address over the decades. Keeping a record of that two-week trip to Lillehammer gave me the opportunity to note how much I envied my friends' bell-bottom trousers, their fashionable jackets, their make-up and their knowledge of the pop scene. But above any material object, it was my envy of their lives with their parents, compared to my life with the Taylors, that comes through most clearly.

> *4 April, Monday*
> ... I didn't leave my house until 7.50 a.m. I thought I would never make it by 8.00 a.m. as I had to get to King's Cross by tube and I also had no one to help with my bags. I managed to get there, however, and found that practically everyone had arrived including mums and dads.

That was the opening paragraph in my journal. The final entry ended where I'd started – at King's Cross station.

> ... at 2.00 p.m. we were at King's Cross watching the rain fall heavily. No one was there to meet me and once more I had to carry my bags – only this time I had an extra basket full of things to carry. Even worse, I just missed a train and couldn't find my ticket at the other end. I got caught in a downpour and got soaked. I arrived home at 2.45 p.m.

As Holloway Road was only two stops after King's Cross, it's hard to imagine how it took forty-five minutes to arrive back at Guernsey Street. I had known that my journal would be read and assessed by my teachers, so I must have been feeling particularly sad to expose just how low my mood was. I do remember that I hadn't relished returning to the Taylors': Kayin and I had started bickering, and neither of us found it easy to settle into the new regime after life at Tufnell Park Road.

The level of detail I provided in my journal about the food on offer in Norway was borderline obsessive, though the reasons for this focus were easy enough to recall. At the Taylors' I was always hungry. Going through an adolescent growth spurt at the same time as disliking the meals on offer had led me to crave the food I couldn't have. In Norway, we could eat as much as we wanted, food literally piled high on huge serving dishes from which we could help ourselves whenever we wanted. Every day. At Guernsey Street, I had to scavenge what I could when an opportunity arose.

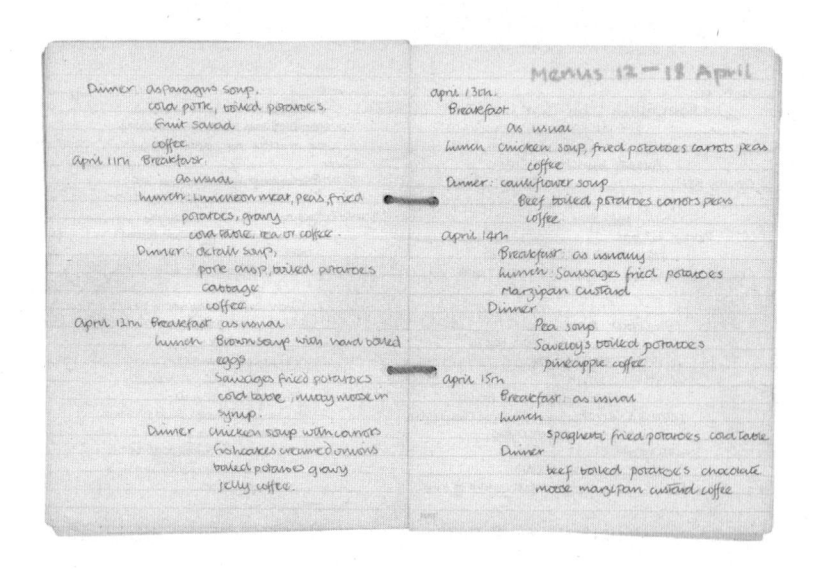

There were only two dishes cooked by Kayin's mum that I liked, one of which was jollof – rice, made with onions, tomatoes and tomato puree – and I would have been happy living on the jollof and the other food I liked – fried plantain. But if Kayin and I didn't eat the pigs' trotters or chicken wings put in front of us, the food would be served up for our next meal.

The kitchen was on the first floor, at the back of the house, and overlooked the garden and the rear of Westerns Laundry. We were often left to eat on our own, so Kayin and I simply threw all the food we didn't like out of the window and into the rough ground between the back wall of the garden and the laundry building. Out it all went. I made up a story about having to feed the monster that lived in Westerns Laundry, which made Kayin laugh, but the truth was I hardly ate anything at mealtimes. Instead, I survived on secret marmalade sandwiches – something that would eventually lead me into trouble with the Taylors.

Kayin likes to remind me that I had form when it came to unorthodox ways of disposing of food I didn't like. The unappetizing mixture of meat, greens and potatoes that Daisy had sometimes served up often ended up in a drawer in the kitchen's Welsh dresser. Then one warm summer's day, I opened it to find it full of wriggling white maggots. I hated having to get rid of that mess with my bare hands. Feeding the monster in the laundry was easier and more fun.

In the early summer of 1966, when I was fifteen years old, Mrs Bould left me and Islington behind. Had she warned me she was moving on? And if she did, had she explained why? If so, I don't remember, and my emotional memory tells me her departure was abrupt and unexplained. A Mrs Walton took over as my child care officer. She wrote to me asking me to meet her after school at Islington Council's offices on the Holloway Road. Without preamble, she told me that the Taylors wanted me to leave. I had been there for less than a year.

Mrs Walton's account of the Taylors' case against me came as no surprise: Kayin's mother's face had already told me that my time in their household might not last. For one thing, notwithstanding Mrs Taylor's tutorials, my bed-making hadn't ever been up to scratch. She had been a midwife at the Royal Northern Hospital on the Holloway Road, but neither Kayin nor I understood why the practice of folding our bed sheets into neat hospital corners should be so important.

The food problem was deeper and of more significance.

They must have realized that I made sandwiches to eat when I was having a bath. I did so without asking their permission, of course, because I was always hungry. The bread would disappear into my stomach every day, though curiously Aunty and Uncle never challenged me about it. It hadn't been my fault, I reasoned to myself, to assuage any guilt I might have: if the bath hadn't been installed in the kitchen, I wouldn't have been tempted every morning, would I? I assumed that this food pilfering was the basis for the complaint they'd made to Mrs Walton, resulting in me being summoned to her office.

I told Mrs Walton about my near-constant hunger, and explained that was why I took the bread. She raised one thin, pencilled-in brown eyebrow and cocked her head. She was surprised by my confession, I thought. She told me that the Taylors had said I'd been stealing, but they'd not been specific, and Mrs Walton hadn't realized that my crime was 'stealing' food.

The hospital corners, the food thrown from the window, me stealing bread – these hadn't been the Taylors' only complaints. Another charge levelled against me was the crime of bad manners; more specifically, helping myself to biscuits or fruit before passing the dish around to guests. I also read in the care notes how Uncle Tolu told Mrs Walton something about me having served up his food on a chipped plate. He claimed I lied about the damage and encouraged Kayin to lie too. I hadn't remembered that at all, but now that I'd read about it several times, I began to think there might be a trace of the incident lodged in the back of my mind. The more I read, the more the line between actual and newly made memories began to blur.

My uncle and aunt thought I was a bad influence on Kayin. But the truth is that she was as naughty as I was. Like me, she enjoyed spending the collection money her mum gave us for church, which we spent on treacle tarts. Ironic, considering Kayin's eventual career destination as an ordained priest in the Church of England. But although Uncle did sometimes tell her off too, and accused her of being an 'exhibitionist' in their account to Mrs Walton, I was the source of disruption in the household.

What I do clearly remember was that Mrs Walton believed what the Taylors told her, and she stuck her own oar in by asserting, 'Mrs Vince let you run wild a bit, didn't she?' I was outraged by this. By accepting the Taylors' version of events, not only had Mrs Walton implicitly tarnished Daisy's name, she'd also accused Kayin and me of being feral. Her attitude and tone, so soon after Daisy's death, made me defensive and led me to mourn the loss of Mrs Bould's sympathetic ear, as well as Daisy.

My departure from the Taylors didn't happen immediately. I remember, at our next meeting, sitting in the Taylors' kitchen with Mrs Walton while she described Park House, a holiday home that sounded very appealing. I could stay there during the summer holidays, she'd said. The Taylors needed a break from me. The feeling was mutual.

Park House, located in Hertfordshire, north of London, was deep in the countryside. I thought it sounded like a place that would rescue me from the unhappiness into which I had sunk at the Taylors'. I was so happy at the prospect of getting away that I wanted to start packing immediately, but Mrs Walton explained that I'd have to wait until nearer the time.

Back in my bedroom, in my mind's eye I saw a film of something that hadn't yet happened, images from the future: I'd be going to a place where other young people who loved reading and walking would be my new friends, adding to those I already had at school. And we'd have adventures – walk across fields and streams and discover an old house like the one in Waterlow Park, where Mum, Kayin and I used to picnic.

In the grounds of this house, I could already see the tennis courts and we'd play every day. Unless it was raining. Then we'd have to make do with ping-pong. Or Monopoly. Or Scrabble. It would be 'A Summer Holiday to Remember' (a good title for a short story). There would be fish and chips on Friday nights, followed by suet pudding and treacle, and custard, with enough cream soda to float a boat in. There'd be a huge library, as big as the one at school, and when the holidays were over, I'd be off to –

There the fantasy came to an abrupt halt: holidays were temporary, and Mrs Walton had said that my stay at Park House, which was located in a village in Hertfordshire, was to be a holiday. So what would happen to me after the summer? When your holiday was over, you went home, didn't you? And that meant going back to the Taylors'. But I knew they didn't want me there. And I didn't want to be there either, but there didn't seem to be an alternative. Because I had no way of articulating how I felt in anything other than negative terms, I couldn't express what I wanted to Mrs Walton. I'd written off the possibility of having a conventional family life, and I didn't want to live in an institution like the one Richie had been sent to. I think Mrs Walton must have been hoping that a break from each other would give us some breathing space and allow us to repair the relationship.

*

Mrs Walton picked me up from the Taylors' in her old car on a sunny day in July 1966. There was another girl already sitting on the back seat. I climbed in next to her, and felt uncomfortable at having to sit so close to a complete stranger. The girl's name was Rosie and she asked me a couple of times what I had done to get sent to Park House, a question I didn't fully understand at the time.

I sat back in the car as we drove up through Holloway, from city to suburbs to countryside. I waved a 'goodbye for now' to north London, and wondered if north London would notice that I'd left.

Rosie and I started chatting again and Mrs Walton observed, 'You two seem to be getting on well,' as she drove through the traffic.

Rosie, possibly spurred on by Mrs Walton's comment, said she wanted us to share a bedroom, and talked as if we were old friends. She seemed very different to me: she was quite the extrovert, and apparently didn't care about books or schoolwork. We drove past fields of long grass and grazing cows, and I wondered how this holiday in the countryside with a new friend would turn out.

Park House was a large detached house, with a gravel driveway. We were met by a tall, slim man wearing glasses, and a shorter woman with clipped, short black hair. Mrs Walton introduced Mr and Mrs Tusker, the houseparents, as Uncle and Aunty. I hated that: they weren't my uncle or aunty. It was a pretence, a sham intended to gloss over the uncomfortable reality of our situation, which only made matters worse. *I'm only going to be here for a holiday, after all*, I thought. It made me bristle.

I might not have been keen on staying with the Taylors but when I arrived at Park House to find I was sharing it with other children and teenagers in care, I was desolate. I quickly realized that nothing about the place indicated it would be anything like the adventure I'd imagined, and I felt stupid for having had fantasies of playing tennis, and reading in a library. It didn't feel like a holiday home at all, bearing no relation to the place I'd pictured before my arrival. Although it felt as if there were hundreds of children, I think there were actually about fourteen others besides me, but these young people – whose lifestyles included robbing pensioners, bunking off school and assaulting other kids – were nothing like the friends I knew from school.

When Rosie had demanded to know what I'd done to get myself banished to the other end of the world, in Hertfordshire, I'd asked myself the same question. We did end up sharing a room, though that turned out to be an unhappy experience.

Having moaned about the unwritten rules intended to govern our behaviour at the Taylors', I now found myself living in an institution governed entirely by regulations and routines: you must have so many hours' sleep at such and such an age, you must eat what you're given, and other similar strictures. You couldn't play your records if staff didn't like your choice of music; you had to 'join in' with everyone else in the playroom; and if you invited friends to the children's home, you would have to sign them in. I certainly couldn't spend all day in my room reading and fantasizing about another kind of life.

Until I read my care notes, part of me thought I must have reimagined my first conversation with Mrs Walton about the move to Park House. For years after that move, I'd been sure that she'd told me I was going to a holiday home. That meant my imagined tennis-playing scenarios weren't as naive as they might have seemed. Then my mature self told me that I'd been wrong, that I'd heard what I wanted to hear: Mrs Walton had said no such thing, had been truthful and told me I was going to live in a children's home.

In fact, my original memory had been correct: the care records contained a number of Mrs Walton's scrawled handwritten notes saying exactly what I'd initially thought – that I was going to Park House for a holiday.

As far as I can gather from the notes, it seems Mrs Walton had no idea where she would be able to place me after the summer holidays. I think she was just hoping that the Taylors would have me back.

However, her hopes were ill founded. After a brief return to the Taylors' at the end of that summer, I moved to Park House with a view to staying there permanently. From the records, it seems that despite my initial reservations, I had been eager to leave the Taylors'. Mrs Walton noted that one morning after I had left for school, Mrs Taylor came home from work to find a packed suitcase in the hallway; I was apparently readying myself to move out, though who knows where I thought

```
                                                        CH/19
                        London Borough of Islington
                            CHILDREN'S DEPARTMENT

                              REPORT ON VISIT
  1.
  N.B.  In the case of boarded-out children it is not necessary to see the children always in the foster-home, but
        when they are seen elsewhere, the foster-home must still be visited within the prescribed periods.

  Name of child:  YOUNG Lola       Date of Birth:        Type of Case  CA '3—  1
  Placed with:    On holiday                             Action reqd. under (4)
  Address:        ▓▓▓▓▓▓▓▓▓▓▓▓▓▓▓▓▓▓▓
  Date of visit   2.9.66         Date of placing         In hand:
  Whom seen:      ▓▓▓▓▓▓▓
                  and Lola.
  Date of last visit                                     Completed:
  19.8.66                                                Initial & Date:

  2. GENERAL REPORT
        Called at ▓▓▓▓▓▓▓▓▓▓▓ and talked first of all to the ▓▓▓▓▓▓▓▓.
  ▓▓▓▓▓▓▓▓ has talked on the phone to the headmaster of the local
  comprehensive school regarding their O-level exams. It seems they
  take the Associated Education Board exam and have nine or ten children
  taking between 7 and 8 subjects at O-level this year. I felt we
  should discuss this with Lola and in the meanwhile ▓▓▓▓▓▓▓▓▓ said
  that ▓▓▓▓▓▓▓▓, their assistant, who would soon be leaving, seems to
  know Lola's family and when her brother-in-law who is on 3 months
  leave from a job as attorney in Lagos came on a visit, he said that he
  lives only 4 doors away from Mrs. Santos. He said that she is in a
  good position and he cannot understand why Lola has been rejected in
  this way for so long. The story he tells is that Mrs. Santos became
  pregnant by Mr. Young who was her husband's friend and since she was
  a widow and he a married man, she came to London to hide the fact of
  her pregnancy. ▓▓▓▓▓▓▓▓ has talked to Lola about her family, but
  the ▓▓▓▓▓▓▓ do not know what was said. We then returned to the
  question of Lola's schooling and recalled her in to discuss it. I
  pointed out the drawbacks of changing schools when the syllabus could
  not possibly be exactly the same and that I felt the journey to
  Parliament Hill Fields from ▓▓▓▓▓▓ would be too tiring, particularly
  taking into account that her school report had shown that she needed to
  work hard if she were to succeed in passing a few O-levels. When I
  suggested tentatively that it might be necessary for her to return to
  the ▓▓▓▓▓▓▓ for a while, Lola became rather tearful and ▓▓▓▓▓▓▓▓
  asked if she might perhaps stay at ▓▓▓▓▓▓▓ and do the journey daily
  for a few weeks to give us time to make some other arrangements.
  Lola thought this was a good idea. Meanwhile, I asked ▓▓▓▓▓▓▓
  to phone the headmaster again and he arranged to take Lola to see him
  on Monday morning. It was also arranged that Lola should go to the
  ▓▓▓▓▓▓▓ on Tuesday morning to collect all her things and I would
  then call there at about 12 noon and bring her to the office where
  she would leave all except the items she needed immediately. The
  other things could be taken to ▓▓▓▓▓▓▓ when somebody was going on a
  visit.
```

I was going? I still don't remember this, and even given my emotional state at the time and my deteriorating relationship with the Taylors, I was surprised to read of the incident in Mrs Walton's notes. I thought I'd outgrown the idea that I could run away.

*

At one point, early on in those summer holidays, just after I'd left the Taylors' for the first time, I remember writing to Jo, my school friend, telling her what had happened, and where I was now living. In just over a year I'd moved three times. Now I was going to stay in an institution – a dreaded children's home, like Richie, only I had nowhere to run back to.

Jo and Sue promised to come and visit me, and I was elated at the thought. Mr Tusker suggested I invite them to tea.

My heart sank as I thought of my two worldly friends observing what it was like at mealtimes in a children's home – eating alongside noisy little kids, bad boys and runaway girls. Not only that, but I got the impression that the cost of their food would be deducted from my pocket money. Their names would have to go into a visitors' book in case something happened to them while they were visiting. But none of these considerations put me off. I was so desperate to see them both – representing, as they did, a link to a more settled past.

Jo and Sue came to tea; I signed them in and we talked about going back to school, and the prospect of exams looming on the horizon. We discussed clothes and music and make-up, and meandered around the grounds in which Park House was set. I've a feeling we were allowed to eat somewhere separate from the other kids, for which I would have been grateful. They didn't seem to mind my surroundings as much as I did – I was acutely aware of the differences between my life and theirs. I'd been to Jo's house and met her family. Her older sister,

Jane, went to art school, worked in advertising, seeking out locations for shoots, and was impossibly glamorous. She'd made me up several times – with false eyelashes, and eyeshadow – and I must admit I did enjoy the care she took, her attention to detail. I looked like a different person, and I wondered whether somebody who looked like the new me could work in fashion or publishing, or even advertising, rather than teach PE.

Seeing my friends as they walked up the driveway of Park House meant a lot to me – knowing that they would bother to come all the way out to Hertfordshire for a cup of tea and a slice of cake.

As if it wasn't bad enough to be living in the middle of the countryside, away from friends and familiar places, after a couple of weeks Mr Tusker suggested that it would be easier all round if, in September, I swapped from Parliament Hill School to the local comprehensive near the village. This was when it became clear to me that my stay at Park House might not just be for the summer. The prospect of starting over at a new school conjured up a nightmare. It wasn't just that I'd lose touch with my friends, it was that going to a local school meant accepting that I would stay in this children's home until I left care at eighteen years old. But I agreed to visit the local comprehensive, to pacify Mrs Walton and the Tuskers, just to have a look. Yes, it would have been a short journey to my new school from Park House, but so what? I'd miss not only my friends but their parents and siblings, some of whom I'd got to know quite well. Fortunately for me, a different exam board syllabus proved to be a persuasive argument against changing schools. In the end, as I had already begun to prepare for my mock GCE O levels, it was decided that I should be allowed to stay at Parliament Hill.

As Jo and Sue and I chatted, I wondered whether they could imagine what it would be like for me to make that long, arduous journey every day to and from school, if I did end up living at Park House after the holidays. Jo says now that all she could think of was how difficult it was going to be for me.

A memory: A walk in the dark

November 1966: *fifteen years and five months*

Six a.m. Time to get up, make breakfast and leave the home, just as everyone else is waking up.

Walk the twenty-five minutes to the station, catch the overground train to Finsbury Park, take a bus to Camden Town, then a bus from Camden Town to Parliament Hill. Reverse that journey when school's over.

The journey was long and tiring, but it felt manageable on my return to school in September and for most of October, when there was still enough light to see me safely back to Park House in the afternoons. But after the clocks went back at the end of October, the light began to dim earlier every day. Soon it was properly dark by 4.30 p.m.

The darkness here is different to London-dark.

The first, short section of the walk from the station, which is closest to people and houses, is well lit. I tell myself that I hate having to walk through an area with street lights and a pavement. During this stretch I have to repeat to myself, over and over again, how much I am looking forward to being the only human on foot on the deserted country road up ahead; cars speeding along, clipping the grass around my feet as I walk; drivers rushing to reach their homes, back in time for their evening meals, in their cosy homes in front of the telly. This is what I tell myself. This is how I'm going to get through this.

To keep going on this road, in the thick of this darkness, I tell myself that the absolute last thing I want to see on a cold, wet, windy autumn evening is a car with bright white headlights that illuminate the way ahead. I force myself to become a creature of the night, craving the solidity of darkness.

Oh, how I hate light, any light. *I really hope there's not a full moon*, I repeat to myself as I walk, quickly as I can. I say this over and over, while a different compartment in my brain desperately hopes the moon will do me this one favour, just this one time, please. Oh no, a car travelling slowly with its headlights on full beam – oh how horrible that is. How I long for the return of that deep, deep darkness.

And the cows whose mooing I think at first is a man coughing, following me along the treacherous road. Would they attack me, a trespasser, if I tried to walk through their field instead of walking in the road? Or maybe someone's lying in wait in the bushes. Is that the outline of a shrub or a man over there, crouching, waiting to kidnap me and do whatever it is they do to Black girls from London who've strayed into the English countryside? I walk quickly, checking to see if there are any shadows following me, trying not to trip over the roots of trees, or slip on the rain-slick grass.

On the worst of these dark evenings, the journey seems

to go on for hours. But it's only the twenty-five minutes of terror. There it is. For the final fifty yards of the walk I can see the glow of lights in the windows at Park House.

How wonderful, I say to myself, *that I get to have this experience all over again tomorrow.*

I want to be brave, and I don't want Mrs Walton to think that by opting to stay at Parly Hill, I've made the wrong decision. I've made up my mind: I can't go back to the Taylors, and I'm not changing schools, so I will just have to put up with the walk until Mrs Walton can find me somewhere else to live.

Seven: Taking the long view

NOTES
Consideration of the 'Welfare' of the child involves taking account of such all-important matters as his attitude to members of the foster family, and theirs to him, and similar things affecting his well-being. Assessment of the child's 'Health' will involve consideration of medical reports, on the interpretation of which the Divisional Medical Officer should be consulted as necessary. In the case of a child who is attending school 'Conduct' includes conduct at school, and 'Progress' includes educational progress.

At the start of the Easter break in 2012, I finally managed to set aside the time to take the long and scenic train journey from London to Cornwall, where the call of the sea and the light beckoned. As we hugged the coast, the train seemed to skim across the waves, and I could almost taste the droplets of salty water suspended in the air outside.

I would be staying in Falmouth for almost a week. I had with me the entire contents of the box file, and planned to read them systematically, free from the pressure of having to dash off to meetings or scrutinize committee papers. I'd invited my son, Gregg, to join me – he had a writing project to work on, and a change of scene would do us both good.

The rugged landscape and the cliffs whose paths begged to be walked proved irresistible. There was also the lure of clotted cream. My love for it harked back to when I was a child and Daisy's daughter, Evelyn, would send a postcard from Devon or from Cornwall, promising that cartons of it were on their way to us in the post. Whenever I pestered Daisy for an update on when the cream would arrive, she would say, 'It's on the way. Just be patient!'

But what does being patient mean when you're nine years old? When other things that are supposed to arrive by post – postal orders to placate Daisy and Evelyn, and birthday cards signed with love and kisses – never did?

We were staying in a former meteorological tower with panoramic views of Falmouth Bay. We set up our laptops on the top floor, where we had the benefit of a 360-degree view uninterrupted by tall buildings or trees. At the mere suggestion of sun outside, light poured in through an expanse of windows. There was so much sky! The clouds lined up, presenting themselves for identification, and a journal had been placed on the window sill by the owners for us to record our observations.

The sight of the weather systems rolling in from the Atlantic was mesmerizing. I allocated 'staring out of the windows' slots in my diary. These offered a break from reading and thinking, and gave me the space to empty my mind and ready myself for the next instalment.

*

Reading all kinds of texts over the years in a professional capacity had been a challenge I'd relished. Book prizes, committee papers, evidence in inquiries, reports, essays and theses, parliamentary bills – all needed different kinds of literacy and analytical skills. My time in the academic world had trained me to analyse and critique, to try and identify and understand what was going on beneath the surface of the written word or the visual image. I accepted that no document offered an uncomplicated record of an objective, unvarnished truth.

I wanted to deal with my care notes with a similarly robust attitude. The piecemeal approach I'd taken up until now wasn't going to work. I was convinced that somewhere in among the barely legible handwriting and the poor, shadowy photocopying, there was a revelatory narrative waiting to emerge, if only I was diligent in my reading. But it's one thing to have your critical faculties on alert when discussing an academic paper or a new law; it's a different prospect when it comes to subject matter of such a personal nature.

As I embarked on a more thorough read, I was finding material that confirmed much of what I'd remembered from my years in care. This was reassuring. No earth-shattering discoveries just yet – more like a few gentle tremors. I started to relax.

When I was growing up, it hadn't occurred to me that Islington officials would attempt to make contact with my parents after the death of my foster mother.

But I was looking at the evidence of it now. In July 1965, Mr Everton, then Islington's director of social services, wrote to my mother at the address I had memorized, to let her know that Daisy Vince, the woman to whom she'd entrusted her baby daughter, had died.

/HOL/HM

21 July 1965

Dear Mrs. Santos,

<u>Margaret (Lola) Young (1.6.51)</u>

I understand you have recently been informed by ▓▓▓▓▓ of the death in June this year of her mother, Mrs. D. Vince, 207 Tufnell Park Road, London, N.7 - Lola's foster mother.

As your daughter has no relatives in this country able to make a home for her, it has been decided to receive her into the care of this Department, under Section 1 Children Act, 1948, and to place her with local registered foster-parents. She has settled very happily and is able to continue at the same school, doing extremely well and entering very fully into the life of the school.

To avoid confusion and misunderstanding with the foster-parents, any communication you may wish to make to Lola should be addressed to this office.

Yours sincerely,

Mrs. O. Santos
10 Taiwo Street
Lagos
Nigeria.

My mother responded to Everton on 15 September 1965.

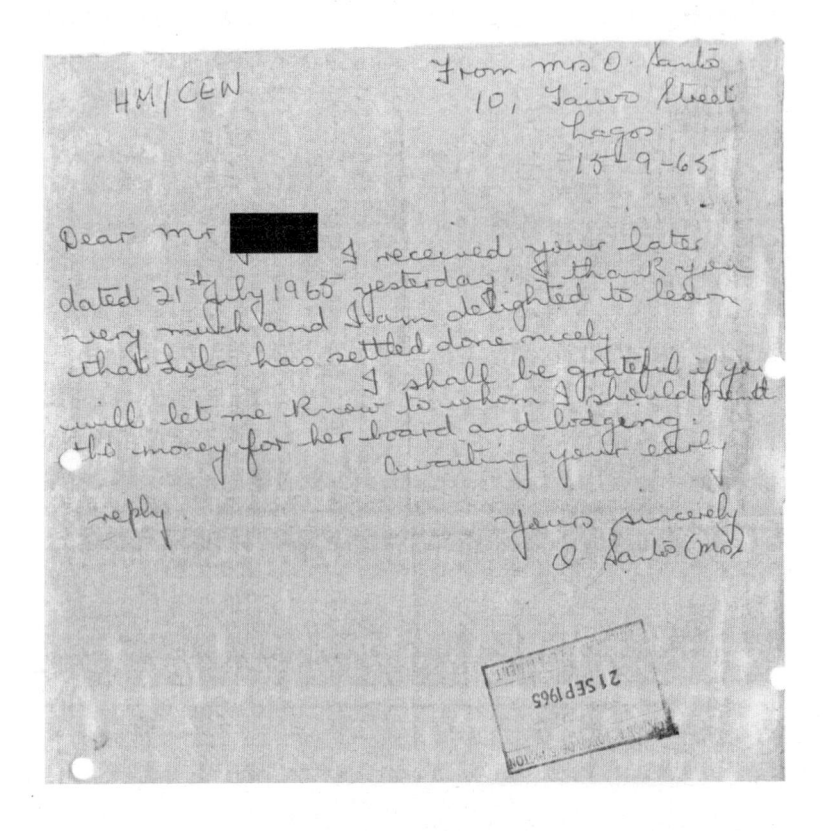

> HM/CEW
>
> From Mrs O. Santos
> 10, Taiwo Street
> Lagos
> 15-9-65
>
> Dear Mr ▮,
>
> I received your letter dated 21st July 1965 yesterday. I thank you very much and I am delighted to learn that Lola has settled down nicely. I shall be grateful if you will let me know to whom I should remit the money for her board and lodging.
>
> Awaiting your early reply.
>
> Yours sincerely,
> O. Santos (Mrs)
>
> 21 SEP 1965

I read and reread my mother's letter as I tried to piece together an explanation for every interaction that had – or, more accurately, hadn't – taken place between us. It didn't work. A part of me had needed to think that my mother had been wronged, abandoned by my father, and left a broken, penniless woman to fend for herself. An imagined scenario that would enable me not to blame her, but rather to pile all responsibility for my past predicaments on to my father.

When I was living in the children's home, there was a housemother, or 'aunty', named Toyin who worked there, who was Nigerian. It took me a while, but I managed to find the courage to ask her if she knew my mother. I explained that she too was Nigerian. Of course, it was a stupid question, rather like, 'My friend so-and-so lives in London, do you know her?'

Aunty Toyin seemed to treat my question seriously though, and asked for some family details. All I could tell her was my mother's name and her address – I remembered it clearly: 10 Taiwo Street, Lagos. I told her my father's name too, but I hadn't known his Nigerian address.

She promised to see what she could find out.

Aunty Toyin. In spite of what I'd thought about addressing people paid to look after us as if they were family, I wished she could have been my real aunty, but I had to share her with a dozen or so other children on the few shifts she worked. My recollection is of a tall, slim woman with a halo of Afro hair. I might well be misremembering her look though: it's just as likely she had relaxed hair, or a curly wig. I thought she was kind because she listened to me, but I saw her so infrequently, I was under no illusion that we had a close relationship.

I didn't remember her ever reporting back to me, and now, as I read the care notes, if that memory was correct, I could see why. The records showed that, apparently, Toyin had spoken to Mrs Walton and the Tuskers about me. She did have contacts in Lagos and they'd reported that 'the family' – that is, my mother's family – were quite well off, so no one could understand why Yele Santos hadn't brought her child back to Lagos with her. If these observations were valid, they would have modified my assumption of my mother's vulnerability, to some extent, though Toyin's 'evidence' had been anecdotal.

I don't recall expecting any contact from my parents in the immediate wake of Daisy's death. But later on, as I entered the maelstrom of the teenager's world during the mid- to late 1960s, I came to resent the lack of communication. I would go over the sequence of events, again and again, wondering why I'd heard nothing from either parent since they had left London. At Mrs Walton's suggestion, I summoned the courage to write to my mother, and actually received a reply the first time. When I followed up with a second letter, there was no reply and I think, after that, I gave up. Memory mingles with Mrs Walton's report here, as I read what she'd written and vaguely remembered the correspondence. The letters were not, of course, in the file, since this had been private communication between my mother and me. The lack of a follow-up from my mother, anticipated by Mrs Walton, must have nonetheless been disappointing for me, because I'd been particularly fixated on my mother. I think I'd assumed that my father was too engrossed in his new family to wonder about my fate. It's possible, though, that by the time I'd reached my mid-teens, when I'd written the first letter, my expectation of establishing a relationship after all that time was negligible.

Forgetting so many of these details is counterbalanced by the shape of what I have remembered. I imagine that remembering everything that has ever happened to you, as well as being improbable, would lead to a kind of insanity. Collective memory is important – that which is repeated and refined in gatherings with family or friends – but for those who've been in care, it can be very different. The loss of memories doesn't make for a comfortable mental experience either. I'd always felt I remembered more than enough of what mattered, but now the reports were adding more texture to my store of memories.

My mother's address took on an air of mystery in my mind, its precise significance elusive: 10 Taiwo Street, Lagos, Nigeria. I had no concept of what a house in a street with that name might look like. The only images we saw of Africa featured starving children in dusty, dry rural areas, or squalid accommodation in sprawling urban settings. Conflict, famine, poverty – the media's portrayal of the region was only emphasized by the news reports from what developed into the Biafran or Nigerian Civil war in 1967.

A further note in the file, dated after the exchange of letters with my mother, and written in May 1966, records the following interaction with the Taylors.

> [...] suggested (for the first time) perhaps Lola ought to be reunited with her natural mother. The [...]s do

still hear news of her from their own friends. It was pointed out that Mrs Santos has a family and life of her own now and has not seen Lola since she was a baby, Lola having grown up in an English and Islington home far from Nigeria.

Although it wasn't, strictly speaking, true that my mother hadn't seen me since I was a baby, in essence the point had to be accepted that there was little to be gained by Islington Children's Services pursuing the possibility of a 'reconnection' between mother and daughter. Mr Taylor made this suggestion just before he told Mrs Walton that he and his wife no longer wanted to look after me.

Taken with the information reportedly gathered by Toyin, reading this snippet was both upsetting and comforting. Upsetting because, even after all I'd achieved, and after the decades that had passed, I could still experience a sense of loss. As a young person, I'd not been able to express or share grief after losing both my birth mother and my foster mother, and I still maintained the hope that my unanswered questions could be resolved, one way or another. And comforting, because it suggested that the threads of my mother's bond with me had been tenuous to the point of non-existent, justifying my dismissal of concepts such as 'family bonds' and 'maternal instincts' during those horrible years.

As I read, I recreated scenes I remembered from the past, the additional information provided by the notes embellishing my original recollections. As fresh details emerged, a series of images flashed before me in quick succession, overlapping with each other, creating a cacophony of sound and vision: me at seven, declining to go with my mother to Lagos; me at ten, saying I hoped Evelyn would die, and her hearing me say it; me at twelve resisting my father's half-hearted attempt to take me away. With each painful memory and sensation that rose to the surface, I had to keep reminding myself what it had taken me to get hold of my care records in the first place: how many times I'd been told by the authorities that I must be mistaken about having been in the care of Islington Council. The effort of getting to this point meant I had to commit to completing the exploration of my care records.

Those images were now augmented by new knowledge culled from the records. My fear of being sent to a children's home when I was living with Daisy seems not to have been a dystopian fantasy. The records note that Daisy – pressured on the one hand by her daughter, Evelyn, who felt that blood relations should be her first priority, and on the other by a social services department concerned that the day when Daisy lacked the capacity to look after me was approaching – had resisted. As an adult, once I learned more about how and why children were taken into care, I'd wondered why Islington Council hadn't acted earlier, and I'm sure that, had social services wanted to, they could have overridden Daisy's wishes. Since she wasn't my legal guardian, her refusal to allow me to go into a children's home would have had no standing.

My mother's coolly expressed 'delight' at my having been placed with new foster parents hadn't been that much of a surprise; nothing in her behaviour ever suggested that she had forged an unbreakable maternal connection with me. However, there was something curious and inconsistent about her behaviour; for example, I discovered that she had returned to work in a hospital in west London, without a word, in 1963. Daisy was alerted to this by my father, of all people, just before he and his family left London. That visit had been some five years after she'd said goodbye and set sail for Lagos. I found it hard to accept that she could behave in this way. I had to somehow remould my presumption of my mother's sadness at leaving me behind. There was just so much new information to assess and assimilate, including the claim made by Daisy that Yele Santos had asked her to promise never to allow me to be cared for by my father, under any circumstances. How was it possible for me to integrate these inconsistencies into the already blurred image I had of this woman? She'd felt able to leave her young daughter on another continent, with a foster mother barely known to her, rather than have the child looked after by her biological father. Yes, these were all fresh insights into the contradictory directions my mother's thoughts had taken, but the information didn't really help answer my questions about my parents' lives before I was born, about what kind of people they actually were. The answers to questions I'd had throughout my life, along with those provoked by the package from

Lagos, seemed just as far away as when I had started on this trail.

Then there was the man himself: my father, the iceman. The enigma who'd also left me behind at the first hint of my dissent, who already had another family before I came along.

> *2.2.62*: Lola's mother sent a cheque last month to Mrs Vince but no letter. Never sends a card or present to the child. Mr Young does not visit now.

> *28.3.62*: School authorities have contacted Dr Young, father of the child, who promises he will visit Mrs Vince once a month. Case is known to Nigerian Government. Father now lives in Balham. Address noted. He promises safe custody of the child and will be taking her eventually to Nigeria where she will be a pupil in a State School.

> *11.7.63*: Mrs Vince has not been to Children's Department. Urged to do so after reading a letter from Mr Young who says one day he will come and collect Lola.

The assurances from my father to Daisy and to the authorities, promising visits, promising safety and security, promising a home in Nigeria, had not been revealed to me at the time. Daisy and Miss Boardman had both been silent on the subject, perhaps concerned not to disappoint me. If so, their concern was misplaced: I had no hopes to be dashed on that score. I had few expectations and no desire to live with a man I viewed as a stranger who had clearly decided where his parental priorities lay.

Though I'd been unaware at the time of the promises he'd made, my perception of my father's lack of interest in me was vindicated many times over in the care notes, from birth through to my childhood and adolescence. He failed to deliver on each of his pledges.

In late autumn of 1966, when I'd been living at Park House for about three months, on one of her regular visits, Mrs Walton told me that a Mr and Mrs Galloway, a police officer and his wife who lived in Barnet, a suburb north of London, wanted to take in a foster child to add to the two they already had. It still wasn't proper London, as far as I was concerned, but it was a lot closer than the unlit, dangerous country roads of Hertfordshire.

At the time, I somehow interpreted Mrs Walton's words to mean that I – at the age of fifteen – could potentially be adopted by the couple. This enduring fantasy, fed by cravings for the family life that had always eluded me, persisted until all hope of such a result had disappeared. It was a clear illustration of just how desperate I was to leave behind the traumatizing walk from the train station to Park House.

Mr Galloway did not, thankfully, wear his police officer's uniform when he first came to meet me at the children's home, but I would have recognized him as a police officer anyway. Tall and broad-shouldered with dark hair, he reminded me of Jack, Daisy's adopted son.

Jack, Gillian and their son, Oliver, had also lived in Barnet, which perhaps strengthened the association in my mind. Either way, it was a comforting thought, a link to a happier past.

The Galloways' Barnet home was set up the way a proper family home should be, with a mother and a father – not a housemother or housefather, or an unrelated aunty or uncle. One set of parents. And a dog. Not a family that I had invented.

I spent the weekend playing with the children – hide and seek in the park and in their garden, and snakes and ladders in the kitchen. On Saturday night, lying in the bedroom, I enjoyed the luxury of sleeping in a room on my own.

I remember that, as I lay in bed, I was awake and dreaming at the same time. The surrounding floor had changed into water and I became frightened, because I thought I was going to drown. The water would rise and soon be as high as the bed, lapping at my feet. I tried to make the water and the feeling of creeping cold and damp go away. If I could only pull the bedclothes over my head and repeat, 'It's only a dream, it's only a dream,' I'd be safe.

Despite my desire to believe in the potential of finding a permanent home with the Galloways, even during that first weekend visit I had an inkling that the price of escaping the children's home would be babysitting and clearing up toys, entertaining the children and providing any other services the Galloways might need.

On the Sunday evening, before I returned to the

children's home, Mrs Galloway said that she hoped I'd stay with them again, because the children liked me. On the whole I had enjoyed my time there – apart from the waking dream, which had been unnerving. Even doing the chores hadn't bothered me all that much; at least I wasn't being taken for granted.

The next time I visited the Galloways' house, I was ready for the experience of feeling wide awake at the same time as being fast asleep. But that night, I experienced only a shadow of the previous dream – flimsy, where the other had evoked something more tangible. Cool wet sand and singing dolphins. I fell into a deep sleep.

I sensed throughout the weekend that the policeman and his wife were not quite so welcoming as the previous time I'd stayed. It was hard to be specific about what had changed, nothing was said, but there was a different atmosphere in the house.

On Monday morning, Mr Galloway informed me he was going to give me a lift to school in his van. I'd never imagined I would be getting a lift into school, and it came as a welcome surprise. I guessed it would be a test run to see how long the journey would take when I eventually went to live with them. Even without a lift the journey would be relatively easy: from Barnet, down to Kentish Town on the Northern line, and then the bus or walking to school from there.

After about twenty minutes' drive, we reached Archway, which wasn't far from Tufnell Park. I'd only been living in Hertfordshire for a few months, but it felt much, much longer, and I was grateful to see that north London was still where I'd left it. We were not far from school when Mr Galloway pulled over and parked at the kerb on Dartmouth Park Hill. He had some news, he said.

He started by saying how much they'd all enjoyed having me to stay with them, how good I had been with the children. Then he went quiet. When he spoke again, he was nervously apologetic. 'I'm sorry, Lola but we've just discovered that my wife is expecting a baby, and what with the other children and a new baby, well, we wouldn't be able to manage another child. It wouldn't be fair on you.'

He may well have been sorry but, more than anything, I thought this was a cowardly act. It seemed to me to be cheating to tell me like that, sitting in his van. Why hadn't he and his wife told me that morning over breakfast, when they would have had to look me in the eye?

We sat there in silence, neither of us looking at the other, the air thick with guilt and disappointment.

He insisted that he'd take me all the way to school, if I liked, but I didn't like, and I politely told him so. He was nervous and relieved all at once when I opened the van door and stepped down on to the kerb. I thanked him for the lift and walked up the hill towards school. It was the same route I'd taken every day from Daisy's house on Tufnell Park Road.

When I came to Mrs Walton's report about the Galloways in my file, it chimed with my initial sense of what they had wanted from me: I'd sensed their unspoken motive. It was noted in the care records that they had known about the pregnancy before they met me, and what they really wanted was a live-in au pair.

Mrs Walton wrote:

> *4.10.66*: Spoke to [. . .], the CCO [child care officer] who deals with the [. . .]s and whom she visited last evening. She said they seemed worried that too much might be expected of them with regard to Lola and what they really wanted was an au pair, or at least someone who would babysit for them.

Great. And especially disappointing to read after seeing the claim for extra financial support they required from Islington to feed this 'large girl'.

Until Islington Council could find a place somewhere for me that was closer to school, I would have to continue to live in Hertfordshire and deal with the challenges that decision posed.

When the move to the Galloways' fell through, I managed to convince myself that I didn't care, asserting that I would never have chosen to live in a police officer's household anyway. Now I think it would have been hard for me to admit how upset it had made me feel, because at that point I was beginning to experience an onrush of hopelessness, my expectations of what the future might bring going into free fall. Whatever criticism could be laid at the door of Islington

Council for allowing Daisy to continue fostering into her late seventies, at least I had experienced stability. The loss of Daisy Vince was a seismic event in my life and, looking back, it seems that nobody knew quite how to help me through it.

At this point, I had struggled with this series of disruptions for just over a year. In addition, no matter how many times I told myself that I could cope with the walk home from the station, I was left in a state of anxiety that was to stay with me for years. Even now, more than half a century later, the memory of that experience comes to mind too easily, and too vividly, for comfort. The impact was immeasurable.

I'd been cheeky and unhelpful at the Taylors', but now at Park House I'd added a short temper, lashing out verbally and physically, and adding sullen and quiet to my repertoire of moods. Somewhere else had to be found for me to live, but Mrs Walton had been looking for a suitable placement for me since the Taylors first asked for my removal in July, and it was now October. There was no longer any point in asking if there was a prospect of living anywhere else: whether in a hostel, a home or with a family.

I've been back to the area just once since 1966, to see if Park House was as I remembered it. There were no surprises, though the detached building looked as though it might now be privately owned. That awful walk from the station to Park House? There's a proper pavement there now. And street lighting.

*

In November 1966, Mrs Walton finally announced that she had found somewhere closer to school for me to live, a children's home on Vicarage Road. 'Closer' was relative, of course: Vicarage Road was in Middlesex. Middlesex was still not London, as far as I was concerned. The prospect of moving to live with yet more strangers in a strange land held no attraction. Nevertheless, I agreed to the move, and that autumn Mr and Mrs Flagg became the latest embodiment of my corporate parents.

Like Hertfordshire, there was little comfort to be had in the out-of-the-way space to which I'd been consigned. Few Black people; no opportunity to go back to a school friend's house unless they had been vetted by the council, and even then, it would have been near impossible because of the length of the journey back to the children's home; and no other children who shared my interest in reading, or art, or even sport.

North London was my home, and I missed it terribly; I knew how to read the signs of trouble back there. Hertfordshire, Middlesex, even Barnet – where the Galloways had lived – were indecipherable. How could I identify friend or foe when there were only shadows and silhouettes on dimly lit country or suburban roads? With rows of identical houses, few shops and no underground, how would I even know whether I was lost until it was too late?

There was no train from Vicarage Road to north London, only buses, so I still had to get up when everyone else was asleep, creeping around so as not to disturb the other three girls with whom I shared a bedroom. I had to leave the home in Vicarage Road by 7.15 a.m.; then it was up to the traffic and an irregular bus service as to whether I arrived at school on time. Maybe there was somewhere they could have sent me that was even further from school? Any vacancies in a home in the Shetlands from which I could commute, perhaps?

From the outside, the home in Vicarage Road was virtually indistinguishable from the rest of the houses on that row, the only difference being that on closer inspection it was actually two houses rather than one. The interior decoration made no impression on me as I can't remember a single detail. In retrospect, I'd say that the decor was bland in the way that most institutions are, the design wary in case something bold and distinctive might somehow provoke the residents into breaking the rules. Of my three roommates, all similar in age to me, I can only recall one, and that was the one I'll call Carmen.

Children moved in and out of homes all the time – I wasn't exceptional in that. Every time I moved – and coming here had been my fifth move since Daisy died – I left some of my possessions behind. Records, books, ornaments, photographs . . . gradually the pieces of my earlier life were reduced to almost nothing. But somehow, I still had the Tony Hancock album *The Wild Man of the Woods*, a comedy record Daisy had bought for us when we lived in Tufnell Park Road. Unfortunately, it wasn't enough to cheer me up, especially as I no longer had a record player.

I felt like an outsider at Vicarage Road from the start. Or maybe that's me rationalizing after the event. Whatever I felt, there are references in the records to the Flaggs expressing to Mrs Walton their doubts about whether I'd fit in with the other kids because I was at a higher academic level than the others. They seemed quite apologetic about the situation, as if they thought it reflected badly on them. These comments made me wonder what the Flaggs had said to the other staff and children about me, prior to my arrival. The exchanges between the Flaggs and Mrs Walton about my academic attainments were only revealed to me once I'd started a deep dive into the care notes. If Mrs Walton had reservations about moving me to Vicarage Road, she didn't express them in writing, and she certainly never said anything to me in person: in any case, she had few options if she was to bring to an end my arduous journey to and from school.

At weekends, we older kids would take the young ones to the Saturday morning pictures, creating a curious sight: a line of small children being shepherded by a mixture of early to mid-teenaged boys and girls. On Saturday afternoons I had a job stacking shelves in a small local supermarket. The rest of my time was mainly spent pretending to study in order to keep away from the others as much as possible.

Despite our mutual antipathy, on one occasion I joined the other older kids in some of that aimless rambling around local streets that teenagers often do. An onlooker might have thought that my roommate Carmen and I looked like two friends out for an autumn stroll. We might even have been walking along arm in arm, as teenage girls sometimes do, though there was no sense of sisterly solidarity between us.

'I don't like coloured people,' Carmen said slowly.

The air around us changed.

'So you don't like me, then?' I asked.

'Oh, no, I don't mean you, you're different,' she replied, seemingly thinking this should have made me feel better. It didn't.

One of the boys drew my attention away from the strained conversation. He dragged a key along the side of a car, a series of scratch marks appearing as he walked. The mood among us was, 'Yeah, let's all have a go!'

I thought about everything that had happened to me in the past year, things I hadn't had any control over; then I just thought, *Why the hell not?*

I dug the key into the car's door and dragged it along the whole length of the car. My reward was the sight of a streak of silvery grey metal that appeared from under the glossy surface.

We ran back to Vicarage Road, having enjoyed five minutes of disorderly behaviour. If the Galloways or the Taylors had seen me then, I wondered what they would have thought. Would I have been cast as a typical bad seed? Or a victim of bad luck?

The day I scratched the car was the only time I made

a conscious effort to try to be part of the teens in my age group at Vicarage Road. Something told me that teenagers who habitually damage property like that, pouring their anger into a rampage, were going nowhere, and I had no desire to go with them.

As the end of 1966 approached, I refused to let the idea of Christmas take hold. Once the holidays were over, I'd be back to sitting on buses for hours to get to school and back. Attempting to prepare for my mock GCE O levels was a joke: the best quality revision time I had was on the 269 bus – for as long as I could keep my eyes open. I'd lost my appetite for studying, in any case; it was hard to see what the point of it was. Nothing stayed in my brain; I read the same notes and textbooks over and over, unable to retain many details.

This would be my second Christmas without Daisy – the first having been spent at the Taylors', which had been surprisingly pleasant. According to Mrs Bould, Kayin and I made decorations and gifts by hand, and Kayin and I both remember being visited by what felt like an endless stream of her parents' relatives. In the Christmases that came before, even though Evelyn had never really liked us, she'd always put on a great feast for us all. The gifts that Kayin and I received from everyone made us feel as though we were on the same footing as the other children – as though we belonged as much as anyone else on that day. A sense of dread hovered over me at the children's home. For the first time, I would be spending Christmas with strangers, in a house out in the sticks.

The antipathy I had felt towards the Taylors was nothing compared to the visceral hatred I came to feel towards the Flaggs. I was in a poor emotional state, and I acted out in various ways, but it's also true that they were horrible to me, and to others too. They made cruel comments, and Mr Flagg didn't seem able to restrain his sarcasm. He behaved like a playground bully. The Flaggs' behaviour resulted in the gradual erosion of a child's confidence. Mr Flagg rarely resorted to shouting: there was no need to raise his voice, as the menace was in his tone. Mrs Flagg's weapon of choice was the withering stare. What a pair.

One child in particular seemed to provoke Mr Flagg's ire. About nine years old, Daniel wore a large hearing aid. Flagg accused him of pretending to be deaf, saying the boy could hear perfectly well when he felt like it. I hated that – an adult in a position of authority picking on a child who had more than enough to deal with, without being accused of being a fraud. And so what if he did occasionally switch off the cumbersome device? I certainly wouldn't have blamed him for not using his hearing aid, with all the noise and clatter and shouting and nonsense going on around him.

Another little boy twitched and looked as though he was in fear of his life whenever Mr Flagg walked by. Some days it felt as though the underlying tensions would come to the surface and hurt us all in some way or another.

*

A surprising discovery in my care notes stirred up painful memories of one particular weekend. Saturday meant no school, so I couldn't make my own breakfast and I would have to sit and eat with everyone else. The porridge was awful, a mass of congealed blobs floating in a lake of hot milk covered with a thin, pale yellow skin. Just the smell of it made me want to retch. I was sitting at a table far enough from the Flaggs to get away with pretending to eat a couple of mouthfuls, then smearing the rest of the stuff around the dish with the back of my spoon. From a distance it looked as though I'd eaten the stipulated spoonful of the revolting food.

'Islington Council's regulations, not ours,' the Flaggs would say.

I found it hard to imagine that anybody had written into the rulebook governing how to run a children's home the instruction that every child must eat at least one spoonful of every meal presented to them.

Mr Flagg was staring at me. He sighed, and with his voice soaked in sarcasm said, 'So, Lola Young is unhappy here.' His pale blue eyes cut through the children and the house staff seated between us.

'She's feeling depressed,' he said in a mock-sympathetic tone. He carried on like this for some time.

The heat from the rush of blood spread unseen from my neck to my face and the roots of my hair. Given the way he treated all the other kids, I shouldn't have been surprised by this outburst.

I wrote and told Mrs Walton what had happened.

> LONDON BOROUGH OF ISLINGTON
> RECEIVED
> 5 JAN 1966
> CHILDREN'S DEPARTMENT

AP

2/1/67

Middx.

Dear Mrs ▮▮▮▮.

Thank you for the toilet bag and contents that you gave me for Christmas. I hope you had a nice time. I was alright over Christmas but afterwards I became rather moody after several little events that seemed to build up. Anyway this morning I was given an ultimatum. I could either stop being moody because I was hurting others, or I could have it out with the member of staff or children causing me to be moody and get it off my chest or I could write to you. This was said at the breakfast table in front of all. ▇▇▇▇▇ said if was being here that was the cause then he could do nothing about it as he was "umbered" with me, so I should write to you. I am sorry if this is yet another dissapointment for you. I ~~can~~ also apologise ~~~~ that I refused

> the ▓▓▓▓▓▓▓ invitation.
> Thank you again for
> my present.
>   love from
>   Lola. xxx

The possibility of finding copies of my own or anyone else's handwriting in the box file from Islington Council had never occurred to me. I'd recognized Daisy's careful script with a jolt. Reading my mother's airmail letter to Islington social services had delivered a different kind of shock; her detachment and lack of affection were crushing. Yet there it was: a letter I had written and sent to Mrs Walton in the winter of 1967. A letter from my fifteen-and-a-half-year-old self to my child care officer. The incident I had remembered in some detail had been corroborated. It would have been impossible for me to know that, fifty years after the fact, my grown-up self would be reading a letter originally intended for Mrs Walton's eyes only. Stranger still to think that I'd be sharing it with countless people unknown to me.

Reading it for the first time, it was as though I'd dug up a time capsule that had been buried for over half a century. The letter reminded me of how much I'd hated every moment I stayed in that place. The tension between me and the Flaggs was horrible, damaging for everyone, and I could read between the lines of the care notes with the odd reference to me appearing 'tired' or 'worried', but explicit references to me being depressed were almost non-existent. The social workers who wrote about me were preoccupied with my physical appearance – my 'large', 'well-developed', 'Nigerian' body featuring on many occasions. For a sense of my mental state at that time I have to call on my own memory to identify the extent to which my younger self was slipping inexorably towards depression.

I had no belief that anything would work out for me, or that anyone could possibly like me. Despite my increasingly negative thoughts, I rarely created a fuss about things that weren't to my liking. I didn't complain or request better treatment and consideration in anything other than polite tones – most of the time, anyway.

My schoolwork was beginning to suffer, and I sensed that I was letting Mrs Walton down. She'd told me many times that very few children in care take A levels and go on to university, and I got the sense that for her and her colleagues there was a lot riding on my doing well at school.

I'd wanted to do something creative as a career, but it was a secret that I wouldn't have dared articulate for fear of ridicule. I knew how it would sound to say it out loud to the pragmatic Mrs Walton, who continued to assume that my aim was to teach PE, as I'd originally told Mrs Bould.

As a fifteen-year-old, for the first time I had a weekly clothing allowance in addition to pocket money, and I tried to channel my fashion aspirations into supplementing home-made clothes with strategic purchases. One time, I'd spotted a girl at school wearing a pair of shoes that I fell in love with – plain but beautiful in their simplicity. They were round-toed with a button-down strap across the middle of the foot. I couldn't get the image of those shoes out of my mind; I could almost feel the smooth leather gliding on to my feet instead of the old, scuffed, regulation black lace-ups I usually wore.

To buy them, I'd have to travel to Anello and Davide, a shop in Oxford Street near the Academy Cinema, which I'd been to with Mrs Bould. That evening out had felt like a century ago, though it had only been the previous year.

At £2 19s 11d, the shoes were very expensive. The shop had a pair in my size in every colour except black or brown, which is what I was supposed to wear to school. When I saw the pair made from lilac suede, I just knew they were the ones for me. Our school uniform was purple and grey, so perhaps I could smuggle them past the teachers who enforced the rules. Anyway, I thought, girls modify their school clothing all the time. And after all, lilac is just a paler shade of purple, isn't it?

I handed over three pound notes, and the next thing I knew the shoes were mine.

Monday morning, and assembly was barely even finished before I was hauled off to sit outside the headmistress's office. There hadn't even been time for my friends to compliment me on my new footwear. The sharp-eyed deputy headmistress, Miss Jessop, noticed my non-regulation shoes straight away and swooped on me as soon as we finished the last hymn. She escorted me to the headmistress's office for a telling-off.

The headmistress, Mrs Landers, pointed out that I had knowingly broken the rules on school uniform. Yes, I knew what I was supposed to wear, but I didn't know how to explain what those shoes meant to me, why it was so important to me that I owned them. And it couldn't have been the worst thing anybody had ever done in school. I used to think Mrs Landers had kind eyes, and that one day she might even want to invite me to her house for tea. Mrs Walton had once been told that Mrs Landers knew someone, a West Indian woman, who might have been willing to take me in, so I was aware that she knew something of my situation. But now the hope of an invitation to tea, or a possible place to live, evaporated.

I apologized and explained that I couldn't afford to replace them with another pair. I reminded her that I lived in a children's home, unashamedly pity-hunting. She didn't need to know that I'd never been so well-off as I was now. To my horror, she offered to lend me the money to buy a pair of shoes for school.

I refused, and so, 'No more lilac suede shoes,' said Mrs Landers. I had to wear my plimsolls for the rest of the day.

When I returned to the Vicarage Road home, I explained to Mrs Flagg about the shoes and what had happened with the headmistress. I could tell that she thought no shoes were worth that amount of money, and she told me to take them back to the shop and ask for a refund. Rubbing salt into my already stinging wounds, she told me that shoes like that were unsuitable for someone like me.

Eight: A sour note

16 December 1966, ▬▬▬: She [PHS headmistress] mentioned a coloured woman who lives in the same block of flats as she does in Kensington. She felt that she might be interested, in which case she seemed willing to bring Lola into school with her each day.

18 January 1967, ▬▬▬: [. . .] said that certainly since Christmas Lola has not been working. All she does is read comics and sketch.

A friend once introduced me with the words, 'This is my friend Lo. She was brought up in foster care and now she's in the House of Lords.'

I'd laughed at the time. That wasn't at all how I would have chosen to remember the meandering path my life had taken. On occasion, I'd planned the next move in my professional life, looking out for a promotion or securing a role by collaborating with people whose strengths complemented mine; sometimes it was a case of having thought about something I'd like to do – for example, wanting to write and present papers at international conferences and work on international projects, contributing to the debates and theories of culture, arts, politics and ideas. There had been occasions when I'd expressed the desire to travel, and then opportunities materialized and I'd have the chance to do so. All of that thinking had been as an adult, when I'd realized I could shape my life as I wanted to live it, not as directed by parents or staff in institutions or anyone else. I'm not a fan of off-the-shelf narrative trajectories, which suggest a straightforward, linear progression from one stage to another.

Now I wondered whether the care records might simplify or flatten my past experiences by suggesting a ready-made storyline that matched my friend's account: from foster care to the House of Lords. I reminded myself that I was in control of the narrative. And whatever information or insights the records held, the Islington Council edit of my story couldn't go beyond my eighteenth birthday, the end of my time in care.

As well as the emotional barriers to reading the documents, there were practical difficulties to contend with. I had suspected that the quality of the handwriting might not be perfect, but even when it was clear, the photocopying was poor, especially where there had been writing on both sides of the paper: a faint but intrusive shadow of the words written on the other side, confusing the eye.

The aim of the week away had been to start weaving memory and the official record into a coherent account of my past by getting a grip on the sequence of events, the locations and the cast of characters. Although I hadn't known what the exact content of my files would be, I had assumed that everything would be 'official'. Notes composed and written up by the social workers I'd been assigned to, with perhaps added commentary contributed by the administrators and decision makers who'd been 'in charge' over the course of my years in the system; that's what I'd expected. To find several letters – about me, from me and to me – had been a shock.

The handwritten ones in particular carried a raw potency that penetrated my defences. I returned several times to the letter I'd written to Mrs Walton, trying to recall what I'd really wanted to say, what I'd left out, and why this statement from the distant past got to me in the way it did. I realized it was painful because it hadn't even been the nadir of my mental state; there might be more to come. It produced a physical reaction, a feeling that I was constantly on the brink of nausea. I struggled to carry on reading.

Stuck in Middlesex, with Christmas behind me, I knew I had to do better in my schoolwork, and I tried harder to revise for my mock O levels. To their credit, the Flaggs did try to accommodate my need to study by allowing me to use the dining room after we'd had our evening meal. That seemed to work well enough, and I began to feel more confident about my prospects. Maybe there was a route out of this mess for me, after all – though the thought that I might have to stay with the Flaggs for another two and a half years did not appeal on any level.

I felt abandoned in Middlesex. I thought that Mrs Walton had forgotten all about me, and that her focus was elsewhere. Reading the notes, I understand that my teenage self had done her a disservice. There is evidence of Mrs Walton making a concerted effort to find me an alternative place to live – but none of her approaches had yet worked out.

Then, at the start of January 1967, shortly after I'd written to her explaining what had happened with Mr Flagg, Mrs Walton called me with some news. The Browne family, comprising mother, father, son and daughter, were interested in fostering me straight away, right up until I left school.

Inwardly, I felt a flicker of excitement. Would this finally mean saying goodbye to the 269 bus and its fickle timetable? Outwardly, I found it difficult to be grateful for Mrs Walton's news of a potential foster home. Determined I wouldn't be lured into the trap of false hopes again, I greeted the information without enthusiasm.

The Brownes lived in an area I was familiar with from my stay at the Taylors', though they were on the east side of Highbury Fields rather than the west. Memories of that time, just eighteen months earlier, were mixed. Life with the Taylors had not been easy: perhaps I'd had idealized fantasies about what living with a family might be like, or perhaps I was simply mourning Daisy's death. Since leaving their home in Drayton Park, the memory I revisited most often was of sitting in Highbury Fields with Kayin, eating contraband treacle tarts funded by the collection money we'd been given for church. It had felt like I'd gained some sort of victory over Kayin's parents as we sat in the sunshine, scoffing food reminiscent of what we'd been used to eating when we lived with Daisy.

Mrs Walton wrote to me with directions to the Brownes' house.

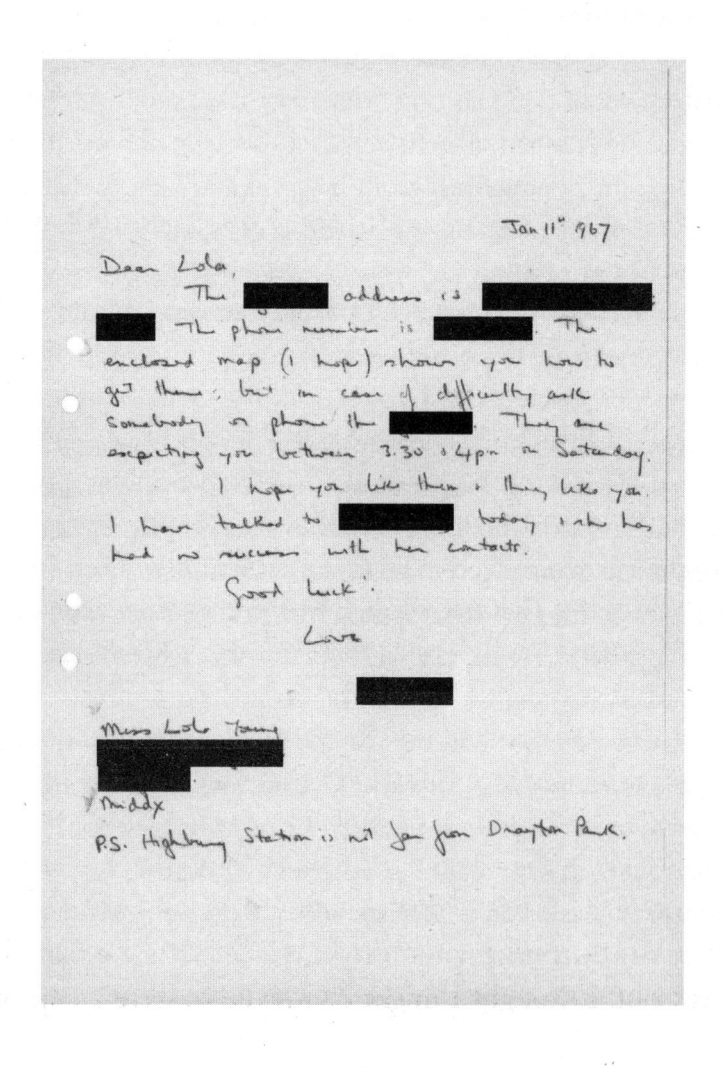

> Jan 11" 967
>
> Dear Lola,
>
> The ▮▮▮▮ address is ▮▮▮▮▮▮▮▮▮▮. The phone number is ▮▮▮▮▮. The enclosed map (I hope) shows you how to get there, but in case of difficulty ask somebody or phone the ▮▮▮▮. They are expecting you between 3.30 & 4pm on Saturday. I hope you like them & they like you. I have talked to ▮▮▮▮▮▮▮ today & she has had no success with her contacts.
>
> Good luck!
>
> Love
>
> ▮▮▮▮▮
>
> Miss Lola Young
> ▮▮▮▮▮▮
> Maddx
>
> P.S. Highbury Station is not far from Drayton Park.

The letter made it clear I would have to go to this meeting with the Brownes on my own – with no adult accompanying me. This had felt wrong, even at the time. My overactive imagination worked on every awful scenario that might befall me. And why the reference to my head teacher Mrs Landers' West Indian contact? I'd long since given up hope of that leading anywhere.

As I made my way by bus to Highbury that Saturday afternoon, I tried to anticipate what kind of reception awaited me. I had little to go on: all I knew was what Mrs Walton had written in the letter, and the sparse details she'd disclosed in the phone call.

A woman I assumed to be Mrs Browne answered the door. My impression was of a grey woman – a bit like Miss Asher, one of the single women who had lived above us at Tufnell Park Road; even if they'd worn bright red, they'd still have been grey. She put out her hand for me to shake and I offered mine. Her grip was limp, so light it was as if she didn't want to touch my skin for too long. She looked me up and down suspiciously. She must have been told to expect a Black girl, so I wondered why she was looking at me with an air of annoyance, with impatience, even though I'd arrived on time.

In my recollection of the afternoon, after her lukewarm greeting, Mrs Browne showed me into one of the street-facing rooms downstairs. What Daisy would have called the front room. The curtains were very thick, unlike those at Tufnell Park Road – which had let the thin, north-facing light shine in, and allowed the heat to drift out. I thought I might be invited to have a cup of tea – it seemed like the sort of house that would have fine china cups and saucers laid out for visitors – but no offer was forthcoming. I don't even recall being asked to sit down.

Was Mrs Browne really so inhospitable, verging on hostile? Or did she gently enquire about the subjects I liked best at school? Or maybe she interrogated me with a view to catching me out? If she had asked, in a tone that suggested she genuinely wanted to know, surely I would have remembered. I would have answered, 'I like art and English literature, but I find it difficult to do much reading where I'm living at the moment.'

It wouldn't have taken much encouragement for me to disclose how horrible it was in the children's home. Perhaps I didn't say enough to make her want to like me. But I didn't want to sound too desperate, so I didn't volunteer any information that she didn't request. I tried not to project anything except the willingness and desire to fit in. If Mrs Browne had wanted to know about who I was, then she should have asked me specific questions, made an effort to draw me out and reassure me.

We must have walked purposefully around the vast house, because I remember seeing several different rooms, and being on the move most of the time. When I cast my mind back, I see myself walking around as though in a fugue state, climbing and descending stairs, past landings and doorways. In the intervening five decades, I must have added several hundred square feet to the house in my imagination. I can see Mrs Browne and me standing in the entrance hall under a light so dim it barely created a shadow; our bodies hovered between the darkness and the light. It was a spooky house; or rather, the house spooked me. At some point, in the part of the brain that makes memories, the architecture of the Brownes' house became conflated with exterior shots from the 1960 gothic horror film *The Fall of the House of Usher*; the two are now for ever intertwined.

Mrs Browne said we'd go and see her son whose study was on the ground floor. She knocked on the door, which felt a strange thing to do in your own house – but then I wasn't used to people asking permission before they came into my room. A man's voice called out, inviting us in. He barely looked up from whatever he had been reading before we entered. Young Mr Browne looked pretty ancient to me. Never mind twenty-seven – as Mrs Walton had told me – he looked more like forty-seven. Tweed waistcoat, a grey shirt and a tie. Fancy dressing up like that on Saturday afternoon, just to sit and study. A young old fogey in his book-lined den.

Mrs Browne told me he was studying for a PhD, but at the time I didn't know what that was and I didn't dare ask. She was talking to him now, ignoring me, so I started looking at the bookshelves, though they were too far away to read the titles, but I could see hardback books and the familiar blue and orange covers of Penguin paperbacks lined up, shelf upon shelf, almost reaching the ceiling. I had a few books myself that I'd managed to keep hold of during my travels, but I had the impression that there were hundreds here in this room. He looked like he couldn't wait to get back to them – although he had smiled when we first entered his lair, he didn't seem to want to talk to me. To live in a house with such a library would be wonderful, but I tried and failed to imagine him sharing his room and precious books with me.

Mrs Browne and I climbed the stairs to the first floor, and she pointed up to the attic. I shuddered involuntarily. They say that if you feel shivery when it's not really cold, it's because someone has walked over your grave. A horrible expression, I thought – even though I didn't really believe in ghosts. Things like that used to scare me. At a friend's house one Halloween we sat in a circle and sang a song in low, spooky voices, with only candles for light:

> Never, ever laugh when a hearse goes by,
> *Ooh, ooh, ooh, ooh, ah, ah, ah,*
> You may be the next to die.

There had been a strange atmosphere in the Brownes' house of dark hallways and never-ending staircases, which may have been due to my overactive imagination, though at the time it had felt real enough. Whenever I looked back over that Saturday afternoon, my memory told me that everything about the house had given me the creeps. Now I'm not so sure. The nightmares I might have expected to experience afterwards didn't materialize. But that may have been because all the bad stuff – the feelings of dread and fear – had moved from my dreams into my everyday thoughts after Daisy died.

Can I claim anything about my encounter with the

Browne family with any certainty? Mrs Browne called out to her husband – she must have done, because I remember that we had a brief conversation, the three of us together. Afterwards, though, I was never able to describe him to anyone or conjure convincingly into existence the shape of his presence in the house.

Did Mrs Browne really point out an attic? I couldn't say. I could certainly imagine Mr Browne up there, maybe clearing out a space for my bedroom.

But my recall of what happened next has been consistent ever since that Saturday afternoon.

Mrs Browne led the way back to the entrance hall, where a pale-faced teenaged girl, about the same height as me but older, was now sweeping the floor. I guessed she was the young Miss Browne. She didn't stop her activity or seem to acknowledge our presence. I noticed that she moved awkwardly with the broom, almost tripping over her own feet.

'My daughter,' said Mrs Browne, by way of introduction. Then, standing rigid beside me, she spat out, 'She's spastic. Nineteen years old, with the mind of a child.'

I gasped. How could the woman talk about her own daughter like that to me, a stranger? There was a nasty edge to her voice, and her cruel way with words reminded me of Mr Flagg.

I summed up the situation in an instant: they made that girl do all the work around the house, because they knew she couldn't complain. This was what the rest of her life would look like, condemned to perform household chores for as long as she lived. She hadn't looked up when her mother spoke; perhaps she'd heard it all before, and couldn't or wouldn't fight back. I felt sick to my stomach. This was how she spent her Saturday afternoons, and it was not fair. Kayin and I had had to do housework at the Taylors', but at least we'd had a Hoover.

If I did move in here, I imagined making friends with the daughter and helping her with whatever tasks she had to carry out. That had probably been Mrs Browne's plan anyway, I reasoned, just as it had been with the policeman.

I despised Mrs Browne for the way she had spoken about her daughter to me, as though the young woman wasn't there, to someone she'd just met. What stuck in my mind about that afternoon was my desire to get away and forget the whole episode. Though the thought was repugnant to me, I resigned myself to having to live in the children's home with the Flaggs for another two and a half years.

But here's the strange thing: according to the official record, Mrs Flagg told Mrs Walton that as soon as I returned to Vicarage Road, I started to pack my belongings on the assumption I was going to live with the Brownes.

When I read the report, I struggled to take this in. It was so at odds with my memory of how Mrs Browne had acted in my presence. Like many others who've spent time in the care system, my experiences had encouraged me to become adept at reading people's emotions through their gestures, vocal tics and facial expressions. Learning that skill had been a matter of survival, especially when I lived in children's homes and had to assess the moods of the other children and the people looking after us. I had sensed Mrs Browne's distaste for me from the beginning. In my mind she'd become Mrs Danvers from Daphne du Maurier's *Rebecca*: all simmering malevolence, and hard-done-by victimhood. That made it difficult to accept Mrs Walton's note in which she described me packing in anticipation of going to live with the Brownes. Assuming the Flaggs were telling the truth, perhaps I had packed my meagre belongings as a symbolic act, indicating the desire to be anywhere but where I was. Or else I was preparing to run away, and I had a 'plan' – something I'd often considered but never executed. If I took the report at face value, it would indicate that I felt much, much worse about living in the Vicarage Road children's home than I'd remembered.

Before we have time to register what's going on in the present, it's already become the past – waiting to be forgotten or reshaped, cast in a mould that fits our individual or collective needs. I wonder if that was what happened with the suitcase-packing episode. Had I misremembered, forgotten or been in denial when I thought back to 1967 and the events after the visit to the Brownes?

But there was a bigger shock in the care notes, lying in wait for me.

14th January 1967

Dear ▮▮▮▮,

I am writing at once to let you know that we do not think we should be able to provide the right environment for Lola. She seems to have been well integrated into a normal working class background and I do not think she would at all happy in a declassé family whose interests are mainly intellectual. I also feel she should be with someone who is at home all day as she has few resources of her own and would need constant chivvying.

Although she is taking Art as an exam subject she seems to have little interest in it; she has read only set books and does not like reading; she talks of being a P.E.T instructor but does not like swimming or walking or bicycling. The one and only interest I could trace was dancing and, although this is all right in itself it doesn't take one very far.

It was obvious that she would need constant nagging about sexual hygiene. I have enough difficulties trying to get my daughter to keep herself and her clothes clean & I do not think I could face two large, lazy, lethargic, girls when I got back from work. I also have a feeling that in a fairly short time she might be getting into trouble with boys, not because she has bad intentions but because she has no positive attitudes and would tend to take the easy line with everything.

If I were not working I would have a try but I don't think Lola really took to us and I think you could find her a home where she would be happier, preferably with other younger members of the family. My husband was particularly emphatic that Lola would not be happy with us.

I am not really a professional foster mother. The Children's Welfare Department asked me to take Ann and it was successful all round but I can only help a special sort of child as things are. If I were not working and could take younger children I would take different types but as things are I can only really help the rather odd intelligent teenager who can fit into our kind of family and benefit from it. A child already adjusted to one sort of atmosphere should really be kept in it unless it has a very enquiring type of mind.

If you have any other children you think would fit in, I will always try to be of help but one can only be a good foster mother if there is a mutual feeling between child and adult that somehow the relationship can be made to work. I am sorry not to be of more help and I hope Lola will find a more suitable home. Yours sincerely

I wish I could claim that in the moment of reading that letter I was not affected by it. But the truth is that to say it caused me anguish would be an understatement. Revisiting the time I'd spent at Vicarage Road was difficult enough – I'd tried to read the content while resisting what people had said about me – but now I'd been ambushed by three sheets of notepaper.

My thoughts spun off in several directions at once as I read and reread this woman's version of my reality. What if Mrs Browne had merely said what others were also thinking? Had Mrs Walton secretly agreed with the woman? What if even those who'd acted benignly towards me had also been harbouring these thoughts about who and what I was? Had the Taylors thought I was negligent about hygiene? And what about Evelyn, and Lynne, and my school friends? Had they thought those things about me? I knew that this depiction of me as unclean – citing my apparent lack of attention to personal hygiene – was underpinned by the racism embedded throughout Mrs Browne's letter, and the entirety of the care records for that matter. But it still made me feel as if I had a layer of grime slathered all over my body.

The many slights and aggressions contained within the files had been gradually accumulating over the course of the week. On two occasions I took a long, scalding shower before going to bed – a kind of self-flagellation to cleanse my past character failures.

The term 'triggering' hadn't yet come into popular discourse when I first ventured into the depths of my care notes, not in the way that it has today. If it had, the concept might have helped me to understand why I'd had such a strong response to the story of the alleged suitcase-packing incident, and an even more intense reaction to the Browne letter.

There was no escaping the vitriol dripping from every sentence, but once I'd achieved some distance from the letter's contents, I could start to see how it demonstrated Mrs Browne's anxiety about her own shortcomings and those of her husband, as well as what she thought were mine. Her confidence in having achieved her own and her family's social and intellectual aspirations were revealed to be as insubstantial as the emperor's new clothes. Whatever short-lived triumph she and her husband experienced as a result of trashing the character of a vulnerable, depressed teenager living in a children's home, I hope they enjoyed it.

Fortunately, I was unaware of the thoughts of Mrs Browne in January 1967, and my own fragile self-confidence survived another rejection. I had to accept that, for now at least, Vicarage Road was my home.

The benefits of the long walks and fresh, home-cooked food that Cornwall offered couldn't fully mask the painful experience of reading through the records, and the toll it was taking on me. The difficulty of deciphering semi-legible documents in the box file caused problems and marred my reading experience, but it was the material – the substance of what was there, and what wasn't – that prompted anguish, physical pain and nausea.

A voice inside said, 'Give it up. None of this matters any more. Stop reading, for the sake of your sanity.' But a louder voice told me that it did matter, it really did. I couldn't erase this version of the past – one I hadn't even known existed prior to reaching my sixties – so I'd better be clear about what it meant for my understanding of who I'd become.

As for Mrs Browne, I had to dig deep to find an iota of charitable feeling towards her. But in my more dispassionate moments I could see a woman unfulfilled who couldn't reconcile what she was with the image she had of herself, her family and their status in society. And as I read the letter once more, I found myself intrigued by the mindset that framed her thinking. Such analysis was a luxury I could afford, since I had defied her damning prediction of what the future held for me. But I felt for her daughter and I hope she managed to find some fulfilment and joy in her life, quite possibly away from that household.

By the end of the week a trapped nerve in my neck was causing me significant discomfort, and would go on to interfere with my life back in London. I hadn't counted on the shock to my body that the experience of reading my care records would bring about, and I made much slower progress than I'd imagined – it would soon be time to return home, and I still had not finished reading all the material. In the end, I realized I would only be able to endure the impact by spreading my reading over a period of several years.

The social workers responsible for my welfare had no

idea that, decades after they'd submitted their reports, the subject would herself be reading them. The legislation that let me access the records hadn't even been on the horizon at that time. There was no need for them to consider what impact their words would have on me as the object of their scrutiny. For better or worse, that much has changed.

The heartfelt letter I'd written to Mrs Walton complaining about the Flaggs had been officially date stamped and put in a file. The same with the letter from Mrs Browne. If only the emotional fallout caused by the rediscovery of these documents could be dealt with so easily. Forcing myself to confront those artefacts from my past was proving difficult. But I was determined not to be defeated, no matter how painful it was, or how long it took to complete the task.

Nine: On the edge

18 January 1967, ▮▮▮▮▮: Talked despairingly to Miss D— who felt it was ridiculous that there was no Islington vacancy to be found in this emergency. She said she would ask around at the various establishments and talk to me again tomorrow.

27 April 1967, ▮▮▮▮▮: Lola still does not seem able to discuss her deeper feelings but it is possible that if she is allowed to stay on with [. . .] she will then feel secure enough to begin thinking and talking about other things than her day-to-day activities, and her future career.

On my return to London from Cornwall I was immediately plunged back into a hectic schedule in the House of Lords. I threw myself into my work, whether on legislation in which I had an interest, or policy-related extra-parliamentary activities. The latter included the Young Review and Agenda, both of which were moving towards their concluding reports and recommendations, and the end of my contribution to the initiatives. I was becoming increasingly involved in the development of modern slavery legislation, owing in large part to my collaboration with activists within the fashion industry. In addition, I was prompted by campaigners working on children's experiences of the care system to look at the forthcoming Children and Families Bill.

The experience of dealing with my care records and sharing my impressions of the care system with others helped to inform my thinking about what kinds of legislative or regulatory reforms were necessary. The policy work involved in both the Young Review and Agenda demonstrated how many people were affected, in so many different ways, once they became embroiled in the care system. Although my experience had been rooted in a different era, many of the testimonies I heard indicated that much remained the same. It was a matter of chance if care records were available at all, and if they were, support in accessing them was down to the luck of the draw. To an outsider, it can be hard to understand what makes these procedures – gaining access to a complete record of a childhood spent in the care system – so difficult administratively. Why is there so much variation in the quality of service from one local authority to another? And why does it matter so much?

It matters because most children have on their mind a variation on the question 'Where did I come from?' For those of us who didn't grow up living consistently with parents or family, that fundamental curiosity is complicated with other, additional questions: 'Why did I live with strangers who were paid to look after me?' and 'What did I do to make my parents not want me?' I thought – as children think – that once I'd received my care records a good number of those questions would be answered. That I'd find clues about the motivations of the key actors in my childhood dramas. But I was beginning to realize the extent to which the records were *about* me, not *for* me.

For all the problems I had encountered – the false hopes, the delays, the revelations – I couldn't help but think of far more difficult experiences that people had shared with me in the course of my work, or that I'd read about in case studies. How might I have coped with being handed a cardboard box full of unnumbered loose papers, with three-quarters of the contents redacted? Page after page of blacked-out names, locations, comments ... Or what about one woman I met whose care notes consisted of a single sheet of A4 paper, only half of it covered with handwriting – and even some of that had been redacted?

There were reasons why local authorities treated the content of care records in that way, I knew. And I recognized how difficult it was for council officials to balance the competing needs of people's right to privacy against the needs of those for whom information might help them to both learn and understand more about the circumstances that led to them being in care in the first place. Even so, understanding and sympathizing with the predicaments faced by local authorities doesn't change the damaging and dispiriting effects of incomplete or non-existent care records.

Colleagues from the Care Leavers' Association, Coram-BAAF (formerly the British Association for Adoption and Fostering), Barnardo's, the South East Post Care Forum and the Association of Child Abuse Lawyers (ACAL) formed the Access to Care Records Campaign Group (ACRCG) and gathered together compelling evidence for a change in the law. Building on that work, about a year after I first accessed my own records I put forward amendments to the Children and Families Bill as it proceeded through the House of Lords, which we hoped would improve the situation for anyone seeking access to their care notes.

The suggested changes reflected earlier extensive discussions about our experiences as practitioners, policy makers and/or care experienced adults. Throughout 2013 and beyond, to the present day, I've been struck by the commitment of so many of the professionals in the statutory services and NGOs to improving the lives of the young people with whom they're concerned. Some of those involved in this evolving campaign have had personal experiences that make my story seem quite mundane. But we weren't interested in competing over who'd had the worst experience in dealing with local authorities. We'd come together to advocate for councils to develop a more nuanced approach to the redaction of personal data. Redaction is often a blunt tool: in my records, there were several instances where the names of children I'd been in care with, and their personal details, had been blanked out, and it was obvious why. They had a right to privacy. Problems arise in less straightforward examples, such as if a birth parent's or a relative's name and actions have been wiped from the record. Again, that person does have a right to privacy – but how far does that extend? Should every detail about that person be expunged from the record? And is their right to anonymity more important than the care experienced adult's right to know their origins and how they came to be in care? These situations make those responsible for processing applications for care records in local authorities nervous.

There's no easy resolution to the problem, but currently the threshold for taking the decision to redact extensively seems to be the default position in too many cases. In addition to advocating for a more consistent, sympathetic approach, giving as much detail as possible, the campaign also lobbied for support for those seeking their records whenever it was needed, no matter the age of the person concerned.

As often happens, the amendments weren't accepted by the government, and without a clear endorsement from the other political parties, I had to make a decision: either I could test the level of support for our suggested changes by calling for a vote, which I would almost certainly have lost. Or I could, instead, request a meeting with senior officials in the Department for Education (formerly the Department for Children, Schools and Families), and negotiate changes to the statutory guidance that government issues to local authorities and other bodies involved in the care system. I took the latter course, which turned out to be fruitful. Of course, to some it was a disappointment not to pursue the proposed changes by taking them to a vote. But simply by tabling them we had provoked a debate and exposed the lack of knowledge among legislators about how the treatment of children in the care system differed from that of adopted children – with care leavers missing out.

Through our collaborative efforts, in 2014 the campaign group was able to work with officials from the Department for Education to amend the statutory guidance for local authorities, enabling care leavers up to the age of twenty-five to access support when they took possession of their care records. Our basic principle was still that whatever age someone reached, they should be able to have access to support during what can be a distressing time. The age issue is an important one, because research strongly suggests that many care experienced adults only feel ready to access their records after the age of thirty.

The Children and Families Bill eventually became law in 2014, and in 2016 the ACRCG launched a report recommending further improvements in the system.

My own care notes were unusual in that relatively little material had been redacted, probably because the focus on me was intense and there's little detail about my parents or other relatives that would have been seen as problematic. One of the aspects of the whole experience I had to get used to in the months and years after accessing my records, was the idea that someone else had written the story of my childhood as part of their job – without consulting me or even appearing to be particularly sensitive to what I was feeling.

The depths of despair I'd reached after 1965 had not

assumed the same significance in Mrs Walton's official write-ups as they had for me. However, she'd recognized that my situation was less than ideal, and finally came up with a potential solution to my plight.

It looked like there might finally be a place for me in a home in 'real' London, not out in the countryside or the suburbs. In Highbury, to be precise – to the south of Highbury Fields, not far from the Taylors and the Brownes. Familiar territory, at last. No new, false promises of a pretend family life, either. I would be going to another children's home, albeit with half the number of children who had lived at Park House and Vicarage Road.

I'd initially welcomed access to my notes as a prompt for my memory, fully aware (I thought) of just how fallible those notes might prove to be. But even taking account of the official records' deficiencies, I was struck time and again by the discovery of just how much I'd either misremembered or forgotten.

Take my memory of my first introduction to this new home in Adams Street, which was run by a woman called Elizabeth Harefield. I have vivid memories of me sinking into an armchair in her sitting room, greeting all-comers with a scowl, trying to give everyone a good reason not to like me. I had been pursuing a policy of sulky non-cooperation in my last days at Vicarage Road, having given up on everything and everyone, and I had convinced myself that I was impossible to like, let alone love. What was the point in making myself amenable, trying to please this 'Aunty Elizabeth' person who was yet another manifestation of institutional 'care'? Sooner or later, she'd discover the real Lola Young, and there was no doubt in my mind that she wouldn't like what she saw.

Memory tells me that Elizabeth Harefield directed me to sit in that upright armchair, in the corner of her tiny sitting room. Mrs Walton was there, and I did my very best to let the two women know that I hated the position in which I found myself. And that I considered it was their fault – if not as individuals, then as representatives of the system and the adult world in general. In the contradictory, self-immolating manner of many troubled teens, I remember willing Elizabeth Harefield to reject me, to hate me, thereby sending Mrs Walton back to Islington Council's children's department to find an alternative to the home in Highbury. By striking a pre-emptive blow, I would save myself the agony of rejection. I would make myself objectionable on my own terms.

The records told a different story, seemingly from a parallel universe – one where I visited the little house on Adams Street and stayed there a couple of times before moving in for the long term, aged fifteen and a half. It was a story where the Flaggs thought I had some good qualities and that it would be better for me and for my O level grades to move somewhere with equally motivated young people with whom I could converse. A story where, eager to please, I rushed to get up and wash the dishes before anyone else could volunteer. The Lola Young who landed in Highbury was a girl who was still depressed, but also desperate to please, to be accepted, and not to be shunted somewhere else in three months' time.

There were four others living in Adams Street who would be taking exams in the summer of 1967, in addition to me. And there were three who went out to work, and they all had social lives that didn't involve roaming the streets committing acts of petty vandalism. Admittedly, a lot of extra-curricular activity revolved around the local church, which I wouldn't have chosen myself, but at least it gave me opportunities to go out and meet other young people, to have a life.

Mrs Walton had informed me before we visited the Adams Street home that it was already at full capacity; built to accommodate seven residents, and I would be number eight. I'd have to sleep in a room with three other girls on a Z-bed, rather than a proper one – a reminder of my intrusion into a settled household. The role of interloper suited my frame of mind at the time; I could characterize myself as superfluous to requirements before I was even admitted.

Despite my best efforts, Elizabeth Harefield did accept me as the eighth child in the home, and soon enough I came to terms with my cramped living quarters, for the home in Adams Street was only a reasonable two-bus distance from school: I would finally be able to see friends socially and at weekends. What's more, I'd never have to eat rice pudding again. All of which helped me to feel better about myself, and that there might be a point to thinking about the future.

The atmosphere at Adams Street couldn't have been more different to Vicarage Road. It felt different to Park House too, though the latter had begun to feel less frightful with every day that passed, putting greater distance between me and that distressing journey to and from school. It had been the journey that had driven me to the brink of deep despair.

Although there were undercurrents of wariness among some of the other teenagers at Adams Street, no one was outwardly unfriendly towards me, which was a relief. I was even given a nickname, almost straight away: Lolongs. At school I had successfully resisted being addressed as 'Lolly', but I did eventually concede to 'Lo', which has stuck with me to this day.

What I found even more striking than having several new companions of a similar age was the discovery that there were two sets of siblings in the home, all of whom had been looked after by Elizabeth Harefield for most of their lives. I experienced a momentary pang of envy, and wondered why a home like this hadn't been a possibility for me before now – especially when I learned it was one of several in the area. There was even one next door, at number 3 Adams Street, a mirror image of number 1.

Elizabeth Harefield placed significant emphasis on our participation in church, in a way that I hadn't experienced since I'd lived with the Taylors. This seemed something of a contradiction, as 'Aunty' Elizabeth never hid the fact that she was an atheist. I'd heard some vague murmuring about going to church being a council edict, but as with the 'you must have at least a spoonful of every dish served up to you, no matter how disgusting' rule at the Flaggs', I struggled to accept this as true.

Perhaps Islington Council really did feel compelled to save the souls of the poor unwanted children in their care. Or perhaps Elizabeth Harefield simply wanted a couple of hours to herself once a week. Time alone to enjoy a cigarette and read another instalment of Dennis Wheatley's chronicles of satanism in rural England. Whatever the underlying motives, she insisted that we attend St John's Church every Sunday, and we were also encouraged to join the Covenanters, an affiliated Christian youth group.

There were times when I attended both the morning and evening services, and also the Covenanters, on the same Sunday. Given that then, as now, I wasn't at all religious, I can't explain this enthusiasm for the church. If anything, it went against my declared political leanings at the time. But it may have been that the dirge-like hymns and the ritualized standing up and sitting down induced a trance-like state and had a calming effect on me. I could feel the difficulties of the previous two years slowly releasing their grip on me. Or perhaps it was the routine and the illusion of a ready-made social life that were so attractive. Now, I think my diligent presence at St John's Church every Sunday was driven by my desire to fit in, to stand out as little as possible.

Deirdre lived at number 3 Adams Street, next door to where I was living with Elizabeth Harefield and the others at number 1. There was an easy flow of friendships between the teens in the two homes, as a result of living next door to each other and attending the same church. Both houses were easily identified as Islington Council children's homes, I always thought, and though I had no knowledge of architecture, I felt they had a certain municipal look about them. That was partly due to numbers 1 and 3 Adams Street, as well as the council flats opposite, being obviously more modern than the old houses that surrounded them.

Deirdre and I chatted as we meandered along Blackstock Road, going over something that had happened in Covenanters a few days earlier. The leader of the church's youth group had claimed that 'yatch' was the correct spelling when I knew it to be 'yacht'. In response, she had said that I probably didn't understand how English words were often spelt differently to the way you'd expect. Well, I'd heard that line before, and so as soon as I got back to Adams Street, I had looked it up in the dictionary, and I was right. I was looking forward to rubbing the leader's nose in her mistake when we met the following Sunday, and I said as much to Deirdre. She didn't care either way – but though these little victories over patronizing adults might seem petty, they can mean a lot.

We were nearly home when Deirdre's face screwed up in disgust, so I followed her gaze to see what she was looking at. 'I hate seeing that,' she said, lifting her chin towards the sight that had reduced her eyes to the size of sultanas in her pale, doughy face.

All I could see was a couple walking along, hand in hand.

She paused and folded her arms across her chest. She was round, like one of those wobbly toys that can't be pushed over that we used to put in the cage for the budgie to play with. Finally, she blurted out, 'White women going with Black men,' referring to the couple walking on the other side of the road.

'I'm not saying which one of them is in the wrong,' she added, which was meant to make what she'd said acceptable.

I'd thought that Deirdre was a bit of an outsider, not a member of the inner circle – the 'in group' – of children's home residents. I'd half thought that we might become friends. But it was the same as it had been with Carmen, who'd told me she didn't like 'coloured people' but didn't include me in that assessment. It irked me that both girls seemed to think that by taking me into their confidence, they were doing me a favour. I didn't appreciate their assumption that they could say what they liked to me, use me to exempt themselves from the accusation of being racists.

Now that my period of exile to the hinterlands had ended, I could go to social events, some of which were unconnected to church. However, while Elizabeth Harefield was more amenable to the idea of my having a social life than the Flaggs had been, there were, it seemed, certain rules and regulations she wasn't prepared to circumvent.

When I went to a classmate's house for the night, I had to produce a note from the parents in question, asking for permission for me to stay at their house. It was worth the mild humiliation of knowing my friend's parents might be quizzed about their personal suitability (and that of their accommodation), just to be granted temporary freedom, away from the rule-bound environment of my corporate parents. To be able to attend these other non-church events, I sometimes had to stretch the truth. By obtaining permission for outings with my school friends, I was able to take part in some genuine, post-council-mandated-bedtime partying. These events were very different to the activities organized through St John's Church.

The first time I asked for permission to stay with a friend overnight while I was living at Adams Street came about when some of my classmates were invited to be extras in a film. I was a few months away from my sixteenth birthday, and I probably wouldn't have remembered the event at all if it hadn't been dutifully documented in Mrs Walton's typewritten report. It all had to be officially recorded, including the handwritten note from my friend's mother.

The Crazy World of Arthur Brown was a 1960s English rock band and wouldn't necessarily have been our music of choice, but when we heard through a classmate that producers were looking for extras to take part in a short film based on the band's eventual hit single 'Fire', we thought it would be a great, unmissable adventure. This was, I think, the event to which Mrs Walton referred.

The reality turned out to be even more exciting – and more incendiary – than we'd imagined. Arthur Brown wandered through the audience with a blazing helmet on his head, and this fell off perilously close to where we were sitting, gazing in awe at the performance. Naturally, these details did not form part of my account of the evening when I gave a rundown to Elizabeth Harefield.

One of the older boys would be leaving Adams Street shortly, having reached the age of eighteen, so if Elizabeth Harefield would have me, I could stay on at the home; I'd no longer be the superfluous one. I coveted the only single bedroom, but I was too far down the pecking order to be granted that privilege. But I'd settled in well: it seemed that Elizabeth Harefield liked me, and to my relief she said she wanted me to stay. In any case, there was nowhere else for me to go.

My time at Adams Street was the longest I'd stayed anywhere after leaving Tufnell Park Road in 1965. The relative peace and stability of my time there was reflected in my notes, which offered very little by way of revelations or material that contradicted my own memory of events. No big dramas recorded here, then: I had even managed to achieve respectable results in my mock exams while at the Flaggs' home, so when I took my actual GCE Ordinary level exams in the summer of 1967 and gained six O levels at grades considered sufficient to continue studying to Advanced level – and then eventually to apply to university – my academic prospects drastically improved.

Elizabeth Harefield praised my revision efforts, which had led to my decent exam results. The other teenagers who'd taken exams had done well too, so she threw a party for all of us who'd enjoyed academic success. Mrs Walton had also been appreciative of the effort I'd put into my studies, and rewarded my hard work with two tickets for any show in town. My companion for the outing would be one of my school friends, Genevieve O'Farrell, because her family had shown me kindness in the past. We'd been tasked by our English literature teacher to report back to the class on a cultural experience, so Mrs Walton's offer of theatre tickets was timely.

I chose to see *A Day in the Death of Joe Egg* by Peter Nichols, and I still have vivid memories of Joe Melia's impassioned performance on stage as Bri, father of a young girl called Joe – Josephine – Egg. Joe lives with cerebral palsy, is in a wheelchair and non-verbal throughout the play. There's a memorable line, often quoted: Bri, Joe Egg's father, describes God as 'a sort of manic-depressive rugby footballer'. It's a bumpy, up-and-down existence, being human – a sentiment to which I could relate.

I remember worrying at the time that Joe could not articulate for herself what she wanted for her future – whatever that might have held. Joe Egg's parents spoke *about* their daughter, not *to* her. Like Mrs Browne – though expressed in less obnoxious terms – it felt as though Joe Egg's parents saw her as a child whose presence was lamented, the parents resenting that they could not live out their dreams through their daughter. Perhaps it's too easy to claim that I felt some sort of solidarity with Joe Egg – as a person talked about, talked at and rarely talked with, or heard. But something in the play resonated with me, and led me to identify with the principal but silent character.

During my time in the home in Highbury, I would develop an unexpected lifelong relationship.

On Avenell Road stood Highbury Stadium, a fabulous art deco building, home to the Arsenal Football Club. Its scale and distinctive architecture stood out among the Victorian terraces and 1950s buildings that characterized the area. On match days I'd see the home fans milling around The Gunners pub, not far from the home, before moving in clumps towards the stadium. I watched wave after wave of spectators leaving after the game, trying to guess how the match had panned out by observing the ebb and flow of the fans' procession to the bus stop, clad in red and white. Elation, quiet satisfaction or despair reflected in the tone and volume of their voices and their movement along the street. The success or otherwise of the Gunners would be absorbed, the fans' emotional response to the result affecting their mood, and being replayed for days to come. Through it all I wondered at the devotion of the thousands of people making the pilgrimage to the stadium, then returning home.

Once a year, the club sent its team to the local church – our church! When I was first told about the special Arsenal service, I thought someone was pulling my leg. Was this a trick to make me feel more enthusiastic about attending the services? I imagined the players coming straight from the pitch to church in mud-and-grass-stained white shorts. I pictured them sitting in the front row in their red and white kit, studying their hymn books and then kneeling next to each other on the little mats. In my mind the scene took on the quality of a fever dream. But the reality was far less odd – in the 1960s and 70s it wasn't unusual for the lads in the squad to have connections to local communities, and be members of a congregation.

In order to see as much as possible of the Arsenal service, I found a seat as near to the front as I dared, close to where the team would sit. One of the younger players helped to deliver our fruit and veg every week, and I craned my neck, trying to spot our greengrocer's assistant, Pat Rice, who played in the reserve team. He didn't say much when he came to the home with his boss, carrying crates full of food, but I suppose I'd say now that he let his feet do the talking on the pitch. Being present at the service catapulted me from being a care home kid, forced to go to church, to being a girl in the presence of heroes; they were famous, these young men, and they were in the same church as me! If only they could come to St John's to help relieve the boredom more often.

The Arsenal Football Club's Highbury Stadium became totemic for me almost immediately. It identified where I lived – even the local tube station had been named in homage to its presence. And by virtue of not being a children's home, or the home of foster parents who'd rejected me, it represented something, it was a special place. Rather than be defined as the Black girl who lived in an institution, I would be the Black girl who lived in close proximity to a famous football stadium.

A strange kind of salve, you might think, but that's what Highbury Stadium represented to me. I can't identify the exact moment when my loyalty to the club was sealed. Perhaps it was after I'd sat a couple of rows behind the team in church. Maybe. All I know is that there came a point, not long after I left the Adams Street home, when I regarded Arsenal as my club. It was a secret loyalty – one I kept to myself for some time, partly because I wasn't in a position to further my interest in the team, and partly because it wasn't something that girls would shout about back then. It's very different now, especially with the rise in popularity of women's football.

As the nature of top-flight football has transformed over the decades since I lived in Highbury, so I have tried to develop a better understanding of how elite sport captures the imagination and emotions of millions of people around the world. As that growth has continued, so inevitably has the complex relationship between clubs, fans, communities, media and finance. I think of myself as an active fan, which means attending every Arsenal home match, and participating in walking football sessions run by the club. The nature of the work I do – and the perspectives I've developed over the years – means that for me it's important to have a grasp of the policy areas that impact on football, and vice versa. Legislation that relates to forced and exploitative labour practices in supply chains is rarely associated with football clubs, yet fans will be aware of the range of promotional products on sale in club shops; these will be as prone to the factors that underpin modern slavery as any other business sector. And it doesn't stop there – working with campaigners against the exploitation of children in and through sport has taught me that the scourge of abusive labour permeates every aspect of our lives. My hope is that clubs will support the work that's taking place to try and eliminate these practices, which can manifest on and off the pitch. More recently, I've appreciated the opportunities the club has given me to learn about the work of the Arsenal Foundation and Arsenal in the Community and their support of, for example, care leavers and children trapped in refugee camps.

Praise from Elizabeth Harefield and Mrs Walton for doing well in my GCEs made me feel good for a while, and temporarily served to distract me from the depression that I'd been sinking into ever since Daisy's death. As I went into the sixth form, I started to think about the potential of carrying on to higher education.

But once the excitement and novelty of being in a smaller home, closer to school and nearer to friends, had passed, my thoughts once again turned inwards. *There must be something wrong with me*, I thought. The words sank their teeth into my rapidly waning confidence in my academic ability, and nibbled away until I felt consumed by something I couldn't name. It was impossible to even start thinking about having a good time. I felt like I was in a game of charades – that I was playing at being clever, when I wasn't at all. I began to resent my schoolwork

> **LONDON COUNTY COUNCIL**
> **PARLIAMENT HILL SCHOOL**
> Highgate Road, N.W.5
>
> Name: Lola Young   Form 4A   Average Age: yrs. mths.
> Term ending: School re-opens:
>
> **REPORT**
>
> | SUBJECT | Examination Result | | |
> |---|---|---|---|
> | SCRIPTURE | 50 | Lola cannot afford to relax her efforts; very thorough revision will be necessary to ensure 'O' level success. | |
> | ENGLISH Language | 57 | Lola has worked well and has written some imaginative well-written essays. | |
> | Literature | 63 | | |
> | HISTORY | 38 | Poor. Lola does not work and therefore she has made little progress | |
> | GEOGRAPHY | 29 | | |
> | MATHEMATICS Divn 2 | 52 | Lola is making steady progress. | |
> | SCIENCE Biology | 55 | Lola is capable of a better result than this. She needs to learn her work more thoroughly. | |
> | DOMESTIC ARTS | | | |

and became increasingly withdrawn from the other young people I lived with. I knew that, even if I wanted to, I wouldn't be able to stay at Adams Street for ever. What would become of me in two years' time, once I turned eighteen?

If Aunty Elizabeth asked me how my A level revision was going, I'd say it was fine, but it wasn't fine; I wasn't making enough progress with my studying. It was too noisy to work in the playroom. But I couldn't ask six-year-olds to be quiet, so I read the same page of *La Peste* over and over. I could no longer read French with any fluency, let alone write or speak it. That was a big problem, given I was supposed to be taking my mock A level

French exam in a few months. Nothing would sink in, and my ability to learn deserted me almost entirely.

Years before, I had written stories – for Kayin and sometimes for myself. I'd no idea what had happened to them; I'd assumed they were lost or thrown away in all the moves I'd been through. It was as though various parts of me had been lost, not just the stories, but whole chunks of my life, and my potential had disappeared along with my possessions. I saw the idea of working in the arts, or doing anything creative for a living, as nothing more than a childish fantasy. I can laugh now, but there was a moment when I thought I wanted to be a forensic scientist, solving crimes, just because I'd watched an episode of the television drama *The Hidden Truth*. It's embarrassing to think I'd actually said to my teacher that forensic science might be what I wanted to study at university. I'd barely scraped a pass grade in Biology at GCE O level.

My school friends had always been precious to me, and I liked them a lot, but I had no expectation that they could like me in return, and it really was a mystery to me why they'd accepted me into their circle. They had no real understanding of what my life was like. How could they, when their experiences of the world were so different to mine?

When I got to know some of them better and met them outside of school in their homes, I realized that they had their own problems, and I understood that nobody experienced a perfect life, whatever that might mean. There were times when I found myself stuck in the middle of family disagreements, which I found uncomfortable and embarrassing, being a witness to their thinly veiled, long-held grudges and disputes. But whatever was going on in my friends' families, it was me, not them, who was falling behind in my studies. And it was me who had packed her bag seven times in two years, always moving from one place to another; me who'd had a family life dangled in front of her, had my hopes raised, only for them to be smashed to pieces. And that's what I couldn't help thinking about, all the time.

On Christmas Day 1968, instead of pulling crackers and playing snakes and ladders, I reread my notes on Guy de Maupassant until my eyes were stinging. It was pointless – hard to think, let alone study, when I felt like that – it was really just for show. I had a large file, with all my notes indexed in it, an effective prop for my performance as a clever, studious teenager, but I believed it was a waste of time. Revising for mock A level exams and dreaming of higher education? All of it a complete waste of time.

It wasn't like it had been at Vicarage Road, or Park House, or the Taylors', where I could point to the adults around me and say that they had created the circumstances underlying my problems, that it was they who had made me feel like this, that the journey to school was wearing me out. I didn't have to look far to see that it was my fault that I was living this life; I came to believe that I was the problem.

Given there were so many children's homes scattered around the Highbury area, I found it hard to understand why it had taken so long to find somewhere for me to live, within a reasonable distance for travelling to and from school. The children's home I lived in was a duplicate of the house next door, at number 3 – that's two children's homes just in the one street. Two more were a short walk away, less than ten minutes. Not far from the local church, there was a National Children's Home. In nearby Highbury Fields, there was yet another.

I've since discovered that there were at least ten homes within a mile or so of where I was living at that time. Then there were the houses in Highbury Fields and Drayton Park that marked my failed attempts at securing foster care. My mental map of the area was dominated by potential homes for the legions of unwanted children who depended on Islington Council for somewhere to live. Every corner seemed to remind me that I lived in a place children disappeared to when their parents had given up on them. I wanted to be someone who was seen as more than that. But my surroundings made it hard to escape that reality.

By February 1969, I had managed to some extent to get back on track with my revision; my ability to deal with the demands of the academic curriculum fluctuated, along with my mood and confidence. My friends and I sat our mock A level exams and sent off applications to universities. Despite my deep and private melancholy, my social life had been steadily growing and, to my surprise, I became quite popular. I found myself a member of a group of confident, intelligent girls, some of whom were sporty too, and all of them competitive. They were interested in politics and world affairs and culture. They'd emerged as a distinct group in our fourth year at secondary school, around the age of fifteen, and they had an air about them . . . it was classy, the way they altered their school uniforms to make them more fashionable, without drawing attention to their creative adaptations, and the way they just about conformed to rules about skirt lengths and hairstyles.

They went to late-night parties, danced to pop and soul music from record labels such as Atlantic and Motown, featuring Aretha Franklin, Stevie Wonder, the Temptations, and the Supremes; some were also fans of Bob Dylan and Leonard Cohen. Interest occasionally stretched to classical music. Film was a big thing, but any form of creativity was admired. Our form teacher had once accused the group of seeing themselves as an intellectual elite, setting themselves apart, assuming they were superior in intelligence to other girls in their year group. Jo, Sue, Anne, Sally and Christine were core members, with others 'in' or 'out' according to what was going on.

The attributes that gained me entry into the charmed circle? I could be quite funny. I had a good sense of humour, in spite of everything, which had even been noted a couple of times in my care records. I enjoyed performing and liked art. I was a decent athlete and gained temporary anti-hero status for being the first girl sent off the netball court for swearing. I had an interest in politics in a general sense – if I couldn't join in discussions about communism, the *Little Red Book* and Mao Zedong, I knew how to listen and rehash the ideas for others to consume in another forum. I was bright enough, if not as confident as my friends appeared to be.

Much has been written about the 1960s and the rise of young people's involvement in political activity. By 1969, as we approached A levels, my core group of friends and I were already aware of injustice and inequality in the wider world. In spite of the school's efforts, the disparities in students' wealth were apparent simply by observing who lived in the leafy green areas closest to the school, and who lived on council estates; who bought the second-hand blazers, or who was entitled to free school meals, or who couldn't afford school trips to overseas locations. Our interests weren't only focused on domestic politics, either. The family of one of our classmates, Abby, had experienced close-up the persecution of anyone suspected of communism in McCarthy-era USA, the rabid anti-Semitism and the attempts to undermine the civil rights movement there. There were also older girls at Parly Hill, the daughters of anti-apartheid campaigners now in exile in London, who had witnessed close-up how racist ideology played out.

I tried to avoid conversations about current affairs: the little I'd heard from my fellow teenage residents suggested we would not have had much in common politically. Anne and I went on a demonstration against the war in Vietnam, protesting against the bombing being carried out on the orders of the US government. We marched all along the route from Hyde Park Corner to Grosvenor Square, where the US Embassy was located.

'Don't watch, join in!' we chanted as we walked. And, 'Hey, hey, LBJ, how many kids did you kill today?' We shouted it out to the people lining the streets staring at us. Some shouted back, but we couldn't hear what they said, and we didn't care. We shouted our slogans at the police, who stood watching as the thousands-strong crowd of demonstrators waved placards and sang songs about peace. I felt the power of being part of a collective protest on that march. In 1968 and 1969, we saw how young people in France, Mexico and Czechoslovakia (now the Czech Republic) vented their frustration at the failures in leadership of an older generation around the world.

Our local church wouldn't have appeared to be a likely candidate as a site of protest, but there was an incident when the vicar used his sermon to ask God to support the USA in the war in Vietnam. A young man who'd been sitting on his own at the end of a pew rose noisily, shouted something, stomped down the aisle and out of the door at the back of the church.

I told myself that I hadn't really been paying attention to the sermon, and so couldn't be blamed for not joining the man who had walked out. But the truth was that I lacked the courage to stand up in front of everyone and leave as he had done. His actions had made me feel cowardly, because marching along with others in a crowd who share the same opinion as you wasn't that difficult. Standing up, as he had, knowing that many of those present thought he was in the wrong – that was brave.

My school friends were all white. Among the 1,200 or so girls at our relatively new, well-regarded single-sex comprehensive school, there were only a handful of Black girls. And maybe a few more girls of South Asian heritage. That was it. A general unspoken consensus was that Britain was somehow relatively unsullied by the issue of 'colour prejudice'. Apart from among extremists and 'the ignorant'. Racism was an American problem, from which South Africa also suffered, whereas Britain, in spite of evidence to the contrary, considered itself to be free of such intolerance.

At weekends, I'd stay the night at my friends' houses in Camden Town or Primrose Hill or Parliament Hill. Elizabeth Harefield trusted me when I said that I'd be staying at Lelia's or Sue's or Genevieve's house. There were times when I plotted with my teenage co-conspirators to stay out all night, each girl claiming they were staying with another. I could sleep over at some place where a party was going on till dawn, or at someone's house when their parents were away, and nobody cared if you crashed on the sofa after going out dancing until two in the morning. I relished my escapes from the tyranny of the rule-bound environment governed by Islington Council, where I had to be in bed by 10.30 p.m. and go to church every Sunday.

Often, I would lie awake wondering about what was going to happen to me once I'd taken my A levels. At eighteen years old, that's it, as far as the council is concerned. You're done with the care system – or rather, the care system is done with you. Stroke of midnight on your birthday, and out you go. The harshness of that cut-off point is recorded in the notes.

I was constantly reminded of my unusual family history during parents' evenings, prize-giving days and school performances. Now there was a new variation on a theme: forms to fill in for university or college, or for grants to attend university or college. All of them required answers to questions about my mother and father, of whom I had no knowledge. But I ploughed on as best I could with the applications, and was happy to receive a conditional offer from Keele University to read social studies. This meant that, assuming I got the grades they'd asked for – three Cs – I'd be heading north to start a new life in the autumn term. But I would still need to find somewhere to live in the summer holidays before my university course started – and I had no idea how that would be achieved.

The results of our mock A levels came in and, despite all my worries, I found myself with a reasonable set of marks in my pocket – good enough to take up the offer from Keele, at any rate. So I was surprised and delighted when I heard my friend Anne's ambitious proposal: after we'd finished our A level exams, we would go hitch-hiking round Europe.

Ten: Getting on track

15 September 1969, ▮▮▮▮▮▮▮: ... Mr McLean [Jo's dad] mentioned something about using influence on Lola's behalf to get into the right job, and both girls [Jo and Lola] were horrified by this, saying that there was something demeaning and dishonest about this. They felt that one must get on by one's own efforts without any undue influence from outside.

20 September 1969, ▮▮▮▮▮▮▮: Lola asked if she was still in care.

The run-up to my eighteenth birthday signalled the final stretch of the care records. As I read on to the end, I found few further surprises or revisions to what I'd remembered. Though it meant accepting I would be left with many questions unanswered, it also came as a relief, as I'd developed an ambivalent relationship with the material in the box file.

Just as I was beginning to gain some perspective on my own experience, the work on legislation became more intense during 2014–15. The Access to Care Records Campaign Group had gained some traction with the

Department for Education, and we worked with officials to refine the existing statutory advice. The improvements the group suggested, and which were taken up, were intended to deliver a smoother, more supportive environment for those seeking their care records, at whatever age.

If they'd been in force at the time, the changes in regulatory guidance might have had a positive impact on my experience of accessing records, but that wasn't guaranteed. The administrative issues that had hit me hardest included the long wait for Islington to acknowledge that they had ever held the notes, and the misdirection caused by the inadequacies of the filing system. In any case, unless services are adequately publicized and properly implemented, those who should benefit won't.

It had been important for me to work with colleagues with an all-round understanding of the challenges faced by older care experienced adults. And I was keen to use my platform in the House of Lords to help draw attention to the need for improvements in the system. Contributing to the campaign group served, in part, as an antidote to the woes I'd experienced when I'd accessed my records.

But while the campaigning helped me feel I was taking back some control of a difficult experience, there was another strand of the story that the policy and legislation work wasn't addressing. One of the silences in my records was the absence of any sign of understanding or accounting for the wider context of my time in the care system. I'm referring to the social and cultural backdrop to my childhood and adolescence in the 1950s and 60s. The omission was predictable – it wasn't as if I'd anticipated a full analysis of the racialized politics of the time. But I had expected a better quality of understanding, and due acknowledgement of the problem.

It was clear to me that I'd been observed through a racialized prism from the first page of the records. It was evident in the many references to my physical attributes. This was as present in my care notes as it was in more general comments about Black people outside the care system. Mrs Browne's diatribe had been more explicit than others, but the teachers and fellow students who called Black people names, who made unsolicited comments about our appearance and who cracked un-funny jokes, shared and contributed to a similar sensibility.

Racist language on television, often justified as humorous and entertaining, had real-world consequences as it emboldened racists in the street, in the playground, in public services – racists who served up their own versions of their TV role models. On countless occasions lines from Alf Garnett and the like were spoken softly or shouted at us as we travelled around the city. Brown-skinned people were seen as legitimate targets for anger and ignorance, sometimes leading to uncomfortable and violent experiences.

I didn't experience the political and social context to my upbringing as a mere backdrop, to be scrutinized through the lens of objective historical analysis. Like others, I lived it. The frequent eruptions of racist political rhetoric – which then, as now, focused on migration, educational attainment and crime – were woven into my consciousness; they were an inextricable part of my lived experience that went largely unremarked on in my records. As nobody talked to me about it, or advised me on how to deal with the various shape-shifting manifestations of racism, I had to find ways of working through the situation myself. It was to prove a long and hard journey.

These external conditions overlaid and emphasized the precarious nature of my predicament, so that the personal and the political have almost always been impossible to disentangle. I was never just a girl, either to myself or to others. I was always the Black girl who lived with a foster mother, or in a children's home. I understood this not only in relation to my own circumstances – or to London and the UK – I'd felt it keenly ever since I first saw images depicting the violent abuse handed out to civil and human rights defenders around the world in the 1960s.

I felt it in terms of trying to understand why and how racism proved to be so durable, so pervasive. This was a white person's world, that was the norm, and within that I had to find a way of surviving without simply accepting that's how it would always be and nothing could ever change. There were some discussions at school, but they always felt to me like I would not be understood if I tried to articulate how I felt about the matter. If I spoke out too much, I'd be characterized as having a chip on my shoulder or imagining the sleights and insults; that was all part of the reality of racism. Who could back me up from a position of lived experience rather than detached observation?

In May 1969 I had just finished my A level exams, my eighteenth birthday was only weeks away, and thoughts on the politics of my identity were not uppermost in my mind. I was focused instead on the adventure that lay just ahead: my hitch-hiking trip around Europe with Anne.

When I think back on our planning for the trip, there's so much that I'm surprised by. I wonder at how we managed to create our complicated itinerary without Google or the internet or mobile phones. Anne's family didn't have a landline installed, so I couldn't call her – and even if they had, it wasn't as if any of us in the home could make free use of the phone. Beyond the logistical element, the idea that I – a self-described coward with low levels of trust in people – had willingly agreed to travel across Europe with just one other girl, a school friend, asking complete strangers for lifts in their cars, is astonishing. I don't recall being warned off the trip by Islington social services, either; on the contrary, Mrs Walton successfully applied for a grant on my behalf that would help with travel and accommodation costs.

The potential dangers of hitch-hiking in mainland Europe had seemed less daunting than the question of where I would stay during my university holidays, should I secure my place at Keele University. Elizabeth Harefield had offered me the option of returning to Adams Street, but that was a complete non-starter as far as I was concerned. It would have made me feel a failure – a sad sack of a girl, unable to make her own way in the world, never to be free of the children's home. Thinking about it now, I have no idea how that would have worked, given the pressure on places needed for children in care.

Immediately after my eighteenth birthday, I moved out of Adams Street to stay with Jo and her parents. Here the notes have come in handy as a reminder of the sequence of events. I remembered my stay with Jo and her parents in their home above the shop that Jo's father owned, in Chalk Farm. Jo's sister, Jane, had recently moved out, which left space for me, and her grandmother lived in the basement flat. Mr MacLean was a photographer, and we'd earn pocket money by colouring in black and white photographs for his clients. Not because colour film wasn't available; it was just the aesthetic preference of some of his customers and their families.

I hadn't remembered until reading the notes what had led to me staying with Jo's family. I didn't remember breaking down in tears at school; it was unusual for me to show my distress in public. But Jo and I had begun to develop a close friendship, and I must have trusted her enough to disclose how I felt. I was worried about having no idea where I would live between the end of exams in June 1969 and the start of university in October of that year. It was evident that no plan had been put in place by social services to see me through those months; that much is clear from Mrs Walton's own notes. Prompted by my tears, Jo had told her parents about my predicament, and they agreed to take me in on a temporary basis. The plan was that I would return to Jo's parents once I'd come back from my European adventure and before travelling up to Keele University, in Staffordshire.

Anne and I discussed the fact that, if all went to plan, we'd be watching the broadcast of the first humans landing on the moon while we were somewhere in Yugoslavia, with a commentary in Serbo-Croatian. It was a strange convergence of events that saw us anticipating the kind of holiday abroad that was still beyond the reach of most working-class families at that time, while simultaneously preparing for the sight of men taking a stroll on the lunar landscape. All things considered, it felt like the effort it had taken for me to go on this adventure across the seas was as significant as the effort it took to land men on the moon. My hope was that the time I'd spent on revision, and my boldness in taking up the challenge of the trip, would be rewarded with three years at Keele University.

And so Anne and I set off on our adventure. I imagine we presented an intriguing duo: the five-foot, pale-skinned white girl with blue-black hair cut like Mary Quant, accentuating her high cheekbones. And me, five foot nine inches tall, a short-haired, gangly Black girl, all arms and legs. We would discover on our travels that we usually picked up rides quickly.

After disembarking from the cross-Channel ferry, we took the train south to our first destination: Dubrovnik, in then-Yugoslavia. Having slept on the train, which took us through France, Austria and Germany, I'm sure I must have longed for the opportunity to stretch my legs.

Once we'd unpacked and settled into our pre-booked youth hostel accommodation, we set off to a poetry festival taking place in the town centre, which we'd known about and which had been part of our carefully planned itinerary. On the way, we came across a van selling little sausages wrapped in bread; they were delicious and would become my food of choice during the time we spent in Yugoslavia. As we approached the festival venue, we could hear the hubbub of the waiting crowd; I was excited about what lay ahead. But when we entered the main square, the buzz of conversation died away and the densely packed crowd parted, creating a pathway for me and Anne. Everyone fell silent.

Hundreds of pairs of eyes popped as they stared at me. Elbows nudged to make sure that no one missed the sight of the young Black woman walking among them. I tried a smile, but received only stares in return. No one smiled back. This encounter set the tone for the entire time we stayed in the country.

At first, I pretended I didn't care, but soon enough I began to dread going out. I didn't want to explore the town or any of its surroundings – everywhere we went, people stopped talking and stared at me. Not at Anne, just me.

The situation deteriorated for me when I had a bad reaction to a mosquito bite on my leg and my right calf doubled in size, the pores open and weeping.

I began to wonder if I'd made the right choice – gallivanting across Europe when perhaps I should have been busy back home, making contingency plans in case I failed my A levels. But it was futile to lament my choices, as we'd passed the point of no return. At least I'd managed to find out the name of my favourite dish – the one we'd tasted on our first evening in Dubrovnik: *ćevapčići*.

Anne could see that the staring was getting me down, and she suggested we move away from the crowded city to a deserted beach. I agreed eagerly. Once out by the sea, we found a spot with no sand – just rocky outcrops – and a sea too rough to swim in. Perfect. We'd take a picnic and spend the day there; we'd be left quite alone. It was a relief to have even a few hours away from the intrusive stares.

Out at sea, a small rowing boat came into view, some way off from the shore. The tips of the little waves bobbing across the bay were bright with diamonds of sunlight. There were two figures in the boat, made small by the distance, but clearly adults. One was a man, rowing the boat, and the other, his passenger, was a woman wearing a hat with a wide brim – to shield her from the sun, I guessed. It was so quiet that, as far out as they were, we were able to hear the sound of oars slapping the water.

A scratchy female voice unexpectedly carried across the waves, her words as distinct as if she were sitting next to us. She spoke with a North American accent, replying to a question we hadn't heard.

'Oh, that's a Negro,' she said. 'We have them in America.'

Yet again, a white person had fixed a label to me that hadn't been of my making. I knew that to describe a Black person as a 'Negro' was but a small step away from the other notorious word beginning with 'n'. 'We have them in America,' she'd said in a proprietorial tone. 'Indeed you do,' I could have said, 'or at least you think you do, because "they" don't belong to you any more – never truly did, in heart and soul.' This was 1969, not 1869. Men were about to step on the moon. Black people refused to accept the denial of their civil rights.

When I was still quite young, I'd read African American authors who'd discussed the nature of freedom and liberation, civil rights and revolution, but it would be many years before I came across the work of Frantz Fanon. In his book *Black Skin, White Masks* – which explores the ways in which colonial thinking has insinuated itself into our thoughts, behaviour and language – Fanon, a psychiatrist originally from Martinique, working in Paris, describes the scene on a bus as a small white child shouts, 'Mama, see the Negro! I'm frightened!' Reading those words for the first time contributed to transforming the way I thought about the psychology of racism. I'd always known that the experiences I'd had growing up as a Black girl in Britain in the fifties and sixties, and the feelings they had evoked, were not exclusive to me. But there was something about the way Fanon recreated the emotional climate of the scene that resonated deeply with me, especially when I looked back on that trip.

Eventually, we hitched our way down the coast to Split, from where we would take the ferry to Venice. On the way to our destination, we were deposited by the side of a road with nothing around us but forbidding rocks that looked as though they'd been tossed up in the air and had fallen around the mountain range in uneven clusters. A steep road comprising terrifying hairpin bends and vertigo-inducing sheer drops threaded its way through the mountains. To add to the sense of dread, we had felt earth tremors under our feet.

We'd been waiting for over an hour for someone – anyone – to give us a lift. Finally, two lorries pulled up and the drivers agreed to take us to the next village. In spite of the language barrier, we understood the situation with them: they insisted that Anne and I travel separately, one of us in each vehicle.

We tried to tell them no, but they made it clear it would have to be Anne in one and me in the other, that was the deal. We either accepted the offer on their terms, or stayed where we were. The latter was a frightening idea as night-time darkness approached.

Reluctantly, we climbed into separate cabs. My lorry was in front, and I anxiously checked the mirrors to make sure that the other driver was following behind along the same route. But it was pointless – the twists and turns made it impossible to see what was going on behind me. And what could I have done if I had seen Anne's driver going off in a different direction? Hulking mountains, narrow roads and sheer drops of hundreds of feet only added to the sense of danger. Each of us was out here on her own, out of reach, a thousand or so miles from home.

What if the worst happened? What was the worst? I had a sensation of impending catastrophe.

There was only one point in our journey when anyone would notice that we'd gone missing, and that would be in Avignon, where we were due to meet our friends Jo and Sal. But we were about three weeks away from that meeting.

All I could think was: if we were going to be attacked and left under a pile of rocks in the mountains, our passports and other belongings stolen, or be mauled to death by wildcats and wolves, then please let it happen quickly.

After about an hour, both lorries came to a halt. Anne jumped out of hers and walked quickly towards me. I wanted to hug her. We were safe! The two lorry drivers had treated us so well that I felt guilty for assuming the worst about them. I almost felt like hugging them, too, but before I could decide whether or not that was a good idea, they'd returned to their vehicles, waving as they left us behind. They'd dropped us off in a village with a hostel, on the outskirts of the mountain range; it took us a little while, but eventually we relaxed, having spent an hour or so tense with the anticipation of a very bad experience.

Knowing who you can trust – it's not straightforward.

It didn't take long for us to be spotted by a group of children in the village – they looked as though they'd just come off a film set after being cast as a gaggle of noisy urchins. A shower of stones rained down, and I realized that this was their charming way of greeting me. I wasn't physically hurt, just saddened by it all.

I couldn't quite believe it when a handsome young man came along and rescued us, telling the children to leave me alone. Tall and blond, he at least smiled as he stared at me, communicating through gestures and broken English. He showed us around, not that there was much to see, and asked questions about London and English people.

Eventually, he asked me to marry him. I declined and he walked away.

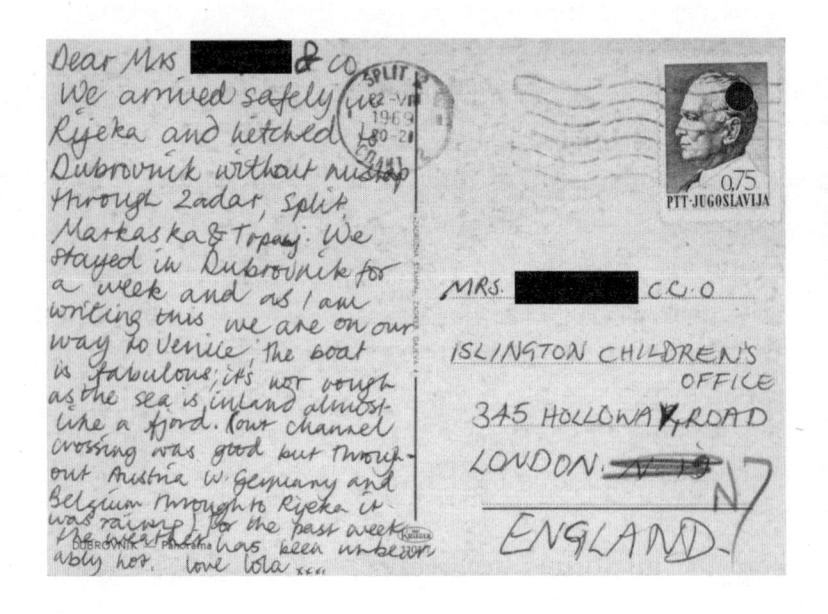

We finally reached our destination: the youth hostel we were to stay in until we left for Rijeka. Here, Anne and I watched as Neil Armstrong took his first steps on the moon. We couldn't understand the TV commentary, but that didn't matter one bit – no interpretation was needed.

On the next leg of our epic adventure, we docked in Venice and were greeted by a picture-postcard sunset. I was grateful to note that the staring had more or less stopped as soon as we landed in Italy, but the damage to my confidence was done. I felt nervous whenever we went out, anticipating hostile looks and verbal abuse, though no such incidents occurred.

After Italy, our journey took us through France to Avignon in the south, to meet our friends. We spent a magical, warm summer night there, catching up with each other's news as we watched ballet dancers performing, listened to music, star-gazed and generally had a fun, relaxing time.

On to Paris, where we would, sadly, have no time to look around, as we had a hovercraft to catch back to Dover. Not quite the same as a rocket to the moon, but still emblematic of the era – and a first for both of us.

As we skimmed across the English Channel on our way home, I knew that there was no more avoiding it. When we returned to London I'd find out if I'd achieved the grades that I needed to get me to university. Whatever the future held for me was waiting in an envelope in Chalk Farm.

The European tour, clouded though it was by the experience of being stared at intensely throughout our stay in the former Yugoslavia, nonetheless provided relief from the stress of waiting for exam results. It also gave rise to a sense of satisfaction. I'd accomplished something significant. For all the discomfort, I had travelled to unfamiliar landscapes, with one friend and few resources, and we'd both returned in one piece. I'd proved to myself that I could act independently, without being chaperoned by Islington social services.

I had survived. But what my next move would be was unclear.

When I returned to London, Jo was still on holiday in France so I went back to her parents' home without her. This felt strange and slightly uncomfortable, as if I were trying to steal her family away from her.

There were two identical envelopes on the kitchen table: one addressed to me and one addressed to Jo. I knew what they contained. Jo was very smart and, if she achieved her predicted grades, she would soon be off to the University of Lancaster. My best friend would be moving hundreds of miles away.

After she read her daughter's results, Mrs MacLean smiled, from which I gathered Jo had done well.

I wished I was somewhere private, where I could deal with the results on my own, but instead I was sitting with Jo's mother in her kitchen. I choked back tears as I absorbed the stark truth: two Ds and an E, when I needed three Cs. It spelled the end of my dream of going to university. The weeks of fun, travelling across Europe, the sense of that achievement, was obliterated in one moment by my poor results. Encouraged to think

I was clever enough, I had fallen at the final hurdle. I felt broken by this, and the contrast between my prospects and Jo's were shown in dramatic relief. The Achiever and the Failure.

Mrs MacLean meant to be kind when she told me it wasn't fair that, without working very hard, Jo had achieved the grades she needed. That was no comfort to me; it just underlined how different we were.

After news of my results came out, there was a flurry of activity: my art teacher queried the D grade I'd been awarded, and Mrs Walton tried to persuade Keele University to admit me with the lower marks. The appeal on my art grade failed, and the social studies course leader refused Islington's request, saying concessions had already been made in offering me a place with three Cs. But all this mobilizing on my behalf meant little to me at the time. I was still coming to terms with what I saw as a freshly confirmed, objective truth: I wasn't clever like my friends.

I took an office job as a temp and entered the world of work.

These days, when I'm asked to give talks and take questions about educational attainment, I reflect on the impact that not achieving the requisite grades to go to university had on me. At the time, I felt hurt and depressed. The decisions that lay ahead weighed heavily on me, and I felt the lack of adult guidance in my life keenly.

It took several years, but eventually I determined that I couldn't let my disappointing A level results be the end of my world. Ultimately, I was able to acknowledge that academic failure was relative. Today, I would say that it was an achievement merely to have survived. And not only to have survived, but to have pushed myself to take the exams that would send me to university, and passed them, even if the results fell short. It hadn't escaped my notice that my grades weren't a million miles off those of the then-heir to the throne of England. I was going to be a temp in an office; he was off to Cambridge University.

I would just have to find another route to making my way in the world.

Mrs Walton came to see me at Mr and Mrs MacLean's home, and Jo was there too. The stated objective of the evening was to discuss what could replace my ambition of going to university.

One thing I was clear about: I wasn't going to retake the exams. It seemed like a pointless exercise – after all, I wasn't going to be any smarter in the months that followed, and my domestic situation was currently even more precarious than it had been previously. No, I couldn't put myself through that level of stress again; my confidence had been dismantled by academic failure.

I'd hoped that Mrs Walton might have something up her sleeve for me in terms of future plans, but that hope was quickly dashed. My memory is that she had only negative responses that evening, as if she'd lost interest in me now that I wasn't going on to further study. When I said I was interested in going into publishing, her response was scornful: publishing was not for girls like me, but for young women with middle-class backgrounds, she said.

There was truth in that: virtually every arts and creative-sector job depended on having the right contacts or having enough financial backing to survive on a low income, possibly for years. But Mrs Walton could have said, 'This will be very challenging because people with your background aren't usually admitted to that profession. But if you decide to take it on, we'll support you.' Or she might have suggested, 'Here's what you need to do if you want a career in that field. Meanwhile, here are some alternatives . . .' But no, she didn't issue a challenge for me to rise to. Her words were a statement of fact, a clear message: don't waste your time dreaming about that, Miss Lola Young. So I didn't.

Jo and her parents sat in on that session too, although I don't recall them saying much. I do remember Jo trying to help me articulate what I wanted to do next, but since I had no idea myself, there was little she could say on my behalf. Here the records augmented my memory of my stay with Jo in an unexpected way, perhaps the last time they did so. Mrs Walton praised Jo for her compassion in having recognized my need for somewhere to stay and for persuading her parents to open their doors to me at that time.

In spite of being the subject of the conversation that evening, I had little to say after Mrs Walton's dismissal of my aspirations. She must have noticed my silence and downcast eyes, but there's no record to suggest any understanding of how crushed I felt, what a wreck I was inside.

I stayed in touch with my friends after leaving school. I knew that I needed some degree of continuity if I were to survive, and my friends represented that for me – something that was lacking in other areas of my life. Kayin and I would see each other every now and then, but she was still at school, and the four-year age gap had reasserted itself in terms of our interests and preoccupations. (Kayin, being both academic and musical, would eventually go to college to train as a teacher.) When I began my temp job at the North Thames Gas Board in 1970, she was preparing for her GCE O levels.

In spite of strong misgivings about being separated from her boyfriend, Jo went to university in Lancaster, but she dropped out after a few months. We briefly shared a flat in Archway when Jo returned to London, until she moved out and married Pete.

Sally – Sal who, several decades later, told me I was entitled to access my care records – went to Essex University to study sociology. Anne had decided to retake her A levels as, like me, she hadn't achieved her hoped-for grades: the retakes delivered the results she needed and she went away to Leicester University.

Mrs Walton suggested again that I should retake my exams too; once she'd got an idea in her head, she wouldn't let go. It was the same when she repeatedly told me I should try again with the Taylors. Perhaps she didn't trust my judgement, but whatever her motivation,

I just couldn't face the thought of it – not to mention the practical difficulties, like having nowhere to live, and no income.

In April 1970, after several months in the role of temporary office assistant, I took on a permanent job as a clerk with North Thames Gas Board in their offices at Kew Bridge. The job wasn't intellectually demanding – I operated machines that reproduced in bulk the paperwork required to administer changes to householders' appliances as a result of the switch to North Sea gas. It was satisfying in its own way, though I'd go home every evening with my hands stained a purple-tinged blue by the ink used on the Banda machine. I was more than happy to be moved on from that repetitive, messy process to work that involved the assessment of reports.

Colleagues helped me find a bedsit locally, just a ten-minute walk from the office. At £4 a week, the rent on the little bed-sitting room I'd found was manageable, but I was hopeless at budgeting, and always seemed to be in arrears with the rent. By coincidence, the tiny house was located near to a football stadium, which I could see from my window. I was even closer to Brentford FC than I had been to Arsenal when I was living at Adams Street, but there was no temptation to switch allegiance to the club that was then in the Fourth Division.

I was convinced that having been in the care system clung to me like a bad smell, and I needed to get rid of it, so I decided that I needed to mark a fresh start. A decisive first step would be to take a 'new' name and move on from 'Lola'. After years of frequent moves and the disappointment of missing out on university, the North Thames Gas Board represented stability; it was almost as good as becoming a civil servant. 'Margaret' was a solid name befitting the clerical work I was initially assigned to do, with none of the exoticism that 'Lola' held in 1970s England. Even so, it was strange to become known by a different name at nineteen years old. I remained Lola with my long-standing friends; I'm not sure I ever told them about being 'Margaret', even though it was officially my first name.

A lingering resentment at the ease with which Mrs Walton had dismissed my desire for a career in publishing settled inside me. I knew, deep down, that I wasn't completely useless, demonstrated by the fact that I'd found a job and somewhere to live and had been able to set up a bank account with minimum help from Islington Council. I felt quite proud of all that. I was independent, which I loved. I was an adult! And some of my colleagues seemed to quite like me too. I was invited round to their homes for a cup of tea or a glass of wine, and learned a little of the ways of the world from women who'd had very different life experiences to mine. I didn't divulge the details of my own upbringing; I was Margaret, and it was Lola who'd had that troubled backstory.

After I'd been in the permanent role for several months, the unit manager at the North Thames Gas Board office encouraged me to apply for a promotion, and when I was granted it my salary shot up to £800 a year. I couldn't help thinking, though, that this job didn't represent the career I wanted.

As I settled into my new home, watching the world from my window was sufficient entertainment for a while. As at Adams Street, I enjoyed watching the fans on their way to and from the stadium, trying to assess the result of the game from the crowd's mood. I'd yet to attend a football match because of the reputation of the game for attracting violent, racist behaviour. When I tired of the entertainment from my window, I had a radio, on which I listened to current affairs, drama and music. And of course, I read, mainly fiction but also some books on psychology: I recall reading R. D. Laing and, at the time, I found his ideas about families and madness intriguing. I even briefly considered taking a course in psychology but dismissed it as fanciful.

I'd kept in touch with Lynne and Len when they'd moved from Kentish Town to Hounslow, near Heathrow Airport, and with me living in Brentford, it was a lot easier to visit them at their flat. They now had a daughter, a toddler called Sheila. Len was all right, as long as I didn't challenge his view of the world. If I did, he'd say something like, 'Well, of course, you're more clever than we are,' intending it to sound like an insult. We mostly argued about politics, and I remember one particular 'discussion' about whether it was right for Britain to sell arms to the country we now know as Zimbabwe, but which was then called Rhodesia, and South Africa, both of which violently oppressed the majority Black populations. Len thought it was all right, because if Britain didn't supply them with weapons, another country would. I thought that was a pathetic argument, and I said so, which didn't go down well.

In December 1970, knowing I'd be on my own otherwise, Lynne invited me to join them for Christmas. In truth, I'd been relishing the prospect of solitude, but I didn't know how to say no, so I agreed. I was dreading more arguments with Len, but I didn't want to lose contact with Lynne, so I made an effort not to engage in any vaguely political discussion with him.

The day passed without incident, and I pretended – or, let's be honest, I lied – that I'd promised to visit the Adams Street home on Boxing Day, to see Elizabeth Harefield. I lied because I knew I wouldn't be able to make Lynne and Len understand that I'd prefer to be on my own. I didn't see myself as being antisocial but I craved solitude, and having had no option in the past but to share with strangers, I looked forward to my time alone.

The next morning, Len insisted on giving me a lift to South Ealing station, which has a large, open concourse, giving them a clear view of me as I entered. Just in case they were watching me from the car, waiting to catch me out in my lie, I pretended to study my route on the map of the underground. Keeping up the act, I took a long, slow walk towards the ticket office, all the time imagining Lynne and Len's eyes burning through the station walls to the back of my head and through to my guilty face. Convinced they were parked around the corner, watching and waiting, I lingered for ten or fifteen minutes, staring at the walls and maps and the timetable of the last trains into central London. Before, finally, leaving the station and walking back to my solitary haven in Brentford.

I promised myself that the following year would be a different story, and when December 1971 came round I would finally, finally do Christmas Day the way I wanted to.

A memory: Christmas

25 December 1971: *twenty years old*

My traditional Christmas lunch is all ready to pop into the oven. All I have to do now is decide what to watch while I eat in delicious solitude.

I've treated myself to a rented television set from a local furniture shop, which I ordered over the phone. I arranged for the set to be delivered after work one evening.

When I answered the doorbell, a man holding a television was standing on the step. He looked at me with a startled expression.

'I thought you'd be Chinese,' he said.

'Really?' I said, puzzled.

'I wrote your name down as Y-u-n-g.'

He was a bundle of nerves: his hands shook as he balanced the set on the edge of the dressing table while he searched for something in his pocket. As he briefly relaxed his grip on the telly, it teetered for a moment, until he shoved it back firmly on to the dressing table. In saving the TV, he dislodged the mirror. It fell to the floor and shattered, spilling glass daggers across the worn carpet.

The man whimpered, and I thought he was going to cry.

'Seven years' bad luck,' he whispered. 'It's happened before.'

I've planned my meal carefully, and have the whole day worked out.

The first clue that something is wrong is when I check the *Radio Times* for a programme to watch while the food is cooking. As I read, the words start to swim before my eyes. Soon enough, they are drifting across the page in jagged movements. I try blinking to get rid of the bright lights flashing behind my eyes, making reading impossible. I switch on the television, turning the dial to the BBC. An old film is on, already partway through. I recognize it as *Tom Thumb*, a fun musical just right for family viewing on a Christmas morning.

Around midday I start to feel sick, perhaps because I haven't yet eaten anything. When I open the oven door to see if the food is ready, the smell of the roasting meat makes me retch, and I slam it shut again. Overtaken by nausea and dizziness, I make my way shakily to bed.

My brain is battering against my skull, as though struggling to escape from its restraints. I know then that something bad is happening to me, but I have no idea what it is or how to deal with it. I am under the duvet, fully dressed. The television is still on and, irritating as it is, I haven't the strength to get up and turn off the tinkling soundtrack. I drift in and out of a sleep which is more like a loss of consciousness, my body trying to rescue me from the pain in my head.

This is how I spend my first Christmas Day alone,

unable to move out of bed until the evening, when the pain begins to subside.

The experience is unnerving and makes me question my decision to stay on my own for the day. It feels like a rejection of the idea that I can exist as an island – a warning against thinking I don't need other people.

Whatever the underlying meaning, I am left with a shrivelled-up turkey and a pile of inedible vegetables.

Merry Christmas.

Eleven: A fresh start

> Whether you're a girl who wants a pleasant job, or a really ambitious career girl, we want you at Westminster Bank.
>
> Advertisement in Parliament Hill School magazine, 1967–68

In 1971, I was coming up to having worked for almost two years at the Gas Board, and I was starting to think about what other opportunities might exist for me in the world of work. One of my colleagues had a sister who was a buyer for a large chain of shops. It sounded like a dream job – she earned good money buying clothes and other lovely products, and she didn't even have to pay for them.

Around that time, I saw that Marks and Spencer was advertising vacancies for trainee buyers, and I applied. After a series of interviews and a visit to a local store, I was accepted on to the training programme, a much-needed boost to my confidence. At twenty years old, I was quite self-conscious about my appearance and other supposed shortcomings that I'd internalized.

But then I learned that being a buyer entailed travelling around the country, negotiating – and socializing? – with businessmen, staying in hotels, sampling unknown food, perhaps being stared at and having my hair touched by strangers in out-of-the-way places. Even in London, my stomping ground, I found it difficult to go into a pub with friends, let alone on my own. Memories of Devon and Yugoslavia haunted me, as did visits to Walton-on-the-Naze, Epping Forest and other places where I'd been stared at, my appearance commented on, and been called names by strangers who'd objected to my presence in their midst. I began to question whether this career would be the right choice for me.

Besides, I was doing well at the North Thames Gas Board. I'd been elected as a staff representative, taking requests for changes in office rules to the head office in Kensington. During my tenure, I was called upon to present the case for women to be allowed to wear trousers to work. It was a qualified success: we were granted permission to do so, as long as we wore a jacket or tunic that covered our backsides. This was in the last third of the twentieth century. Funny how the men at head office had not issued edicts about the length of miniskirts.

Around this time, Kayin – who was now sixteen – and I decided to join the Islington Players and entered the world of amateur dramatics. Having been brought up with popular culture at the centre of our world, with entertainment on the gramophone, on the wireless and on television, both of us had an interest in the performing arts. We could recite whole episodes of *Hancock's Half Hour*, which we'd listen to on Sunday afternoons with Daisy. As well as imagining that acting would be a fun thing to do, I thought that by being forced to project a personality on stage, I might find something of myself.

The artistic director was constantly flummoxed by how to use us in his productions. Always keen to play up the theatrical credentials he'd earned with the Royal Shakespeare Company, he had to contend not only with Kayin and me, but also another Black woman in the drama group, a bit older than us. When he came to direct Dickens' *A Christmas Carol*, he saw the three of us as historically anomalous, and inserted a brief prologue so that we had something to do in the production.

In the end, I decided to turn down the Marks and Spencer traineeship. But I still couldn't see a life spent working at the Gas Board. Soon enough, however, a new opportunity presented itself. In a place, and with people, that I was familiar with.

I think it was Elizabeth Harefield who alerted me that there was a vacancy at the Adams Street home. I'd kept in touch, occasionally visiting her, and she was aware that I wasn't exactly thrilled by the prospect of working at the North Thames Gas Board for the rest of my life. So I applied for a position as a residential child care officer – the new title for the likes of the Tuskers, the Flaggs and Elizabeth Harefield. A job where I could eventually train to become a field child care officer, if I wanted to. Mrs Walton and I would be colleagues then – now there was a thought. I weighed up the pros and cons of staying for a while longer with NTGB or moving on – which was also, at the same time, moving back – to a new career in a familiar world. I relished the freedom to make my own choices in life.

An application form, references and a couple of interviews later, and I found myself returning to Adams Street, to work in the home where I'd been a resident two and a half years earlier. I didn't see it as a backward step. I would be working alongside Aunty Elizabeth (that's how I'd continued to think of her). And I knew that some of the kids I had lived with then would now be in my care. I realized this might feel strange at first, but I was so much older than them, and I hoped it wouldn't be too awkward.

Back to Highbury. To the place where I'd spent two years wondering if I'd ever be able to leave care in any meaningful sense. Back within sight and sound of Arsenal Stadium. Among the crowds of fans, celebrating the victories with them as they flowed out through the gates. Back to what was familiar. Did that make me a failure, a coward? I didn't know.

I hadn't felt sad at the thought of leaving the little mouse-ridden bed-sitting room in Brentford, but it was a chore to think that I would have to search for somewhere to live yet again.

Someone suggested that I contact Dr and Mrs Bishop. I'd known of them when I first lived in Adams Street; they had been active members of a church congregation, and the subject of some uncomplimentary gossip. One of the criticisms levelled at them was their self-confidence, bordering on arrogance. But a flat in the Bishops' vast north London terraced house was available for rent – and conveniently close to Adams Street. I became their lodger, taking up one of the two empty bedrooms in the upstairs flat, and was told to expect a new flatmate before too long.

On joining the Adams Street home as a member of staff, I shed the short-lived 'Margaret' tag, and adopted yet another new identity: Aunty Lola.

The teenagers with whom I'd been in care had left, and space had been created for new residents. A couple of children had recently arrived from the Flaggs' in Vicarage Road, where we'd briefly crossed paths. I was saddened and angry to hear them share more tales of humiliation from their time there. Altogether, there were four girls and three boys, some of them related to each other. Out of the seven children in the home, there was one Black child, a boy named Bobby Martin. I'll return to him later.

Activities for the children living at Adams Street were still based around the local church, Sunday school and youth club, as they had been when I was a resident. Now that I'd been in the outside world the vista seemed even more narrow than it had first time around. I understood better than most how important security and stability were to children in care – and how rare those commodities were. But the tight parameters also limited horizons and thwarted ambition, and that hadn't really changed since I'd left. Through friends at Parliament Hill, I'd had glimpses of other worlds, where exposure to cultural life was the norm. I wanted the children in the home to know about the existence of those worlds too.

After reading about the exhibition in a magazine, I decided I would take five of the younger kids from the home to see treasures from Tutankhamun's tomb at the British Museum. I knew that going to exhibitions and museums was something that middle-class families did regularly, while children who were fostered, or in a home, wouldn't necessarily have such opportunities. It's something I've thought about a lot since – how we can make sure that care experienced children and young people don't miss out on the kind of cultural enrichment that many take for granted.

I knew that we were going to a blockbuster exhibition. But it was still a shock to see the length of the queue to get in. I asked the kids if they'd rather go to a park, or head back home instead, but they said they wanted to stay. None of them complained as we shuffled along what felt like miles and miles of pavements.

After hours of queuing, we finally reached the entrance, and were admitted. The exhibition was cleverly arranged to build anticipation: the route to reaching the final display was constructed in such a way as to suggest the journey undertaken by the archaeologists who had first revealed the treasures to the Western world. We seemed to burrow underground, finally, to discover the funerary mask, in all its gold and lapis lazuli glory. The children revelled in the experience – fully transported by the spectacle. I was equally seduced by the beauty of the exhibits, on loan from Egypt.

We were just six people out of the 1.6 million who visited Tutankhamun at the British Museum in 1972. In those days, I hadn't yet learned about the links between culture and colonialism, and the plunder of treasure from overseas. The cultural heritages of the children who explored the exhibition with me covered a spread of countries, and there were artefacts on display in the British Museum and elsewhere in the UK that came from those same countries. Museum practice was a subject that I knew nothing of at that time, and I didn't start fully to engage with it until the late 1990s. Up until then, I'd had no understanding of how the long tail of colonial history and conquest was a key component of archaeological practices in former British territories.

When I first joined the staff at Adams Street, Elizabeth Harefield had briefed me on the children's backgrounds. She told me that Bobby Martin was highly intelligent, and I remember him as being very good at reading and schoolwork. He was small for his age, but physically tough in a wiry sort of way, and generally well behaved. Though my memories of our interactions in the home are vague now, I would think about Bobby Martin for a long time after our paths diverged. Perhaps it was because I was a young Black woman in a position of relative authority in the home where I'd been a resident myself just over two years earlier. Perhaps I over-identified with him because of the rejections he'd endured, and the treatment he'd received from people who should have known better. But I remember that I was well aware of the dearth of Black people working in the care system, and I was wary of becoming a focal point for him, raising his expectations of what I could offer to him specifically. He'd been badly treated emotionally, and I didn't want to be another in the long line of people who'd let him down.

Several months into my stay at the Bishops' house, the long-awaited flatmate finally arrived. Mrs Bishop appeared in the kitchen with a ghostly young woman with pale, tissue-paper skin and a dark brown wavy bob. I'd been sitting reading *Honey* magazine. She was holding an edition of the *Church Times*.

Mrs Bishop introduced the girl and I nodded in greeting, telling her my name. Mrs Bishop turned to her and asked, 'Do you mind sharing the flat with a coloured girl?'

The young woman said no, she didn't mind at all.

I sat and seethed, and stared so hard at the magazine that I half expected to see singe-marks on the cover. I'd recently read an article about a Black girl in a flatshare who'd discovered that her white 'friend' would scrub the bath immediately after her brown-skinned flatmate had used it. I should've asked Mrs Bishop when she was going to check whether I minded sharing with a white girl. But, overwhelmed by anger, the biting comment came into my head too late.

Mrs Bishop had previous form on the subject of discrimination, so I probably shouldn't have been surprised by her question to the prospective tenant.

'Why did you go to the Jews' side of the practice?' she

had asked me one day, on learning that I had signed up with her husband's medical practice, but not with him. As if it was any of her business who I chose as my doctor.

We had little in common, that young woman and I, and we rarely crossed paths except in the kitchen, the setting of our first encounter. I was into fashion still, avidly poring over the pages of *Honey*, *Nova* and the like, searching for ideas for ways of enhancing my modest but growing cache of clothes. I got the impression that shopping for make-up, getting dressed up to go out with friends – these weren't a priority for her. She was dedicated to her faith – attending church with the Bishops – and to her profession as a radiographer. I think we had one conversation about her work but that was about it. She was always polite and friendly, but we never confided in each other or became close.

I spent a year and a half working in the Adams Street home.

I'd begun to find it too constraining, a little claustrophobic. It was nothing to do with the children; they were well behaved and, by and large, coped well with their situations, at least on the surface. But I felt powerless to provide them with the tools they needed to navigate the world beyond care, and that was a source of frustration. I also knew that I wanted to stretch myself mentally, to challenge myself in a different way, so I decided to take a course in social work. This was partly because it was clear that changes in the organization of local authority services, resulting from the 1968 Seebohm Report, were coming into play. One of the ideas was that the role of residential social workers – the 'aunties' and 'uncles' in Park House and Vicarage Road, which were both run by married couples – needed to be rethought and developed, giving the job a similar professional standing to that of child care officers like Mrs Bould and Mrs Walton. I thought an in-service training course would enhance my social work career prospects, at the same time as providing me with the chance to redeem what I thought of as my poor record of academic achievement.

It felt good to be studying again, and participating in discussions about the shortcomings of the care system and current thinking about how to address them. But I found it hard to relate the theory part of the course to my own experiences, or to that of the children for whom I was responsible. In the end, my growing restlessness wasn't to be remedied by a course in social work.

For all its limitations, becoming a member of the Islington Players had sparked something inside me. Soon after joining, I admitted to myself – if nobody else – a secret desire to become a professional actor. I considered my options. Drama school felt too risky – it would give me nothing to fall back on if things didn't work out the way I hoped. But maybe I could study for a teaching diploma in English and drama. That way, if I never landed a stage role in my life, I could still get a job in secondary schools – I had experience with children now, after all. In 1972, I applied and was accepted on to a three-year course at the New College of Speech and

Drama, which would lead to the London University Diploma in Dramatic Art and a teaching certificate. I handed in my notice at Adams Street, and said a final goodbye to Elizabeth Harefield, who wished me luck and asked me to keep in touch. Now I was ready for the exciting possibilities that lay ahead.

While I waited for the course to start in the autumn term, I worked full-time in The Burgundian public house on Finchley Road. This required me to withhold the exact nature of my 'waitressing' job from the Bishops, who were vehemently teetotal.

I had found this out fairly early on in my stay with them, when Dr Bishop and I were exchanging polite words in their kitchen. As we spoke, he'd lifted a wine bottle – given to him by a grateful patient – high above the sink, and poured its contents down the plughole. But no amount of performative abstinence could disguise the often moody atmosphere in the household. For example, why was it that one of the children would only eat unhealthy fast food? And why did Mrs Bishop sometimes wear dark glasses on dull winter days, and even indoors at times?

Mrs Bishop hurled abuse at me when she discovered I'd been working in a house of sin – or, as I thought of it, a pub. Kayin came to help me pack up and move out. When she saw Kayin's cross on a chain around her neck, Mrs Bishop begged her to pray for me. I don't think Kayin appreciated the assumptions being made by Mrs Bishop, and she certainly didn't recognize the condemned sinner being shouted at by my about-to-be-former landlady. Dear Kayin. I was very grateful for her support.

I said goodbye to Mrs Bishop, and suggested she use her prayers where they were really needed.

Kayin and I had quite a laugh about the woman as we took a taxi loaded with all my possessions to my next north London address, this time near Archway.

For all that I could laugh off some of these experiences – use them as fodder for entertaining anecdotes, or inspirational life lessons learned along the path to serenity and success – they stack up, and require a conscious, sustained effort to keep them in a place where they cannot prompt too much disruption of my psyche.

Having said goodbye to the Bishops, I was ready to embark on my second or maybe third reinvention – from Lola the care kid, to Margaret Young the Gas Board clerk, to Aunty Lola the social worker, and now on to independent, freewheeling Lola Young, aspiring Black actress.

I felt as though I was finally shaking off the shackles of the care system. Logical as it had seemed to me, my decision to resign from a secure job in the children's home must have come as something of a surprise to my friends – though I don't recall any of them trying to dissuade me. A fresh start beckoned, and I was determined to move towards the creative life that had so far eluded me.

I was aware, of course, how few parts there were for Black women in theatre and television. But I wasn't going to allow that to deter me. The sense of having missed out on opportunities can embitter people, eating away at any joy in their lives and those around them. I didn't want to end up like that. I wasn't daunted by reports of how tough the acting business would be: after all, I hadn't exactly been cocooned in privilege up to this point. In retrospect, I think I might also have felt attracted to the nomadic lifestyle of an actor in repertory theatre – that was a precariousness with which I was quite familiar.

The time I'd spent in care had been an education, no doubt about that. My situation had provided endless opportunities to try and work out why people were the way they were; why I was the way I was. Would I always be the girl who had been raised in foster care and children's homes? Yes, of course, but I also had to believe that I wouldn't forever be defined by that experience, and I wanted to explore what else I might become.

Back in 1969, when the course convener had asked me in my interview why I'd chosen the BA in Social Studies at Keele University, I'd said it was because I had wanted 'to give something back'. I had believed it too, even though I hadn't been entirely sure what that 'something' was.

It hadn't taken long for me to stop viewing the world through that prism. After eighteen months of working in Adams Street, I had begun to reappraise my time in care and my motivation for entering the field. I realized that I didn't owe the care system anything: it was a service that I'd needed, and I was grateful for having had that safety net. But that didn't mean that I had a debt to pay for the rest of my life.

*

Joining the student body at the New College of Speech and Drama was a shock to the system. Even into my second year, I was still getting used to being surrounded by, as I saw them, a bunch of rich kids. They were also younger – at the age of twenty-two, I was officially a 'mature student'. I remember being astonished to hear one student say they'd never had to cook a meal in their life – not even made their own breakfast. And then there were those who acted like they couldn't afford to buy new clothes and proudly paraded their threadbare jeans and jumpers, when it was clear Mummy and Daddy kept the funds flowing. Although I knew I didn't want to be like them, I found it hard not to envy their financial security.

It may sound counter-intuitive but the idea that people might like me has often left me feeling puzzled. The early part of my life – the abandonment – was all the evidence I needed to confirm that I wasn't likeable. At school, I worried that classmates only liked me because they didn't know me or because they felt sorry for me. I would feel the same at New College, where I was surprised to find that a cluster of people wanted me to hang around with them. When an idea like that lodges in your brain – that people only like you because they can't see the kind of person you really are – it's hard to shake off, and it can become a self-fulfilling prophecy. Fear drove my suspicion of people who acted friendly towards me. But for all my distrust of others, when I was approached by Charles, a student in the year above, suggesting I'd be great in the role of producer for the next second-year revue, I accepted straight away.

Charles explained the New College tradition: each year, a second-year student was chosen to put on an original piece of work to entertain fellow students and guests. The student who produced the show had to identify the next revue director, and so after he'd completed his stint, Charles had picked me.

I was so pleased to be asked that I said yes without any understanding of the task or knowledge of how much work would be involved. I only thought to ask Charles what I would have to do after I'd agreed to do it. He might well have chosen me because I stood out as the only Black person in the whole year. Or maybe he could see that I was likely to be more competent than those of my fellow students who didn't know how to boil an egg for breakfast. Whatever the reason, I took on the role with great enthusiasm.

Putting on the show was an exhausting, exhilarating experience. I had to conceptualize, devise, write, audition and cast, direct and produce the whole event. In essence it was a satirical, portmanteau piece, which strung together a series of sketches, accompanied by music and dance. I'd never felt so worn out in my life – I remember drifting off to sleep one evening after rehearsals in the local cafeteria, a forkful of food in my mouth. It was worth it, as the experience was invaluable; I was forced to make decisions and accept the consequences, as happens in any creative collaborative endeavour. The production seemed to be well received, but it was hard to tell, since the show was a student tradition – there was even a joke about a Stradivarius violin that had to be included every year – and the audience was as much a part of what went on as the production. I don't think anyone watched through the eyes of a detached cultural critic.

There had been so much to learn since the start of my degree – not just lines in plays, or how to move on stage. There was the theatrical terminology; the complex instructions given by directors that made my brain fizz as I tried to work out what I was meant to do, where I was supposed to stand. And there were many things I'd never known I could do. I made props, stage-managed and acted in Lorca and Shakespeare; I even co-wrote a song – a spoof blues number called 'Let Me Cook a Meal on You'. The songwriting led me to the discovery that I had a talent for singing, which was a useful skill to have.

There were so few men on the course – about seven or eight out of sixty students in each year – that if you were male, you were virtually guaranteed a decent part in every production. But if you were female, you'd be lucky to get on stage as a non-speaking extra in a crowd scene. And of course, because I was everyone's favourite historical anomaly, apparently I couldn't be cast in any play set in the past, unless it was in the role of a prostitute or a witch. With one notable exception.

Flora Telford, one of our drama teachers, had a long-standing theatrical ambition to cast a Black woman as Desdemona with a white male Othello. Flora had been on the admissions panel for New College and present at my audition, which I thought had been a disaster because I'd dried about halfway into my piece. The lines I'd memorized just floated out of my head, and I stopped speaking. The assessors had stared at me in an embarrassing silence until I'd said, 'Um, line please?'

Despite that uninspiring performance, Flora decided that I would be the one to fulfil her dream of being recognized as a Shakespearean iconoclast. So, usually depicted as a physically imposing, dominating warrior with a mesmerizing baritone voice, this version of Shakespeare's tragic protagonist cast Alan, a slight, pale-skinned, mild-mannered Scot, as Othello. And there was me: a brown-hued Desdemona whose skin was supposedly 'smooth as monumental alabaster'. Unsuspecting Shakespeare-loving audiences must have had quite a shock.

After Othello, it was back to walk-on parts and the chorus. But I didn't mind – I had other priorities in my extra-curricular activities. I'd joined a band, the Strutters, as one of a trio of female singers alongside six instrumentalists. A student in Charles's year had put my name forward, I'd auditioned, and that was it. I couldn't read music but I was already familiar with some of the songs, and seemed to be able to pick up others quite quickly. We performed at universities and colleges and pubs in London and in the north of England, at one point almost every weekend. I think we even supported the Troggs once – in 1966 they'd had a big hit with 'Wild Thing', and were still popular years later.

I was thrilled the first time the Strutters were invited to play a gig Upstairs at Ronnie Scott's, the legendary club in Soho. On the night, I walked to Frith Street thinking about the first time I'd visited this part of London with

Mrs Bould. That had been less than ten years ago, and so much had happened since then. It was a sign of how much had happened, and how far I'd travelled, that now here I was, about to sing with a band, in a nightclub famous around the world.

When we walked on to the stage and the lights came up, just enough so our facial features could be seen by the audience, I felt the adrenalin begin to flow. The band began our signature musical introduction and all eyes were on us. We channelled our emotional connection with the music to the audience as they shook off their inhibitions – dancing and shimmying to the beat. Making music: it was all about the connection.

A memory: A visit with my father

Autumn 1974: *twenty-three years old*

'I'm staying at the White House,' he says, when we finally connect on the phone.

Sounds impressive, doesn't it? As if he were the president of somewhere. But it's just a hotel not far from Euston station.

I should have asked him then why he wanted to see me. But right now, standing self-consciously in the hotel lobby, the most urgent question on my mind is: what does he look like? With barely any memories, and no photographs, how am I supposed to recognize him?

I feel the eyes of the hotel staff in their stiff uniforms on me. I have no idea what to do in this situation. I decide I'll call Joy, my friend and fellow student. She'll know how to handle this. It has taken me some time to trust this privileged white South African I met at New College, but we're good friends now. She's socially competent and she'll know how to deal with difficult situations in posh hotels. I'll call her. I ask at the desk and the receptionist points me in the direction of a pay phone booth.

I know her number by heart but check it in my address book anyway. Now's not the moment to risk being connected to a wrong number, wasting precious time and money. She has to be at home, please let her be in. I picture her lounging on her sofa, surrounded by her mates, the South African crew, the boys in another band I've sung with.

Almost immediately, she picks up. Her voice, lightly dusted with a trace of cigarettes, calms me down. I explain my dilemma: how will I find this man when I don't know what he looks like?

'Relax, Lotus,' she advises. 'Just go to the reception desk and ask them to page him.'

Obvious, really. I ring off and return to the front desk, wait while the receptionist picks up her phone to call my father.

The last sighting I had of him was ten years before I started at drama school, in 1963. He's written to me once in the intervening period, I think – to tell me off for not being sufficiently warm in a letter I'd sent him. Maybe it was my fault. I remember my fifteen-year-old hand hovering over the pale blue Basildon Bond notepaper, not knowing how to start the letter I'd been advised to write to him. My fingers refused to make the movement with the pen on the paper that would produce 'Dear Dad'. I just couldn't find it in me. In the end, I started with 'Dear Father'.

I have no idea what I did with his response, a rare document indeed. I might have done something dramatic, like screwing it up and throwing it in the bin. Or I could have tossed it over the wall and into the mouth of the Westerns Laundry food monster, as I believe I had been living with the Taylors at the time. What I do remember clearly were the first few words of his reply. My letter was, he wrote, 'cold, cold as the north wind'. Tellingly, I can't remember what it was that chilled him so; it might have contained a request for some funds, which had repulsed him. In any event, the sentiment behind his words was clear enough: don't bother me with your dreams.

But now I am here in this hotel because Kayin's mother has been determined to get my father to show an interest in his second daughter. And she knew the right person to put pressure on him: a highly respected member of Nigerian society, Lady Olayemi. (Some years later, I read that she had been among those who had fought for Nigerian women's political and economic autonomy for decades.)

Contacting this dignitary had been an interesting move on Aunty Iyinoluwa's part, as Kayin's mother was distantly related to my mother, which is how Kayin and I got to be cousins several times removed. Perhaps Aunty Iyinoluwa saw my mother as a lost cause – I'd certainly given up on her – or perhaps she thought Lady Olayemi had more traction with my father. I'm not sure what my exact familial relationship to Lady Olayemi is, but I do know that her name is always spoken with awe and respect.

I've long since stopped speculating about what talents or character traits I might have inherited from either of my parents. As far as I'm concerned, my love of the creative arts has been generated within me, by me. I wonder if my father has been made aware that I am attending drama school with the aim of becoming an actress. Kayin's mother knows, but perhaps she has left that bit out of her talks with Lady Olayemi, focusing instead on the teaching qualification element of the course.

Whatever has gone on behind the scenes, the pressure on my father bore fruit. And now, ten years and eight addresses since we last saw each other, he has called me and asked to meet – my number having been passed on through a chain of hitherto unknown relatives.

A tall, slim man – about six feet tall – wearing a dark grey suit, walks into the lobby. It's him. My father.

He extends an arm, whether to show me the way to the lifts or to embrace me, I'm not sure. I don't feel like being touched by this stranger, and I shrink from him. He doesn't seem to notice or, if he does, he doesn't show it.

His room is smaller than I thought it would be – pokey, really. And the air in it is too thick, I feel it as soon as we go in. It's claggy. Stuffy. The only furniture is a single bed with an eiderdown, an armchair and a small television. He gestures to me to sit down.

There's horse racing on the TV, and he doesn't switch it off, which I think he should, even though the volume is low, just about audible. The tiny black and white images on the screen are distracting, but then I suppose that's the point. Something to look at, something to listen to that isn't me. While I'm relieved that his focus is on something else, and directed away from me, I am outraged that he hasn't switched the bloody thing off.

He asks me if I want something to drink, pointing to

a row of small bottles on a shelf above a little fridge. I decline. The memory of a weekend drinking competition, involving me, a bottle of student-cheap red wine and a hangover that made me want to die, is still fresh in my mind. I never want to drink alcohol again. Not for a week or two, anyway.

He mumbles as he talks – about his work, his social life, his family. He's a judge in the Ministry of Housing, he says. A perfect fit, I think; passing judgement on others, while failing to examine his own behaviour. It's hard for me to work up any enthusiasm for his tales of Lagos society. Just as difficult as it is for him to pretend interest in my life since we last saw each other a decade ago.

There's something missing; there should be a more obvious emotional connection on show in this room, like you see on the telly, when relatives separated at a young age are reunited and can't stop crying. It's not like that at all though. The tension in the room is so thick I'd need a chainsaw to cut through it. What's going on here is a parody of kinship. I'd wanted an authentic version.

My eyes flick from his face to the telly, and back again, unable to say anything. I find it hard to believe that we have any biological connection at all.

He glances at the TV screen often too; perhaps he has a bet on and is waiting for the result. Or perhaps the figures on their horses are really quite captivating, when you can't look your estranged daughter in the eye.

We've each taken a vow of silence, it seems, and I say nothing of what I'm thinking, and neither does he.

Nothing about what happened between him and my mother. I want to know but I am so scared he'll tell me that I keep very still, not wishing to disturb the air, or draw attention to my presence. He doesn't explain or apologize or try to justify his light-touch approach to paternal care.

When I can't stand it any longer, I say I have to go – I have rehearsals, lines to learn, *The Winter's Tale* to read.

My father says he has something for me. He hands me a ten-pound note. What's this supposed to be for? That's what I want to say. *What the hell is this for?* But I don't have the courage. Instead, because I am broke, I take it greedily, assuming the role of a willing participant in my father's fictional generosity.

Twelve: An invitation

> As far as the South African Government is concerned, white Equity members can perform in South Africa. Black Equity members, however, cannot perform in South Africa. The ban we seek, then, is not only in protest at the obscene and racist policies of the Vorster regime. It is also in defence of members of our own Union who are discriminated against in South Africa...
> VOTE FOR A COMPLETE BAN IN THE COMING REFERENDUM
>
>   'Take A Stand Against Apartheid':
>   Equity referendum, 1976
>   Published by Performers Against Racism

Looking back, my one wish during that meeting with my father is that I'd had the courage to confront him with the story of my life during the years when he – and my mother – disappeared from view. I wanted to be able to tell him everything that had happened to me. And then ask, 'What the hell were you thinking of, leaving me here like that? Do you have any idea how that made me feel?'

Instead, our encounter had been unsatisfactory, an

anticlimax if ever there was one. Fortunately, my father exited my life as rapidly as he had done a decade earlier. I was left feeling strange, a bit moody, I didn't feel like socializing, and threw myself into studying. There were exams coming up soon, and I wanted to do well. I still hadn't rid myself of the idea that I was an academic failure. Acting, directing, studying – this was my life now, and I had to work hard to ensure I didn't mess it up by worrying about a father who'd been absent for so long.

I was also aware that pursuing an acting career – or for that matter, singing in a band – wasn't an accepted pathway to securing family approval with middle-class Nigerians, so I was grateful to have at least avoided any critical scrutiny that might have come my way if I'd been in regular contact with my mother or my father.

Not long after joining the Strutters, I made a surprising discovery. Esther, one of the other singers in the trio, was related to someone who knew my mother. I couldn't believe it at first. But it was true. Esther's cousin had once been involved with the Ministry of Health in Nigeria, when General Gowon was in power, and she'd known and worked with my mother for many years.

The cousin's name was Chief Mrs Arden, and Esther said she would put us in touch. I learned that Chief Mrs Arden had known my mother well – as her cousin, friend and partner in a healthcare business. Several decades later, I discovered that Chief Arden had her own Wikipedia page, and is referred to as the first Black nurse to work for the NHS.

Our initial meeting was in her flat in Baker Street, central London. Mrs Arden came to the capital frequently, she'd said, so it made sense for her to buy a flat rather than staying at the White House Hotel – that place again! – as she had often done in the past.

We probably met three, maybe four times at the most. Some of the names she mentioned to me were familiar from conversations with Kayin's mother, Aunty Iyinoluwa. Lady Olayemi was one of the names I'd heard before, though when Mrs Arden referred to a Lady Fashola, I was unclear about whether she was related to either of my parents.

Mrs Arden would have been in a position to know the details of my parents' relationship and break-up, so I was keen to hear what she had to say, even though I didn't always know what to make of our meetings. I'd become accustomed to the privilege I saw among some of my fellow students, but the level of wealth and the political connections of these newly acquired relatives and 'family friends' forced me to acknowledge a number of contradictions that emerged from what I learned in these meetings with Chief Mrs Arden. My growing understanding of, and interest in, the causes and ramifications of inequality and various social injustices, were now to be considered alongside my family's activities and interests. I was used to thinking of my parents as existing in a parallel world; now I had to accommodate a mental picture of yet another, different universe, where I could have become one of the spoilt rich kids.

While I focused on becoming an actor, Mrs Arden

attended to her business and family interests in London, the USA, Switzerland and Nigeria. My role in our conversations was that of listener: I wanted to find out what I could from this woman who had links and contacts across the globe, as well as the in-depth knowledge of local connections – from London to Lagos. As I sat sipping tea with her in her living room, I would look at her and wonder what basis we had for a shared conversation.

One of the most striking pieces of information Mrs Arden divulged concerned my mother, who in the year of my birth – when she'd been in London, in 1951 – had written home to Lagos saying that she'd had a baby. It was Maxwell Young's child. Yet when my mother arrived back in Lagos alone, Mrs Arden claimed no one enquired about the absent child. I asked her how that had happened – why had nobody said anything? Mrs Arden implied that my mother had been considered too fragile to be pressed on the subject, and so the child slipped out of view.

Without further details, it was hard to process what all this meant. It had taken some time for Mrs Arden to gather herself to disclose the information and I found it difficult to piece together the various parts of the rest of the story. Still, it was more than anybody else had divulged, and although the relationship between me and Mrs Arden was quite formal, she offered a gateway into understanding the complex family dynamics that had led to me being taken to Daisy Vince and Tufnell Park Road.

At the end of our meetings, as I was about to leave,

Mrs Arden would invariably hand me a ten-pound note. That would be my rent covered for another week.

After graduating from the New College of Speech and Drama, my life as a professional actor began in Coventry. Repertory theatre was still thriving in the 1970s and so was theatre in education – known as TIE. Gaining a foothold in acting was, and still is, highly competitive – with rejection built into the cycle of auditions and screen tests. And it was especially so for Black women in the 1970s.

I'd focused on the performance aspects of the New College course over the theoretical academic ones. While I'd found little in the curriculum to stimulate any dormant intellectual curiosity I might have had, I was also protecting myself from the possibility of failing again academically after my inadequate A level results. There came a moment, though, when I realized that this wasn't much of a strategy for proving my sceptical self wrong, and I began to study in earnest. I passed my exams and obtained my teaching certificate too, having been assessed as also competent in that area. After graduating, however, I began to learn of other, new ways of thinking.

This next phase of my learning developed in informal contexts. What were to me at the time new concepts such as feminism, socialism, colonialism, capitalism – all these ways of explaining the politics of class and inequality and more – were fiercely debated during car journeys, backstage, in green rooms, over drinks in bars, curries in restaurants and living rooms in Coventry, Nottingham, Liverpool and London. I did a lot of listening in those days, aware of my lack of a historical and political education. As I tried to assimilate the ideas being discussed, I looked around me, observing how many of these bright, articulate people had been to private schools and elite universities. I marvelled at how confident and articulate they were. It wasn't until later that I would come to recognize the limitations of having a strictly intellectual understanding of the world, without the ability to empathize on anything other than a theoretical basis with the experiences of those from underprivileged backgrounds.

In spite of my low expectations of finding work in the theatre, I was doing quite well, at least outwardly, with one acting job leading almost seamlessly to the next. But a new obstacle presented itself: the depression that had marked the years following Daisy's death had returned by stealth. It started towards the end of my time at New College and gathered momentum when I left London for Coventry. I felt, once again, the need to hide my feelings of worthlessness – which, seven or so years after leaving care, had never quite left me.

After sharing a rented house with other actors for several months, I took the opportunity to move into one of the flats above the Belgrade Theatre, in Coventry's city centre. I'd hopes of entering a new, positive phase in my life, encouraged by achieving my first professional acting job ahead of several of my peer group from New College. But with no cash to spare, and few real friends, life felt pretty grim, no matter where I lived. Most of the time, I was too broke to travel back to London, and at weekends I would stay in bed as long as possible, to avoid revealing to my fellow actors just how down I felt.

During all this time spent away from home, I kept my London bedsit, as well as paying for accommodation wherever I was working at the time. When I was really low in mood and funds, I'd do something crazily expensive like catching a first-class sleeper train to London, if no one was driving south, just so I could spend eight hours in my home city. Part of this was connected to missing my friends – but that didn't account for the whole story. There were several occasions when I travelled back to London on a train at great expense, for just one night, and deliberately avoided seeing anyone.

I might have envied some of my friends during my childhood, but part of growing up meant recognizing that nothing and nobody was simple and straightforward in the way I'd imagined. Now I acknowledged that each had their own lives, with their problems and tragedies, so how would it help them to have to see this miserable version of me? I was poor and depressed, but determined to keep up the outward appearance of someone who'd overcome a difficult start in life and was currently thriving as a performer in repertory theatre. In reality, I'd swapped one itinerant, insecure confidence-sapping lifestyle for another. Still carrying traces of low self-esteem, I made some bad choices and slid further into debt and depression.

In the mid-1970s, in order to perform in legitimate theatre and on television, it was necessary to join Equity, the actors' union. I did so, and very quickly became actively involved. I joined Equity's Afro-Asian committee, and from the moment I began to take part in the meetings, something shifted in my understanding of the casual, everyday racism I'd experienced all my life. The manner in which Black women, in particular, were denigrated and confined to a narrow range of parts, and my observations of how those who'd had a privileged upbringing held an advantage in every aspect of life, began to come together.

I'd been listening so intensely, and for so long, to others; I'd been reading books and newspapers and watching current affairs and documentary programmes – it was as if I'd been revising and was now ready to sit the examination. And this time around, I passed. I had, as they say, begun to find my voice.

Sitting alongside others who'd had similar experiences but had still managed to carve out a career in theatre and TV, all the while maintaining a campaigning spirit, I found that I could speak out. Attending auditions for the tiny number of roles available to Black women, and becoming an active member of Equity's embryonic attempts to make the profession more inclusive, meant seeing the same core group of Black actors, over and over again. At last, I was able to share my thoughts with others without having to explain what the fundamental issues were. We knew what we were trying to deal with, and we trusted each other in pursuing our individual and collective goals.

Now I could pick up on discussions about representation and stereotypes, and collaborate with others with similar ideas and ambitions. For example, we lobbied and protested against the engagement of Equity members with entertainment organizations in apartheid South Africa. We organized and we campaigned for more and better representation on stage, in front of the camera and behind it.

Through my participation in these activities came the revelation that I wasn't academically or intellectually lacking. I found a skill I didn't know existed, let alone one I had myself, one that few others seemed to have a wholehearted desire to develop. Committees became my strength, and whether as a member or, later, as chair, I got stuck in. The qualities required to be an effective member of a committee seem obvious to me now, but in the late 1970s I had no real idea of what it meant at all. Essentially it requires time, energy and commitment, as well as being good at working collaboratively. As there is often a demanding pile of papers to read and follow, being well organized helps, especially if the subject matter is complex and technical. Chairing committee meetings entails the qualities already mentioned, plus being able to motivate committee members; encouraging and acknowledging their contributions is important. In other words, being on or leading a committee is similar to working in a leadership role in many other professional contexts. I was well prepared in the most obvious way – I always read the papers and organized my thoughts by thinking about the questions that arose from them before the meeting.

The work gave me a taste not only for developing a

deeper, more nuanced understanding of Black cultural politics, but also for collective working for change. The more I found out from fellow campaigners, the more I discovered that my knowledge of history – particularly that relating to the long, consequential tail of Europe's continuing impact on former colonies – needed a great deal of work. That would have to wait, though, because at that time it seemed even more urgent to understand what was going on right then, in 1970s Britain, rather than what had gone on in the past. In my defence, I can say that eventually I learned the fallacy of that kind of thinking. The history matters.

I had naively assumed that the further I left my childhood behind, the better I would feel about myself. But I was also conscious of what was going on in the political arena. The context was one in which anxieties about race and migration were harnessed by politicians to pad out their uninspiring manifestos and bolster their election chances. As the 1979 general election approached, I grew more concerned as the government proposed changes to the law on nationality, making me nervous about my status as a British citizen. The thought of what my fate would be if laws were introduced to 'repatriate' Black people haunted me. It was no coincidence that this period also saw a growth in far-right activity.

After a decent run in repertory theatre, and a couple of small acting roles on television – parts as a nurse, and a prostitute – I returned to London to work in theatre in education, at the Curtain Theatre. I also thought that with my experience in the band, and after roles in musical productions in regional theatres, I might be able to get a part in a bona fide West End musical. There were so many around; *Hair, Godspell, Company, Jesus Christ Superstar* were just a few examples of hit productions during the 1970s. Surely, I could squeeze my way through an audition and on to the stage of the Theatre Royal Drury Lane? I kept my eyes open for notices of forthcoming productions and hoped I'd get lucky.

When news circulated that a West End musical requiring an all-Black cast was coming to town, there had been a buzz of excitement. I was sure virtually every Black actor and actress who could sing and dance even a little bit would be keen to perform in *Bubbling Brown Sugar*. I went along to a couple of singing auditions and passed through the initial stages, and was then invited to watch a performance so that I could get the hang of things before going through to the final test.

In the midst of all this excitement, out of the blue, I received a communication from my father. The last I'd seen or heard from him had been at that horribly uncomfortable meeting at the White House Hotel, some six years earlier. The letter was unexpected, and unsettling. While I never forgot about my parents entirely, neither did I spend days and nights wondering what they were doing or whether they thought about me. I was beyond all that, I thought, having decided that my new self was born in 1973 at the age of twenty-two, when I started at the New College of Speech and Drama.

My half-sister, Shade, who would have been about

thirty years old at the time, was to be married in Lagos — and I had been invited to the wedding. My father would, he'd written, pay my fare: he'd send the official invitation and the aeroplane ticket shortly. This time he did fulfil his promise, and just after Christmas 1978 the official invitation to Shade's nuptials, along with a BOAC ticket valid for several weeks, arrived at my bedsit in Archway.

After the initial shock, I wondered what had prompted the invitation. I half thought it must have been a mistake. Given our history, I found it hard to believe that my father would have voluntarily sent me a return ticket to Lagos. Maybe it was down to Lady Olayemi, using her status once more to persuade him to do what she considered the honourable thing. I wondered if there would have been some social stigma, had I been left out. Thinking about it now, it seems more plausible that social stigma would have been a reason *not* to include me in the celebrations.

Perhaps Shade had insisted that I be invited? I didn't think so, even at the time. It wasn't as if we'd ever been able to build a close relationship.

There had been two or three occasions in the 1970s when Shade had visited London to see her old school friends, and we'd met, had a coffee or maybe lunch. I had never been sure what she got out of seeing me. Once or twice, I thought we'd managed to make some sort of peace between us, but then we'd go off the rails and start bickering. I was convinced she thought me sulky and lacking in sophistication, and had said as much. For my part, I thought her a spoilt moaner, always claiming exhaustion and the unfairness of what she had to put up with in Nigeria. Shade seemed to view me as the privileged one, living a charmed life in London. She had been uninterested in a conversation about what I'd been through over the years. Her lack of curiosity about how I'd managed during those bleak years left me cold. The 'half' attached to our sisterhood meant a question mark always hovered over the meaning of our relationship.

More recently, I've tried to see beyond her status as the beneficiary of our father's largesse and acknowledge that she didn't have an easy time herself.

When my father had asked me if I wanted to accompany him to Nigeria – back in 1963, when I was twelve – I'd said no. As spurious as that choice had been when posed to a child in my circumstances, at least there'd been the opportunity to refuse the offer. Shade had had no choice in the matter. Perhaps she'd been as distraught at leaving behind her friends in London as I had been at the thought of such a move. She was the fourteen-year-old girl who had been separated from her school friends and whisked off to Nigeria with her (our) father. And that must have been tough. I wondered if there had been gossip about our father's behaviour with my mother, in her new life in Lagos. Had she been teased or bullied because of him? Or because she had been 'too European'? Once, she'd admitted that the other girls at Queen's College, Lagos had called her *ojeun bota*, or butter eater – a taunt directed at Nigerians who were judged to have adopted European ways.

When I heard that I hadn't been successful in getting

past the latest round of auditions for *Bubbling Brown Sugar*, I wrote to my father to let him know that I would travel to Lagos for Shade's wedding.

I prepared carefully for the event, trying to be as organized as possible: it felt like an even bigger undertaking than the hitch-hiking trip across Europe. There was so much at stake, especially in terms of the possibility of renewed family connections. There was no indication in my father's letter of what I should wear at the ceremony, so I bought a straw hat and made myself a chic wrap-over dress from a subtle floral fabric bought at John Lewis. I'd been designing and making clothes for myself and a handful of friends for several years, so the complicated Vogue pattern held no terror for me. I added a pair of white leather sandals that I already owned. I was happy with the look: very cool, very London.

There were a number of obstacles that prevented the planning of my trip going as smoothly as I'd hoped. Obtaining a new British passport was not straightforward, as I couldn't find my birth certificate, which I'd last seen years before in a drawer in Daisy's old Welsh dresser. I managed to sort that out by using my old passport from my Norway trip as proof of identification, but then I had no money for the renewal fee. I was absolutely flat broke, so I borrowed the sum needed from Anne, my old hitch-hiking partner. Then there was the visa required for entry to Nigeria. The long queues at the Nigeria High Commission meant waiting for hours on end. With no acting jobs on the horizon, I was temping in an office and every minute spent queuing meant wages lost. More than once I had to return to my workplace because I could see that I wasn't going to reach the head of the queue before the High Commission closed.

A great adventure beckoned, a first trip to the land of my forebears, so I would just have to be patient and queue without complaint. A couple of years before the proposed trip, I'd read the bestselling novel and watched the television serialization of Alex Haley's *Roots*. Although the protagonist's story was different to mine, and had a historical significance beyond the life of its main character, I could relate to the desire to know. I needed to understand the narrative that had brought me to this point in my life. I promised myself that if there were relatives present who were ready to fill in some of the gaps in what I knew of my parents' lives, I'd be prepared to listen. I'd be open, if they were.

Now, as I reflect on the period of my life leading up to this journey, to a country that had only existed in my imagination, I am aware of how much my younger self must have been counting on the idea of obtaining some kind of resolution – although whatever I imagined that to be isn't clear to me now. I had no thoughts that I can recall about whether I might meet my mother. I think the concept of 'my mother' was so alien to me that I simply assumed her absence. I was going to stay with Lady Olayemi for some of the time, and with my father and Shade, and possibly with Chief Mrs Arden, all of whom would be among the prominent figures present at the wedding. Clearly, the guest list would not have included my mother.

The trip was freighted with expectations that were as much political as they were personal. Challenging social conditions could make going about our daily business difficult for so many people in Britain in the 1970s. For many Black people, being highly visible and invisible at the same time was nothing new – and for some of us, it resulted in lives laced with the threat of violence. While we could be the object of intensive scrutiny and identified as a threat, at the same time we could be ignored when it mattered: for example, in health or education policies that led to inequalities. I want to draw attention to this aspect of life in Britain as it's integral to my story and that of thousands of others. It wasn't apparent to me at the time when I was about to travel to Lagos, but it became something that I would analyse extensively later on.

Until I went to Nigeria in 1979, I hadn't known what it felt like for my 'blackness' to blend into the background, not to be 'Black' but to be seen as a person. Yes, there were white people who declared they didn't 'see' anyone's skin colour, but I'd always received such pronouncements with suspicion, wondering how that could possibly be the case in British society. In retrospect, I can see that I wanted to test the extent to which Nigeria had something to offer me. I wondered if it might tempt me to stay there, or at least to become a regular visitor.

Whichever way I looked at it, there was a lot riding on Lagos, 1979.

Thirteen: A wedding

> . . . technically *Aso-Ebi* means 'family cloth'. A type of uniform dress, *Aso-Ebi* serves as a piece of identity, displaying unity among a group – such as friends of the family at a celebration or event.
>
> Luluyetha Howell,
> V&A Blog, 8 April 2021

As I boarded the plane leaving Gatwick Airport for Lagos, an air hostess asked me to sit with an unaccompanied ten-year-old girl named Sophie. She was going to see her father for the first time in years, and I felt for her. It was such a young age to have to deal with that kind of situation, as I well knew. She was nervous about flying on her own and so I hid my own fears and hoped that we'd both be able to relax.

Sophie asked me what work I did. She seemed interested to hear I was an actress. Close to landing, I gripped the armrest. The air hostesses took their seats and one of them, a posh-sounding blonde woman, started talking to me.

'I've been to Lagos many times – these Nigerians, they're primitive people, you know.'

Shocked to hear her say that to me, I wondered who or what she thought I was.

After landing at Murtala Muhammed Airport, I emerged from the frigid air on the plane into a warm, wet blanket of tropical heat. For a moment, it felt great. Finally, I was in Nigeria. On the continent of Africa.

Almost immediately, I was ushered into a holding area and questioned for some time – once I'd told the official that my father was a judge and dropped his name heavily, I was released and allowed to leave the airport. After that nerve-wracking experience, during which I'd been told I might be sent straight back to London, I wondered whether Nigeria could ever feel like home: I wasn't sure if it would even serve as a place of temporary refuge, should the situation in the UK deteriorate.

This time, I recognized my father as I exited immigration. He asked me why I was so late, and I told him. His driver greeted us, and stowed my luggage in the boot of the car. My father and I slipped into the back seat.

As we sped along the motorway, I observed an assortment of buildings and structures, old and modern, jostling for attention. Dwellings, offices, shops, fields, roads, building sites, petrol stations; the architecture was strange and familiar at the same time. The setting – the light, the colour of the sky, the greenest of green foliage, the patchy brown grasses – these were the elements that marked the view as distinctive from what I'd been used to.

Lady Olayemi's Victoria Island villa was our first stop,

where I'd be staying for a while. Lady Olayemi had manoeuvred my father into meeting me at the White House Hotel – after prompting by Iyinoluwa Taylor – and she had contacted Mrs Taylor again, before I left for Lagos, to say that she was very much looking forward to receiving me as her guest. This was a woman who could get my father to do things, never mind if they were twenty years too late. As far as I was concerned, she'd been a hero for having understood that the prolonged estrangement between the father and his youngest daughter wasn't entirely that daughter's fault.

At the wedding, Shade wore a floor-length white dress with a long train, in the traditional European style. She'd looked like royalty, or a model for designer wedding gowns, and I felt a twinge of envy, not because of her newly acquired marital status but because of the adulation and attention she appeared to receive from her friends and relatives, mostly from the upper echelons of Nigerian society, who filled the church and gazed at her with admiration. I knew little about the groom, other than he held a position of sufficiently high status to satisfy our father's exacting demands for his elder daughter's suitor. I was told that the man in robes who officiated was an archbishop.

The reception was held at the historic Yoruba Tennis Club, a parade of glistening vehicles making its car park look like a Mercedes showroom. As I observed the obvious wealth of the two hundred or so guests – epitomized in the leaning tower of wedding presents, showing off kitchen appliances, bed linen and the like – I wondered who they were and if I had familial connections to any of them. Clusters of people wore clothing made from similarly patterned material in different styles, women looking particularly striking in their *bubas, wrappas* and *gele*. The fabric had a similar function to tartan: a way of recognizing who was and wasn't in your clan. So why was I not wearing *Aso-Ebi* – the same traditional fabric as the rest of the Young family? Because nobody had thought to mention it to me, that's why. The clearest of statements about my true status in the Young family. Some of the guests must have been wondering who I was – the young woman dressed in European clothes that marked her out as unrelated to the bride's family.

Something felt out of kilter; I was upsetting the balance on this happy occasion. I watched as guests danced around Shade, and stuffed banknotes into her clothing. I was told it was a tradition for guests to give the bride money in this way.

The day after the wedding, Shade said goodbye. She left Nigeria for her honeymoon in Benin with her diplomat husband. I would be left to my own devices, staying with my father and his wife, Joan.

With the wedding over, and no more safe topics left to discuss with me, my father couldn't understand my moody responses to his efforts to strike up a conversation. One balmy evening we sat on chairs on the porch, like actors in some cheesy drama set in the Deep South of the USA, and had one of our turgid exchanges. I looked at this man – the former iceman and still the stranger – and thought to myself, *poor old father*. I was finding it hard to stomach his many references to the importance that Nigerians placed on family and community.

My dress for the wedding had left me with a large 'O' for 'Outsider' stamped on my forehead, and my clothes in general drew disapproving comments from my father. One morning I agreed to go with him to his office to see the wheels of justice turning. When I came downstairs, ready to leave, he looked at my outfit in disgust. He claimed I was deliberately trying to embarrass him, in my sage-green cotton dress, and sent me back to my bedroom to change. This resulted in me accompanying him to his office at the law court with bad grace, ready to argue the point on whatever topic he chose.

Even with the car's air conditioning, he must have been sweltering that day in his three-piece pinstriped suit, white shirt and tie. I read this attire as a sign of his stuffiness and inherent conservatism, and I hoped he felt uncomfortable. When we reached the court, he lined up his staff to be introduced to me: they saluted him and bowed to me. This reverence for those regarded as social superiors didn't sit right with me. It was uncomfortable, a class thing, mistaking deference for respect that had been earned. To add to my discomfort, I wasn't able to ignore the way that my father's driver had been made to sit in the car waiting for us for nearly three hours. My father made it clear that I had no right to judge the situation. 'Don't bring your Western psychology over here,' he'd said, when I commented on the driver's disconsolate look as we returned to the car. 'It is irrelevant, you know nothing about our culture.' His comment was true enough: how could I know?

My ignorance of history as well as culture magnified the difficulty of these encounters with my family, friends of family, servants, drivers and traders. Some of the answers to the questions raised by these histories – individual and collective, of colonized and colonizer – would have been on offer in the university education I'd never had, and I realized that I would need to do some reading and learning once I returned to London.

Chief Mrs Arden, the woman my fellow singer Esther had put me in touch with about four years earlier, had invited me to stay with her for a few days after the wedding was over. I was glad to be out of my father's house. We'd had little to say to each other, my father and I, and I know I'm probably being unfair, but I was tired of feeling as though I was suspected of some unnamed wrongdoing. I filled my evenings reading and watching television, especially enjoying the long-running soap opera *Village Headmaster*.

It was the rainy season, and the sunshine was punctuated by heavy showers. I didn't mind too much but it meant that my movements were constrained by the weather, as well as by the rules concerning where it was safe to travel and with whom. Hailing taxis was considered unsafe, partly because you never knew who you'd end up sharing with, as drivers would stop and pick up as many travellers as they could fit in their cars. The one time I admitted that I'd broken the rule about taking a taxi, I was castigated for doing so. I did not dare defy the order not to go out and about after sundown, which was around 7.00 p.m.

It was just as well I was used to my own company – I was happily living in my Archway bedsit alone – since I rarely had anyone to guide me around this sprawling city and the surrounding landscape. So far, my stay hadn't been a whole lot of fun.

A memory: A visit with my mother

Spring 1979: *twenty-eight years old*

The room in which we're sitting is a wide, open space. European-style heavy, dark wooden furniture sits alongside thick-pile rugs, masks, carved figures and animal hides from across the African continent. It's the Fashola residence. This morning, Chief Mrs Arden informed me that her driver would be taking me to Lady Fashola's house for lunch with Lady Olayemi. Having been her house guest before Shade's wedding, I am happy to see her again.

At eye level, on one of the shelves, there is an invitation to tea with Queen Juliana of the Netherlands at the Dutch Embassy. This is just how rich people live, I suppose. Tea with a queen. Maybe I hadn't been socially ambitious enough in my childhood adoption fantasies.

After lunch, Lady Fashola summons her driver, Joseph, and then the two ladies and I are on the move. One of the few outings I've had on this trip was with Lady Fashola's daughter, Abebi. We had the same driver, and travelled into the bush; I relished the opportunity to see a bit more of the huge country in which I'd been staying but of which I'd seen so little.

They are physically similar, mother and daughter; tall

and comfortable in their bodies. Now in the Fashola family home, although Abebi hasn't joined us for lunch, I am struck by how similar Abebi's and her mother's voices are as Lady Fashola issues instructions to Joseph. Both women are softly spoken, their words carrying with an effortless authority; their accents convey the confidence of their class and education.

I've no idea where we're going, and Lady Fashola and Lady Olayemi don't disclose our destination – I hope I'm finally going to see some sights.

The car is about the size of my London bedsit; a classic Daimler, fit for royalty. The luxury motor's soft leather seats and the vehicle's suspension mean that we barely notice the bumpy rain-rutted streets. The weather changes swiftly, from hot and sunny to a dull grey light and warm rain. Surely this will put an end to our sightseeing? But we keep on going, and I'm beginning to feel nervous about what might be waiting at the end of this drive.

A woman with part of her face missing holds a begging bowl to the car window, her eyes and the empty container telling us everything we'd rather not know about her life. We all look straight ahead so the woman understands she is being well and truly ignored. I don't know how anyone can feel comfortable, living with what I'm seeing around me from a leather-clad seat in a chauffeur-driven Daimler.

At Lady Fashola's instruction, we turn off the main road and pull up in a narrow street.

I stare at the street sign, disbelieving. It's the return address written on the back of my mother's airmail letters sent to Tufnell Park Road from Lagos, over twenty years ago. We are outside number 10 Taiwo Street. My heart is thumping, and I want to leave the car and run away. A strange stifled sound leaves the back of my throat but doesn't quite make it out of my mouth. I start to pull myself out of my seat, ready for flight. But of course I am going nowhere, apart from number 10 Taiwo Street. My mother's home.

Steamy heat engulfs us when we step from the car. A bad feeling lodges in my stomach, unrelated to the food I ate for lunch. I wonder if I'm going to be sick.

When we enter the modest house, we're greeted by a woman who looks about sixty years old, of similar height and build to me. There are no hugs or kisses. Just a flicker of acknowledgement, through our briefly held eye contact, of who and what we are: mother and daughter. Yele Santos ushers us into her living room and invites us to sit down. As we take our seats, Lady Olayemi and Lady Fashola both look towards me, and I look away, unable and unwilling to indulge their satisfaction at bringing mother and daughter together after so many years apart. My mother apologizes for the groaning we can hear from the back of the house, explaining that her mother is unwell.

Mother, daughter, granddaughter – three generations of women connected by blood. A family reunion to celebrate after decades of distance. That's how this story is supposed to go. But blood alone isn't strong enough to bind us together. Too much of the past is creeping into the present, creating a palpable tension.

My mother is the root cause of my disorientation. Or more accurately, the fact that nobody warned me that this meeting had been set up, or even thought to ask me whether it was something I wanted. Ladies Olayemi and Fashola – and perhaps Chief Mrs Arden too? – have obviously connived to set the stage for this dramatic encounter. My mother must also have been expecting our visit, as she doesn't seem surprised.

We wait for my mother to return from the back of the house. Re-entering the room, she looks at each of her three guests in turn and then sits down.

Another distant low groan from my grandmother interrupts my thoughts. It isn't quite the sound of pain, more a rumble of resistance, a wish not to be disturbed or moved. I look around, careful to avoid my mother's eyes.

I tell myself that as long as I don't have to go and speak to the old woman, I can cope. I hope she's not in pain, but I have never met any of my grandparents, and kinship is an alien concept for me. The idea that I have any ancestors at all has never really crossed my mind. The sound of rain tapping on the roof and at the windows provides a backbeat to my grandmother's soft moans, made otherworldly by not being able to see her. Now my grandmother seems to be hovering in some in-between place, and her groans bring back memories of Daisy Vince – who I still think of as 'Mum' – as she lay, so poorly, on her couch. My maternal grandmother is either clinging to or letting go of the last moments of her life.

The smell of anxiety, the humidity, the unfamiliar sounds, the exchange of unsettling looks – I can't think straight. Will the last gasps of a dying woman I've never seen define the story of my stay in Lagos?

When I'd accepted the invitation to Shade's wedding, I'd worked hard to shut out the possibility that I might meet my mother. Now I stare into the space in the middle of the room, and try not to throw accusing glances at everyone. I know it must be difficult for my mother too – even if she had been told beforehand that I would be coming.

She asks, 'How is the weather in England?'

I hear myself answering. 'A bit colder than usual but fine when I left.'

I wonder if my mother had really wanted this meeting to take place. She surely has other, more important things preying on her mind. The conversation limps on, largely going over my head. Ladies Olayemi and Fashola conduct the proceedings, every now and then turning to me for comment, though I have little to say.

Eventually, my mother brings things to a close by saying, 'I hope you will be coming back. It's been nice seeing you.'

'Yes,' I say, not knowing how to respond to her, or how to be myself in her company, with Lady Olayemi and Lady Fashola looking on.

There are goodbyes, light touches and, when we part, I know we won't be seeing each other again.

Fourteen: Home

> People are really rather afraid that this country might be rather swamped by people with a different culture and, you know . . . people are going to react and be rather hostile to those coming in.
>
> Margaret Thatcher, 1978

Glad to be returning to England after three weeks of emotional and physical discomfort, I didn't care that it would be cold and dreary back in London. It hadn't mattered that I had no work lined up, or auditions to prepare for. I was going home.

As we grazed the sky in our little aeroplane, high above a thick layer of clouds, I thought back over my stay in Lagos. On the flight out from London, I'd sat next to ten-year-old Sophie, travelling on her own. She was on the same flight home as me, too, but now she was unwell and was being kept isolated. I hoped she hadn't caught anything serious. I missed her lively chatter, which had been helpful in distracting me from the visit. I sat silently throughout the journey to London. The six-hour flight meant there was too much time for reflecting.

There had been moments during my stay – like when

I'd stood on the beach at Victoria Island, wondering if I really was on the same planet as my friends back in England – when I'd felt totally disconnected from the experience, from what was happening all around me. The feeling of being there but not being there was in stark contrast to experiencing moments of overwhelming emotional intensity, felt most keenly in that encounter with my mother.

As our plane prepared for landing, there was an announcement: Britain had just elected its first female prime minister. Margaret Thatcher's Conservative Party had won the general election. And an unexpected cold spell was casting a chill across the country, with snow in some parts, despite it being May.

The pilot had sounded a bit too pleased to my ears, both about the election result and the late unseasonal weather. The new Conservative government promised it would be radical, and would restore the country as a global economic power.

The emotional stress of the visit left me with little room to record details such as the names of all the people I'd met, the places I'd visited. My memories of this brief stay focus on the emotional landscape, because that's the nature of how the flow of my unconscious works, forgetting being an essential component of memory, and there'd been so much I needed to forget.

I'd travelled to Nigeria with the idea that I was seeking an exchange with this family – the chance for my relatives to give me an insight into my life, past and present, and for me to learn more about theirs, especially their accounts of the history of the country I was now leaving behind. I had hoped I'd feel liberated enough by this Nigerian experience to live more in the present and stop looking back. Now I realized just how much I had to process. Firstly, there was something I'd known already but which had now been confirmed: family wasn't only about blood relations – there had to be more. Belonging, community were all easy enough to invoke, but much harder to enact in any meaningful way.

But I'd learned something else too. The trip had brought some kind of resolution, though not in the way I'd anticipated or hoped. While I'd discovered nothing more than what I'd already known about my mother and father's relationship, or what had happened before I was born, I had come to the realization that I needed to know more about *everything* – history, culture, representation, how the world worked. And I also wanted to channel more of my energy into campaigning for equality and inclusivity in the arts and cultural sectors. I might not want to be an actor for ever, but inspired by what I'd seen while participating in Equity's Afro-Asian committee, I wanted to be more deeply involved in policy-making, as well as the practical, academic and theoretical aspects. And then there was all the reading I planned to do – plenty of work for me there.

The depth and range of the emotional surges I experienced during those three weeks in Lagos reached their peak in the aftermath of the visit to my mother's house. I can bemoan the lack of preparation for that encounter, but what would preparedness for such an experience have looked like? It's not something you can train for.

While I was staying with my father he gave me some Naira to spend, which I'd gratefully accepted, and promptly went on a shopping trip to the premier department store in Lagos. I found it curious that my father seemed willing to hand over spending money to me when we met face-to-face, yet hadn't ever felt compelled to contribute to my upkeep when it had really mattered. It made me wonder what he really thought about me. Did he perhaps feel that this generosity with money was some sort of compensation for a parental attachment that had never had an opportunity to flourish?

I'd written to a couple of friends while I'd been away. I'd tried to skate over the more painful parts of the trip, instead focusing on the kinds of things you put on a postcard sent from an exotic holiday location: the sea, the beach, the heat, the rain – all of that, and probably something about the wedding. That had been an exercise in connecting to people I knew, making sure there'd be a place for me to slot back into when I returned.

Having resisted pleas from Lady Olayemi and Chief Mrs Arden to stay in Nigeria, I now found myself returning to a situation in the UK for which I had little appetite. And yet, embedded in the anxiety of returning there was also a sense of hope and relief. Whatever the newly minted government might say about ancestors, alien cultures and bloodlines, I knew for sure that London was the place where I belonged.

Fifteen: Unresolved endings yield fresh beginnings

7 August 1952, ▮▮▮▮▮▮▮▮▮▮: Strong healthy baby. Walks. Says words.

Watched by friends and family from their seats in the viewing gallery, in July 2004 I was formally introduced to the House of Lords. Several months after the brief ceremony, I waited nervously to deliver my maiden speech. As I looked across the House of Lords chamber to the opposition benches where the Conservative Party sat, I recognized Lord Norman Tebbit. This was the former member of Margaret Thatcher's government who had urged the jobless to 'get on their bikes' to find work. He had also pressed settler communities to take the 'cricket test', to show their support for the England cricket team, rather than those of Pakistan, India or the West Indies. I remembered how his suggestion had been met with a mixture of derision and anger – his remarks seen as a typically simplistic pronouncement on culture, allegiance and patriotism. Now here I was, about to comment on the Labour government's equalities legislation while he chatted quietly with Baroness Thatcher, the former prime minister who had spoken of British people as afraid of being 'swamped' by alien cultures.

There were other major figures from the previous government in my eyeline too. And when I looked to my left, I recognized many faces who'd previously been shadow ministers and were now in government. These, then, were a selection of my new colleagues. People who'd reached the pinnacle of political achievement. I pondered the ways in which each of these high-profile politicians had responded to the challenge of wielding their power and influence in the service of wider society.

Power – who has it, and how to get hold of it – is something activists, campaigners and allies frequently discuss. Gaining access to platforms that enable us to hold those who abuse their power and influence accountable was something I looked forward to when I was first appointed. And while I'm in favour of reforming the House of Lords, for as long as it exists, I'm committed to supporting campaigners demanding changes in policy or legislation. It's satisfying to feel useful, though the nature of the policy areas in which I have an interest means these are long-term struggles for change. That certainly applies to the care system, and to combatting exploitative labour practices, and all the other areas where equity and fairness, human rights and environmental justice apply: in one way or another, these have been live subjects for debate and activism for centuries. The acceptance and acknowledgement that challenging injustice and discrimination is lengthy, and often intellectually and physically draining, is not the same as saying we must be patient, or conceding and giving up.

When I first told my son that I'd been made a member

of the House of Lords, Gregg said, 'Remember, Mum, you're now part of the problem.' But I'd always known I'd find it impossible simply to bask in the glory of a peerage, and not then use the institution's unique platform to try to effect systemic change. Whatever my criticisms of the House of Lords, I'm acutely aware of the privileges that such a position affords me in terms of access and influence, and a certain amount of power. However, nearly all the work I undertake is rooted in understanding drawn from my past experiences.

It's always useful to be reminded of my obligations though. So thanks, son.

As a child, there was no way on earth that I could even have conjured up a fantasy of occupying a place in parliament, with titles and awards to my name: I hadn't been able to see a future where even my more modest dreams could materialize. After Daisy died, and that bewildering, dispiriting phase of my life began, I felt as though I was in transit, constantly on the move – if not literally, then metaphorically. That's another way of saying I couldn't settle, physically or psychologically.

As I grew older and looked back on my earlier life, I realized that my determination not to be beaten by my circumstances hadn't diminished – but the emphasis on figures who had loomed large in my childhood and adolescence had faded into insignificance. That included my mother and my father. At one stage, in my late teens and early twenties, I'd harboured the idea of a plan to enact revenge on them by being really good at something. I would do so well that my mother and father would clamour to 'own' me, and I'd reject their advances out of hand. If I'd allowed that to be my sole motivation, then I would have lost the battle to be who and what I wanted to be.

The various routes I've taken in my search for self-fulfilment and contentment wouldn't work for everyone. In some large part, my strategies for survival and beyond have been a product of the time in which I grew up. With little recognition of adolescent depression, and as good as no understanding of how racism might impact on a Black girl seemingly travelling solo through the world, I felt I had little option but to embrace the identity of someone who could construct her own road map. Reaching out for more formal help and support is a positive action, not shameful; we should know that by now. But there wasn't much by way of professional support around for young people in my position, as far as I was aware. Society still discussed mental ill health in the most disparaging terms and demonstrated scant sympathy for most of those who lived with it.

The episodes that comprised my most depressed, hopeless years combined initially with my material situation to shut down paths to academic success and personal fulfilment. Or so I thought at the time. Now those years seem remote. Embarking on this creative adventure, where I've been forced to confront those scenes of hopelessness, has revealed a rich repository of experience, if not actual wisdom.

As a child, my response was to create my own bespoke mental guide to making my way through the world, composed of what I read in fiction and non-fiction books, what I saw on television and heard on the radio, and the slivers of everyday life I observed on the occasions when I socialized with friends after school. At first this was an unconscious activity, as life got rough and I moved from 'home' to 'home'. As I entered adulthood, my sources of guidance grew wider and the construction of the road map more deliberate.

The 1950s will seem like ancient history to some readers, as will the 60s and 70s. It's hard to attempt a summary of attitudes towards ethnic and cultural difference over those decades, with all its variations, so I've tried to focus on presenting a snapshot of how it felt for me. Many people have told me that nothing's changed on this front. I'd say that there's been plenty of change, though not all of it good – historic forms of racism manifest themselves today. Or, put differently, there's both continuity and discontinuity in the struggle to make progress in diminishing the impact and pervasiveness of racism, and all other kinds of discrimination.

When I received my care records, I was keen to see the extent to which changing sensibilities on the subject might be reflected in the documents. I was especially curious because the period from 1951 to 1979 was a time of intense, contradictory social and political shifts, spanning a period that covered post-war optimism and the start of post-industrial angst.

Would there be references to the so-called 'race riots' in 1958 in the care notes? I wondered. I couldn't recall dwelling on what had happened in Notting Hill and Nottingham at the time, though I'd read accounts of the disturbances. These events took place around the time my mother was preparing to return to Lagos, so perhaps I had other matters on my mind. And so, it might have been for her that I was a distraction, not real to her, the distance between her visits indicative of other priorities. Living as she had done in the Notting Hill area, perhaps she'd been scared by the febrile atmosphere, while to me Notting Hill was as distant as Nigeria.

The newspaper headlines of the day have led me to wonder what had been documented about my parents – were they seen as exotic, these aspirational colonial subjects from Africa? Were they seen through the same prism as Caribbean settlers and their children? There were few clues relating to any of this, and whatever my expectations had been in this respect, they were dashed by that absence. It's important to remember, though, that racism wasn't then, and isn't now, the sole determinant of our lives. But it was there, around us, then as now.

Every time I see an article or report relating to the care system, I try to make sense of what it means to all those who've lived it. There are plenty of us. At the time of writing, there are approximately 84,000 children in care in England, the majority of whom are in foster homes.

When the first lockdown was imposed as a result of the pandemic in 2020, I wonder how many people thought about how children and young people in care would be coping. Those young people who'd just turned eighteen and had moved to independent living would have been particularly vulnerable, isolated during an extensive period of lockdown. As research has made clear, existing inequalities in our society and globally were exacerbated by the pandemic. Given that the outcomes for the care experienced continue to be poor, relative to their peer group in the general population – they are more likely to become homeless, to experience mental health issues, more likely to end up in prison, significantly less likely to enter higher education, and less likely to complete their degrees if they do – we can only speculate about how the cohort most affected will fare in years to come. That's on us as a society to urge our policy makers to do more – and do it much better.

The feeling of dread I experienced as my eighteenth birthday loomed, when I had been so unsure of what would happen next, is described today as approaching the 'care cliff'. From some of the conversations I've had, it seems as though the emotional upheavals I attempt to describe in this book will still be all too familiar to far too many of the care experienced community.

When I've given talks in schools, children experiencing difficulties in their birth or foster families often relate to the story of my time in care. At one school I visited, a girl almost leaned out of her front-row seat to hear what I had to say. I mentioned the child's eagerness to the teacher who had been present, and they confirmed that the child had a troubled background and was living in a children's home.

The list of care system missteps, resulting in care

experienced people facing huge challenges, isn't the whole story though. Yes, we have all the statistics at hand, but we should always remember that the numbers are composed of individual, different and nuanced stories – stories of triumphs, large and small, of overcoming barriers, as well as pain and disappointment.

Sometimes I wonder what kind of life Bobby Martin – the smart boy who'd lived in the Adams Street home when I worked there in the early 1970s – might have had if Islington Council had found him a decent, stable foster home. I caught up with him when, curiously, we found ourselves facing each other in the Houses of Parliament, around the time when London was readying for the 2012 Olympics. It was one of the moments when my enthusiasm for ploughing through my care records was at a low point. Bobby was there, advising MPs and the police on Black youth and crime.

We arranged to meet properly, and Bobby promised to send me an extract from the autobiography he was writing. I was eager to read it before we met again, but I found it harrowing. Judging by the chapters that Bobby'd sent me, his life as it unfolded in *Life Has a Funny Way of Turning Out* had been a series of brutal encounters. It's all there – the physical and mental pain he'd experienced, and which he'd inflicted on others. A tough read. Knowing that he eventually found redemption and happiness kept me going through the more upsetting chapters, although they managed to infiltrate my dreams on several occasions.

'You shouldn't worry about it, you know.' Bobby

reassured me that he was now in a good place, thanks to having found God and family and a community.

We both knew of the many different ways in which a history of being in institutions can worm its way into your brain, too often wreaking havoc there, and about the emotional turmoil of searching for an elusive family life.

Bobby died in 2018, aged fifty-three, and the knowledge that he was unable to complete his autobiography was deeply saddening to me. But he'd put his experiences to use by mediating, advising and helping out on projects that supported others who'd spent time in institutions, who'd been damaged by parental neglect and the systems meant to provide safe places for vulnerable children. I'm glad I got to see him as an adult. No matter how long it took for him to reach that point, he made a difference to many people, as was evidenced by the presence of those crammed into his memorial service. Different people have different routes and road maps, some of which lead into ravines or up mountains. It might have taken him many years, but Bobby served as a role model, a guide and a mentor, and he found a way to peace and success on his own terms.

A recurring thought that I used to have up until my father died in 1994 – a final, lingering fantasy – was that there might be a dramatic deathbed scene.

The ailing old man, Maxwell Fela Young, voice barely more than a croak, is wearing an old-fashioned nightgown (à la Dickens's Scrooge?) and lying in a four-poster bed swathed in mosquito netting that's swaying gently in an air-conditioned room. There's a glass of water nearby and he signals to me to pass it to him. I hold it to his lips and he just about manages a sip, though even that brings forth the kind of cough that has taken up residence in his lungs a long time past. His eyes water, and he makes a final supreme effort to sit up, even as I gesture to him not to attempt it. A word is ejected on his exhale, 'Lola,' and his hand briefly touches mine as I take the glass from him and place it on the bedside table. 'Lola, please. I'm sorry, please forgi—'

I flee the scene to avoid hearing his intended plea.

Of course, there had been no such scene, or anything even remotely resembling it. I never did get that call to his bedside: when it came, the end had already happened. I was invited to my father's funeral, but declined to attend, due to being booked in for a medical procedure; I'm not sure I could have faced going anyway. I wouldn't have wanted to encounter a similar set of circumstances to those I'd endured at Shade's wedding.

In reality, news of my father's death was relayed to me via a friend of Shade's, who lived locally in north London. We'd met several times, had been friendly, eating at each other's houses, discussing politics, the state of the world and so on. On receiving the news, I experienced sensory overload, a flood of unwanted memories – of emotional pain and social awkwardness – that took me back to 1979.

That whole deathbed scenario was later upended by an unexpected development. Several months after my father's death, I received a message from a distant relative who lived locally, to say that she had some correspondence from Lagos for me. This correspondence turned out to be a copy of a will in which Gregg and I were mentioned as beneficiaries. Some cash, a rundown bungalow and jewellery left to me by my paternal grandmother – the jewellery was never delivered, but Gregg and I eventually sold the bungalow.

My father's will revealed that he'd owned several properties, most of which were more substantial than the bungalow we'd inherited. For us it was all a bonus, though, having never expected the windfall. My feelings wavered: I was initially stunned by the idea that my father had remembered me, to the extent that I sat staring into space for several minutes when I'd finished reading through the document. Then I thought again about what it might mean regarding his feelings towards me. The very least I can say is that, ultimately, he didn't deny my – or Gregg's – existence: but anything more than that? I'll never know, will I?

I'd had no equivalent fantasies of maternal deathbed confessions – only questions. They rattled around my head: two subsets of the main conundrum, the puzzle that had motivated me to search for my care records in the first place. How could my mother have left me in the care of an elderly stranger, in a foreign country, at the age of eight weeks? One part of me says I should think about how desperate she must have been – how, for whatever reason, she couldn't think of another way out of her predicament. Another part of me says, how could she even contemplate leaving her baby like that? Then there are trains of thought that lead nowhere. For example, what if I had taken one of those trips to Lagos with my mother or father? Pointless to speculate. At least neither of them had left me in a basket on someone's doorstep; as a registered child minder, Daisy's home in 207 Tufnell Park Road was considered a safe place. The fact remained, though, that in spite of what I saw as half-hearted attempts to persuade me to travel to Lagos on both their parts, their lack of contact over the years had made for a difficult childhood, adolescence and young adulthood.

News of my mother's death would come just over a decade after my father's. I'd been down with the flu at the time, but a deadline for the submission of a research report meant I was sitting up in bed, tapping out the document. Once again, it was Shade who relayed the news to London; this time via my son and his father. I was surprised when Gregg dropped round, that morning in 2005. Sitting on the end of my bed, he told me in the gentlest way possible that my mother had died. I felt sad that he'd been given this task, but I didn't cry – or react very strongly at all. More of an 'oh' than an outpouring of grief. In truth, I didn't know how to react, thinking I ought to feel sad, should be mourning a relationship that had never existed.

Sometimes, we do that – chase something we've wished into being, something that was never really there in the first place. That's not to say I didn't find anything worthwhile in the process of combing through that box file of care records, because I did. The jigsaw puzzle I was trying so hard to assemble had an infinite number of pieces, and the small section I set out to construct will contribute in a tiny, tiny way to that whole picture. It's clear enough to me now that the record of my time in care could never have provided all that I'd desired, or contained the information I wanted. Neither could the mysterious package that turned up on my desk, nor the anecdotes from relatives passing through London. Perhaps even my mother and father couldn't have told me exactly what was in their minds on the day they handed me over to Daisy Vince, in late July of 1951, when I was just eight weeks old.

Being able to access my care notes was the final encouragement I needed to believe that there might be a point to putting parts of my story into the public domain. The records have been valuable as a resource with a longer life than I'll have: when I'm not around, that record will still be there, the originals lodged with Islington Council, in an archive somewhere for the foreseeable future, along with the records of the thousands of others who've been in a similar situation. Hopefully, they'll be stored far away from leaky washing machines.

I'm sure there are answers to questions I haven't even conceived of; answers that others may glean from the text. Finding the nice neat ending that will provide closure is not always possible in the form we imagine we want – the version of an ending that provides a neat resolution. For my own part, I think I'd given up on the idea some time before I reached the end of my reading – and I'm at peace with that. The demand and search for neat endings can be just as destructive as no resolution at all. I see the gaps as an incentive to keep looking for more information and understanding, in the knowledge that the search for the whole truth, the full breadth and depth of individual and collective histories, can never be complete.

As for history, who knows if some day, someone might come along and say to you that they have the definitive story of your parents and other relatives, and what they tell you is nothing like your own account? That's history for you – always in flux, never fixed, as we look back while moving forward, making new discoveries about what's gone before, and incorporating them into our understanding of the past, the world as we experience it today, and the future it informs.

Acknowledgements

Thanks to everyone who has given love, support and encouragement, especially . . .

Ola, for all the shared memories; Jo, Anne and Sal, aka the Parlets, sixty years and counting; Barrie – just the forty years, eh? Anthony Gordon, for your invaluable early insights; Ana Fletcher and Helen Garnons-Williams at Fig Tree, Penguin Random House, for your patience and support during this long process; Hattie Grünewald and Rory Scarfe, The Blair Partnership, for your belief; Michelle Gayle, for your support from the very beginning; Maurice, you suggested it – remember? Angela, for three decades of sisterhood; Susan, Colin and Patrick, for permission to use the photo; and most of all, thanks to you, Gregg, for keeping me going and making it feel worthwhile.

Resources

Access to Care Records Campaign Group (ACRCG)
https://www.accesstocarerecords.org.uk
info@accesstocarerecords.org.uk

AFRUCA
(safeguarding children from abuse and modern slavery in African diaspora communities)
https://afruca.org
info@afruca.org

Agenda Alliance
https://www.agendaalliance.org
adminsupport@agendaalliance.org

Anti-Slavery International
https://www.antislavery.org
media@antislavery.org

Archives and Records Association (ARA) UK & Ireland
(Developing guidance for record-keepers and care professionals)
https://www.archives.org.uk/care-and-adoption-records
ara@archives.org.uk

Arsenal Foundation
https://www.arsenal.com/thearsenalfoundation
charity@arsenal.co.uk

Arsenal in the Community
https://www.arsenal.com/community

Association of Child Abuse Lawyers (ACAL)
https://childabuselawyers.com

Barnardo's
https://www.barnardos.org.uk

Become
(advocacy by and for care experienced young people)
https://becomecharity.org.uk
advice@becomecharity.org.uk

Care Leavers' Association
https://www.careleavers.com
info@careleavers.com

CoramBAAF
https://corambaaf.org.uk

Free Loaves on Fridays: The Care System as Told by People Who Actually Get It
(featuring the voices of ninety-two children and adults from care, edited by Rebekah Pierre)
https://unbound.com/books/free-loaves-on-fridays

Mission 89
(combatting the trafficking of children in and through sport)
https://mission89.org
info@mission89.org